THEOLOGICAL INVESTIGATIONS

Volume IX

Also in this series

THEOLOGICAL INVESTIGATIONS

Vol. I
God, Christ, Mary and Grace

Vol. II
Man in the Church

Vol. III
Theology of the Spiritual Life

Vol. IV
More Recent Writings

Vol. V
Later Writings

Vol. VI
Concerning Vatican Council II

Vol. VII
Further Theology of the Spiritual Life 1

Vol. VIII
Further Theology of the Spiritual Life 2

Still to be published

Vol. X
Writings of 1965–67 2

Vol. XI
Confrontations

THEOLOGICAL INVESTIGATIONS

VOLUME IX

WRITINGS OF 1965–67 I

by

KARL RAHNER

Translated by

GRAHAM HARRISON

NEW YORK
HERDER AND HERDER

HERDER AND HERDER INC
1220 Avenue of the Americas, New York, N.Y. 10021

A Translation of the first part of
SCHRIFTEN ZUR THEOLOGIE, VIII
published by Verlagsanstalt Benziger & Co. A G., Einsiedeln

First published 1972

Printed in Great Britain by
Western Printing Services Ltd, Bristol
Nihil obstat: John M. T. Barton, S.T.D., L.S.S. *Censor*
Imprimatur: + Victor Guazzelli, V.G.
Westminster: 15th May 1972

CONTENTS

TRANSLATOR'S NOTE

I wish to express my gratitude for the help and suggestions given by Fr Edward Quinn, without whose kindness the translation would not have been possible; and also for the friendship of the staff and students of the College of the Resurrection, especially Fr Benedict Green, C.R. Thirdly I must thank the Reverend Mother, S.H.T. and the Sisters of the Company of the Lord Jesus, Ascot Priory, for the warmth of their hospitality during part of the work.

College of the Resurrection
Mirfield

Graham Harrison

PREFACE

VOLUMES 9 and 10 of my collected theological lectures and papers contain pieces of work which originated between 1965 and 1967, with the single exception of the 'Small theological treatise concerning Indulgences'. There are considerable differences as to the literary genre, the mode of thought and the style of language of the individual papers. This is determined largely by the concrete occasion which gave rise to each particular study. A detailed list showing how each one came about has been appended to this volume. Since the origin, the aim and the place of publication were to be included, the best course seemed to be to provide as accurate and complete a 'list of sources' as possible. Some of the essays originated as tape-recordings of informal lectures, which were then remodelled and extended in various respects. Many papers were originally sketches for addresses or visiting lectures. Many were written for books or periodicals which were not meant for theological professionals alone. On the other hand not a few of the larger studies are in the nature of extensive and detailed monographs and are intended (in the best sense) for the theological specialist (e.g. 'Atheism and implicit Christianity', 'The Sacrament of Penance as Reconciliation with the Church', 'Towards a modern authoritative Church doctrine of Indulgences', etc.). Correspondingly, the notes or the critical apparatus also have quite different functions in the individual studies: in the case of remodelled lectures and essays, where only a limited period of time or limited space was available and where neither the writer nor the listener (or reader) could countenance repetition, I have taken the opportunity of making it easier for the reader to see the more precise realisation of and the deeper connection between the developed lines of thought by copious cross-references to other writings of mine. This being the case, no claim is made to have supplied a scholarly apparatus or the otherwise usual comprehensive list of sources. On the other hand, however, the theological papers in the more strict sense are intended to supply the most accurate and universal documentation possible. I would therefore like to ask the reader to bear this in mind when he finds that I quote my own works a great deal. The explicitly limited aim of these references is obvious. In any case many people (especially in other countries) have requested pointers of this kind.

As previously, Volume 9 of the *Theological Investigations* fulfils the aim of collecting together chiefly my theological essays and smaller studies. During this period I also published larger studies elsewhere and I would like to mention them because together with what is published here they constitute a whole: the *Handbuch der Pastoraltheologie* II/1–2 (Freiburg 1966), *Mysterium Salutis* II (Einsiedeln 1967) 317–420, and the commentary to Chapter 3 on the 'Dogmatic Constitution on the Church' in the *Commentary on the Documents of Vatican II* Volume 1, ed. H. Vorgrimler (Herder, New York/Burns & Oates, London 1967), 186–218 (tr. Kevin Smyth). Besides these I would like to mention the articles which have already appeared in Volume 7 of the *Investigations* and the many contributions to the international lexicon *Sacramentum mundi* (English edition 1968 ff.). In addition three large studies are in preparation for the series *Quaestiones disputatae.*

Before being included in this volume all the lectures, essays and studies have been thoroughly overhauled stylistically, more clearly arranged, and trimmed down or extended according to necessity. Since the first publication more precise references to the latest literature have been added to many of the articles. These changes – often considerable – throughout the course of several stages of publication have not been individually noted in the list of sources.

The untiring and learned assistance of Dr Karl Lehmann was of the greatest service to me in revising and overhauling the material. I take this further opportunity of thanking him most warmly. I thank my new colleagues in the History of Dogma Seminar of the Faculty of Catholic Theology of the University of Münster for their careful and thorough help in reading the proofs.

Münster Karl Rahner

PART ONE

The Shape of Contemporary and Future Theology

I

THE SECOND VATICAN COUNCIL'S CHALLENGE TO THEOLOGY

THE question raised here cannot long be suppressed by equivocation: does the Second Vatican Council signify a decisive orientation for present and future theological undertakings or not? It is not just that the Council documents now appear side by side with other statements of the Church, or that a thorough and more precise investigation of the history of this Council has been initiated, and so on. The Council's inner call to the Church can be soon smothered and the Council rendered 'harmless'. There is already a certain tendency to represent the conciliar decrees as being only of 'pastoral' relevance, and thus to relegate them to a particular and circumscribed area, so that practically everything else may remain the same as before. With this in mind we ask how it is that the Council has set inescapable tasks for today's and tomorrow's theology.

I

There can be no doubt that the Second Vatican Council has created a 'challenge' to Catholic theology; that is, it has provided it with new tasks, given it a more dynamic impetus and wider scope for free movement. First of all this Second Vatican Council is of importance for Catholic theology in that the positive teaching of its decrees has in itself great theological significance. For what many Roman theologians had planned prior to the Council, and what many others had feared, did not happen, namely that at the Council the statements were to contain only what had been the received and express teaching of prior official papal doctrine, and that of the professional theology – of neo-Scholastic provenance – of the last hundred years. If this had been so, theology – courteously but firmly directed to these conciliar texts in new Denzinger numbers – would simply have had to pass on what had been taught previously.

The Council was certainly very careful and circumspect in all its doctrinal statements; indeed, it avoided any new definition. But it said a great deal which was not simply a part of the assumed repertoire of professional theology. Of course, a Council can only, and only *intends* to say what has always been, in some manner, in the Church's awareness of faith, even if in very different modes of awareness.[1] In this respect what the Council teaches cannot be absolutely 'new'; even so there is by no means any need for it to belong to the repertoire of the professional theology of the last century. In actual fact the average person's awareness of faith and religious practice draws its life from a professional theology which is decidedly a 'received' theology, with its particular selection of matter and historically determined perspectives. A small example: in no text-book or dogma or catechism of the recent past can one find any reference to the fact that the sacrament of penance is itself – among other things – a 'reconciliation with the Church';[2] and although this truth is in accordance with the plainest original tradition, it plays no part in the *lives* of contemporary Christians. Therefore it is of the greatest importance that the Council should have now broken through the usual themes of the text-books and catechisms of recent times and set free living realities and truths which were present as such neither in yesterday's awareness of faith nor among academic theologians.[3] The really decisive thing is not so much that many questions which were until now matters of dispute have been taken up and – to some extent – decided, setting theology the task of thinking through and justifying the decision and clarifying what still remains obscure; what is much more important in connection with these teachings of the Council is the fact that many themes have been raised which, although they were not really matters of controversy in official theology, did not form part of its clearly-defined subject-matter and therefore found little or no place in the official catechisms and in people's everyday awareness of faith. In this respect the Council provides theology with significant tasks and topics, and it implies the obligation of

[1] For the distinction between what is changeable and what is really changeless in theology and in the field of discipline, cf. K. Rahner, 'The Pilgrim Church', *Theological Investigations* VI (London and Baltimore, 1969), pp. 270–294.

[2] cf. the conciliar constitution *Lumen Gentium*, No. 11. For an exhaustive commentary on this passage and the historical background cf. the author's study 'Das Bußsakrament als "Versöhnung mit der Kirche"' in the *Festschrift für Kardinal Ottaviani: Das Volk Gottes. Sein organischer Aufbau im Alten und Neuen Testament* (Rome, 1967) (containing further references to literature). Cf. 'The sacrament of Penance as a reconciliation with the Church', *Theological Investigations* X.

[3] Besides the concrete references in the study just referred to cf. K. Rahner, 'Forgotten Truths concerning the Sacrament of Penance', *Theological Investigations* II (London and Baltimore, 1963), pp. 135–174.

extending and – consequently – restructuring to a considerable degree the whole thematic compass of theology in many areas and aspects. More express mention will be made of this later. Furthermore, however, the Council is of great importance in a dual aspect: the Council has *consciously* left open many questions, has revealed them as such for the first time or has expressly recognized them as requiring further theological investigation. These are not only questions which have in any case no real implications for the concrete life of the Church or for man's Christian existence and are only theological subtleties, the private business of the theological specialist. For instance, the question of the collegiality of the bishops was a matter of such violent dispute not because it would have been possible in all earnestness to doubt the issue,[4] but because it was suddenly discovered what were the *concrete practical consequences* of this doctrine. If particular mention is made of these topics of the Council at a later time, many of them will be of direct significance for the concrete life of the Church, as can be seen in the Constitution on liturgy for instance, where a broader and deepened theology of the Christian cultus and concrete liturgical measures mutually stimulate and benefit each other.

Above and beyond this broadening and deepening of the scope of theology, the Council's whole attitude shows a spirit of freedom, the desire, as Paul VI has formulated it, to study first and then to make a decision, an awareness of problems and respect for specialists (yet without timidly wishing to let them have the last word in their 'professional' and specialist capacity). All this converges on the realisation that the theological routine which has been really very widespread in the Church in the last hundred years, according to which everything of real importance in theology had already been settled, belongs to a theological manner which has been overcome, provided, that is, that theology now really takes the opportunity offered to it by the Council's attitude. For it seems to me that, however praiseworthy it may have been on the whole, the quantity and extent of technical study in the field of Mariology in the last few decades is *also* (although not *only*) a sign of the tacit assumption that, apart from the field of history of dogma which works retrospectively, progress is only possible in peripheral areas of theology. A dogmatic historian of the stature of Landgraf gave this as his candid opinion in private conversation.[5] Indeed, one may even be inclined to think that the

[4] For the assertion that episcopal collegiality was a factor even in the proceedings of Vatican I, cf. the author's remarks (and further references) in the *Commentary on the Documents of Vatican II* ed. H. Vorgrimler (New York/London, 1967), Vol. 1.

[5] Here it becomes very plain that the highly-prized 'freedom from presuppositions'

Encyclical *Humani generis* was informed somewhat by this mentality in its quite legitimate defence of theological terms, regarding theology as certainly the product of an evolution, but as now being simply 'complete', apart from peripheral areas: the historical evolution of concepts is recognised, but once they have been developed, they are taken as in every respect beyond improvement. This kind of 'monolithism'[6] has disintegrated. At least in its ecclesiology and in the Constitution on Divine Revelation the Council has shown that this attitude can no longer be justified. The Council has assuredly offered theology a more acute awareness of problems and a wider scope for free theological study.

II

Besides these formal aspects of a general theological approach the Council has given something further with regard to theology. The Council has opened 'dialogue' with the world. It has not already carried it through and of course it could not do so itself in any case. But it has begun determinedly to be aware of the world of the modern human spirit, that is, the world of a pluralistic, scientifically and technologically orientated society with its immeasurable breadth and diversity of insights and tendencies, the world of a split and diversified Christendom and of the world religions, the world of an immense future in process of being planned. And this confrontation is not a confrontation with a world in which one merely *happens* to live, whether joyfully or disconsolately, carrying on in adherence to the old traditional activities and aims, but with a world in which one has to be engaged in an open dialogue, the result of which is not a foregone conclusion; it is a world which the

---

of historical investigation is a problematical matter in theology too. 'Speculative' theological study and historical investigation are always mutually fruitful and reciprocally stimulating. In particular Landgraf's view and interpretation of early Scholasticism bears witness to a narrowing of the historical perspective as a result of dogmatic presuppositions: since Landgraf saw in High Scholasticism largely the unsurpassable perfection of theological thought, he was able to see the multifarious theological situation of early Scholasticism only teleologically in terms of its apogee and flowering in High Scholasticism. Thus it is clear that the dynamic quality of this particular mode of theological thought – and it is in itself highly variegated – which is perhaps especially interesting for us in our present theological situation, was not adequately represented by him.

[6] For a more precise understanding of this concept cf. K. Rahner, 'Kirchliches Lehramt und Theologie nach dem Konzil', *Stimmen der Zeit* 178 (1966), pp. 404–420, esp. p. 407 and note 4; cf. in this volume p. 86 note 4.

Church has to help to build and in which tomorrow's Church too will exercise its moulding activity; and that not merely under sufferance from the world, but in a way which the Church itself fully desires. This situation, seen and accepted by the Church, does not mean merely a new, additional and partial region of study for theology – although it does mean that as well; that is, in practice, study of the task clearly set out and delineated by the Pastoral Constitution on the Church in the Modern World. Rather this dialogue situation with the world, consciously initiated by the Church,[7] implies a situation and a task for theology in all its regions and subjects, even those which seem its most esoteric. The whole of theology needs to be aware of this situation. What this means in detail must be said later.

At the same time something came to light at the Council which, it seems, has not yet been a matter for theological reflection and clarification at all. The Church issues a Pastoral Constitution on the Church in the Modern World: in it she even describes this situation to which she wishes to take her stand, and the task which confronts her. But in this way she shows that she must have and must acquire a kind of knowledge, essential to her activity, which, however, does not spring from divine revelation but from human experience. The Church shows that this necessary profane knowledge by no means arises simply out of everyman's plain, everyday experience; at first sight, at least, this would not perhaps be a particularly stimulating theological problem, since this general everyday knowledge is always available. This profane knowledge which she possesses is won from a secular experience, scientifically and systematically gained through modern history, sociology, scientific psychology and futurology. This is a totally new kind of profane experience, previously nonexistent, and loaded with all the dangerous, dubious and provisional qualities which are associated with strange, scientific, 'empirical' manipulation. It could be said that the Church is no longer merely being involved with the world which God created and made available to simple (although still profane) everyday experience, but also with that world which man is building as *his* work, as an embodiment of *his* decisions, dreams, utopias and of his scientific reflection. This is a most strange and dangerous thing, and it has not so far been thought about at all in terms of an ecclesiology.[8]

[7] For the fundamental necessity of this dialogue cf. in detail the presentation and relevant literature in the *Handbuch der Pastoraltheologie* II (Freiburg, 1966), II/1, pp. 102 ff., 265 ff.; II/2, pp. 203–267.

[8] cf. K. Rahner, 'Zur theologischen Problematik einer "Pastoralkonstitution" ',

Proceeding from these presuppositions the attempt will now be made to say something of the tasks of post-conciliar theology. In doing so we are aware of the fragmentary and subjective nature of the following observations. We know too that the mere issuing of demands is a thankless business, that it is easier to give advice than to follow it, and that the *true* principles are given only by those who actually show the application of them.[9]

III

First of all as far as *historical theology* in general is concerned, it must be strongly emphasized that it must be extended and developed further. If Catholic theology (I am not including biblical studies here, about which something will be said in particular later) made great strides in the last century, this was chiefly, if not almost exclusively, in the realm of historical theology; the history of doctrine and theology, the history of patristic literature, textual edition, the history of canon law, etc. Doubtless there remain tasks enough in these areas. No intellectual discipline, above all at the present time, can dispense with studying its own history. And theology, on account of its own sublime dignity, owes itself such study. Where talent is forthcoming in this field – and there are men of talent for whom this should be more or less their only field – it should be encouraged. It would not be amiss if the Church authorities were more magnanimous financially in this respect (for such things as the edition of texts, the publishing of special historical monographs, etc.). But surely it need not necessarily be derogatory to the dignity and the truth-seeking impartiality of this historical theology if in future it became better aware of its function and responsibility in respect of the kind of theology called 'systematic' (including 'practical' theology), which in turn can only understand itself correctly as long as it is the servant of a truly living proclamation of the Gospel and of contemporary Christian existence, and is inspired by the awareness of the crying needs in the practical care of souls. If one considers the most accomplished figures of historical Catholic

Volk Gottes. Festschrift für J. Höfer, ed. R. Bäumer/H. Dolch (Freiburg, 1967), cf. 'On the theological problems entailed in a Pastoral Constitution', *Theological Investigations* X.

[9] As in what follows a fragmentary programme of this kind is to be set forth, the author may be permitted to draw attention in the notes to his own sketches of various topics, lest the impression be given that we are merely dealing here with a number of abstract ideas, incapable of being thought through in concrete terms. Of course the tasks concerned can be tackled differently by other theologians. But reference to many other works would have enlarged the notes disproportionately.

theology in the last hundred years, F. Ehrle, H. Denifle, O. Bardenhewer, M. Grabmann, F. Pelster, A. M. Landgraf and many others, one must conclude in all honesty that their great and scholarly work was practically worthless as far as the proclamation of the saving Gospel of Christ today is concerned, even if one is prepared to take into account highly anonymous and indirect influences. This historical theology was retrospective theology. It need not be so. There are today examples enough to prove this. Consider Y. Congar, M. D. Chenu, H. de Lubac, J. Daniélou, to name just a few. Historical theology today must no longer be as a whole so antiquarian and retrospective. More than before it must be prospective, retracing its steps in order to go forward into a new future of theology and evangelism. Historical theology must not simply ask what *has* been; it must inquire of the past in order to find the answer to the question, what *will* be, what is to be proclaimed tomorrow? In historical theology as well there must be as many theologians as possible who sense the demands, the unease, the burden and the danger of theology today for the proclamation of tomorrow and who bear and suffer these things along with their fellows. In the face of tomorrow's tasks presented by the times and by the Council, historical theology must indeed inquire with all precision and impartiality into what was, but it can no longer afford to maintain the art-for-art's-sake view of a boundless historical curiosity for everything and anything, but must ask the past what are the life-and-death questions which future has in store for theology,[10] even if it means that many *quaestiones quodlibetales* of second- or third-rate mediaeval theologians have to remain unedited and undiscussed.

Naturally, in order eventually to become a fruitful source for systematic theology, historical study cannot dispense with giving the past this opportunity of speaking without prejudice, irrespective of whether what it has to say seems interesting and 'existentially' significant at the first glance. Without the patience required for receptive listening, historical study would ultimately only hear what it already knew; it would learn nothing new. It must certainly not just try to discover justifications to bolster up already developed theses which are already more or less of interest. In order to hear new things it must be able to listen patiently to those traditional things which are apparently wearisome and over-familiar. But this by no means implies that the historical theologian who,

[10] Thus it becomes clear how necessary is an epistemological sketch of the function of the historical mode of thought within theology. Many preliminary studies for this subject can be found hidden away among the works of modern philosophical and historical hermeneutics.

qua theologian (i.e. more than a historian of religions), must always listen to the past within the perspective of faith of the present Church's understanding, may only think of the *present stage of development* of this understanding. He must be sensitive to the *evolving* awareness, heralded both in the promising and in the distressing aspects of the imminent future.[11] In the field of history as well as in other areas the theologian of today should not be demonstrating his scholarly competence by writing books about questions which interest no-one but himself. He should not merely be showing that people in earlier times also knew – in some fashion – matters which later came to be defined.[12]

There is moreover no need for this to be so. A historical theology can make a very considerable contribution towards the necessary expansion and broadening of present theology's awareness of problems, even if one hardly expects to find ready-made answers in the past for today's questions. If the historical theologian is inspired by his interest in the issue itself and its future and not only by interest in its past history, he will often find in the past – instead of confirmation of a later dogma – only interpretations of the dogma which were and are controversial and which therefore remain *theologoumena*.[13] He will seldom succeed – although even that is possible – in finding a consensus in the past in favour of a doctrine not already defined officially by the Church such that he is able to recognise this doctrine as of categorical relevance for *present* systematic professional theology.[14] But even if this is not the case, historical study can be of service to contemporary systematic theology: it sharpens one's awareness of problems and reveals how authoritative dogma originally arose as a concrete response to the demands of a difficult and problematical situation.

[11] cf. in this respect the parallels in the field of history in R. Wittram, *Zukunft in der Geschichte* (Göttingen, 1966).

[12] So long as historical thought in theology only results in study of this kind, a real 'historical consciousness' in the modern sense has not yet been attained. Because people on the systematic side have been too rigid to accept new configurations of questions and changed situations, it is often the case that the only thing that remains in view is the critical and destructive side of the consequences of historical investigation, not, however, its productive capacity – which is no less characteristic of it. This implies a hermeneutic self-criticism of the previous conception of history; cf. esp. H. G. Gadamer, *Wahrheit und Methode* (Tübingen, 1965).

[13] cf., for instance, the rich and varied history of the different theological presentations concerned with the creation of the human soul by God. For details cf. R. North, *Teilhard and the Creation of the Soul* (Milwaukee, 1967).

[14] In the first instance one of the historical theologian's important tasks will be rather to examine the sources more closely to see what are the concrete theological conditions (and limits) of such a 'consensus'.

This makes it possible, within the broad possibilities of more accurate interpretations, to perceive new interpretations in the present intellectual and spiritual situation. Historical study teaches us to distinguish more clearly between 'dogma'[15] and the theologoumena[16] which always accompany it.

Today this applies above all to the field of the history of moral theology and of canon law. There is still much highly useful and indeed necessary work to be done here by historical theology, as contemporary examples have shown, to reopen the debate – with a clear *historical* conscience as well – upon certain too simple and too calmly assumed traditional arguments in systematic theology, and to prepare better, more appropriate and more finely balanced answers.[17] Perhaps what has been said ought also to be referred to ecclesiastical history, however difficult it may be to apply it. At the Council it was sometimes possible to gain the impression that very many leading churchmen had heard little of the historical nature of the Church, her institutions and even of many of her teachings, or that at least they had learned little from this.

IV

Biblical studies have found new tasks in the wake of the Council. Not because the tasks did not exist beforehand but because the conditions for solving them have become better and, above all, calmer. The Constitution on Divine Revelation was certainly very careful and conservative in its exposition of doctrine. That is of great positive importance, since it is true in the field of biblical studies as in other fields that the latest thing need not necessarily be the most true and enduring. In the coming decades we shall need courage to stand fast by the undiluted faith of Christendom, which always remains an offence and a focus for temptation, in order, not to defend merely traditional positions, but to resist the scepticism and the tendency to disintegration which seem inherent in the

[15] For this concept and its change of meaning cf. K. Rahner/K. Lehmann, *Mysterium Salutis* I, ed. J. Feiner/M. Löhrer (Einsiedeln, 1965), pp. 639–707 (with literature).

[16] cf. K. Rahner, 'Theologoumenon', *LThK* X (Freiburg,[2] 1965), cols. 80–82.

[17] In the area of the history of moral theology we refer only to the studies by M. Müller, J. G. Ziegler, H. Klomps, J. Fuchs, J. Stelzenberger, L. Brandl et al. For a historical discussion with regard to the magisterium cf. J. T. Noonan, *Contraception. A History of its Treatment by the Catholic Theologians and Canonists* (Cambridge, 1965); also his study, 'Die Autoritätsbeweise in Fragen des Wuchers und der Empfängnisverhütung', *Diakonia* I (1966), pp. 79–106.

methodology of any modern historical science. These features, unaccompanied by any genuine religious experience, are rooted in the assumption that the living totality which is the reality of faith can be deduced from its individual parts and historically determined presuppositions, or that, if this cannot be done, the obligatory character of dogma or its meaning as affirmed by the Church is necessarily rendered null and void.

But the Constitution on Divine Revelation has actually sanctioned the development which already began with Pius XII (in *Divino afflante Spiritu* and certain statements of the Biblical Commission). The methods which were first developed in Protestant biblical studies, form-criticism in particular, may be used in exegetics and in biblical theology of the Old and New Testaments. This is possible because the techniques do not essentially bear implications unacceptable to dogma.[18] Even if one were to maintain the 'historicity' of the four Gospels, this rather indiscriminate characterization can and must be mellowed by the Constitution on Divine Revelation, and this is basically what happens when one acknowledges the *vario modo historicum*[19] and the influence of post-Easter theology on the record of the pre-Easter Jesus.[20]

The most immediate task of biblical research itself will be to show that there is a profound difference between the historical Jesus and the Christ of Faith and yet that there is at the same time a real connection between them, and a connection which is adequate to the demands of Catholic dogma. Thus it must show how men of today, with all their enlightened historical knowledge and their sensitivity to differences and developments, looking with the eye of faith may see in the story of Jesus more than merely the tragic fate of a religious enthusiast.[21] This is not only a work of defensive apologetics of the kind undertaken by Grandmaison about forty years ago. Making clear the distinction between the intrinsic interpretation of the historical Jesus and Church dogma (which does not

[18] For a historical and factual account of form-criticism cf. K. Koch, *Was ist Formgeschichte? Neue Wege der Bibelexegese* (Neukirchen, 1964); J. Rohde, *Die redaktionsgeschichtliche Methode* (Hamburg, 1966); for the Catholic side cf. the splendid study by A. Vögtle, *Das Neue Testament und die neuere katholische Exegese* I (Freiburg, 1966).

[19] cf. the conciliar constitution *Dei Verbum*, No. 12, and the relevant commentaries.

[20] cf. ibid., No. 19 and the presentation by A. Vögtle, loc. cit. (cf. note 18), pp. 68–96.

[21] For the latest developments in the study of the historical Jesus cf. the large report on the literature by W. G. Kümmel, 'Jesus-Forschung seit 1950', *Theologische Rundschau* NF 31 (1965/66), pp. 15–46 and subsequent issues.

destroy the substantial unity and identity of both) can be of positive value for dogmatic Christology,[22] namely in compelling it to take radically seriously what it says about the true humanity of Jesus, his human subjectivity and setting in history[23] and to make even plainer than heretofore that the 'Hypostatic Union' does not diminish the humanity of Jesus but starkly declares it at its high point of autonomy and distinctness from God.[24] In order for biblical study to attain such a positive value for dogmatic Christology, much closer co-operation is required between exegesis and dogmatics than we have been accustomed to in recent decades.[25] But in this working-together the dogmatic theologian must not expect results from the exegete which the latter is unable, in all historical integrity, to give. The dogmatic theologian must show better than before that, within a correct understanding of Christological dogma (purified of mythological accretions), the exegete's genuine results are quite adequate as a point of departure and a foundation for dogmatics. So this co-operation is of the greatest practical value for evangelism today, for only in this way can Christology so develop as to satisfy today's conditions of faith.

Furthermore the Decree on Priestly Formation[26] in the future has provided Catholic biblical studies with a larger and more fundamental task than merely the furnishing of proof-texts for theses which have already been selected for exegetical study. Biblical theology is commissioned to determine, as a result of its own studies, what are to be the themes of systematic theology, i.e. not merely to insert the appropriate biblical material into a given scholastic framework (as is clearly the case, for instance, even in von Ceuppen's *Biblical Theology*). As opposed to the previous analytic and scholastic method (whereby a thesis is propounded, analysed according to its concepts and then proved from

[22] For an example with particular reference to the title 'the Son' cf. the author's own discussion in *Mysterium Salutis* (Einsiedeln, 1967), pp. 356 ff.

[23] With reference to the question of the self-awareness of Jesus cf. the historical study of the problem by H. Riedlinger, *Geschichtlichkeit und Vollendung des Wissens Christi* = *Quaest. disp.* 32 (Freiburg, 1966).

[24] cf. K. Rahner, 'On the Theology of the Incarnation', *Theological Investigations* IV (London and Baltimore, 1966), pp. 105–120; also 'Current problems in Christology', *Theological Investigations* I (London and Baltimore, 1961), pp. 149–200; B. Welte, 'Zur Christologie von Chalkedon', *Auf der Spur des Ewigen* (Freiburg, 1965), pp. 429–458; F. Malmberg, *Über den Gottmenschen* = *Quaest. disp.* 9 (Freiburg, 1959).

[25] cf. K. Rahner, 'Exegesis and Dogmatic Theology', *Theological Investigations* V (London and Baltimore, 1966), pp. 67–93.

[26] cf. the Decree on Priestly Formation, No. 16.

'sources'), there can be no doubt that an *a posteriori* and synthetic method will facilitate a considerable enrichment and change of perspective of the compass of dogmatic theology. Themes such as a Theology of History, a Theology of the Word, the Hermeneutics of Theological Statements, will then automatically find a place in systematic theology. Or to give a small but important example: up to the present day there is probably not a single official Catholic ecclesiology which expounds a theology of the local church as a concrete actualization of the Church as a whole,[27] a theme expressly recommended by the text of the Constitution on the Church. However, in a dogmatic ecclesiology whose subject-matter had been dictated by biblical theology it would have been assumed at the outset. It is now the business of biblical studies to do justice to this officially commissioned task of being, in a sense, the mistress and not merely the handmaid of dogmatic theology.

V

Something more must be said concerning 'systematic' theology, i.e. chiefly dogmatics and moral theology. First of all it is clear that the Council has rightly proposed many tasks as a result of its express teaching. Theology will have to concern itself above all with the Council's *ecclesiology*. The Council has naturally formulated its teaching according to tradition. But that does not militate against the fact that it has moved many themes in ecclesiology to the forefront of our theological awareness which will reward and which require further consideration, and which have in addition thoroughly practical consequences. We mention here only a few of these themes, in no systematic or logical order: the more precise relation of papal primacy to the whole episcopate;[28] the nature of

[27] In detail with respect to the Council cf. K. Rahner, 'Das neue Bild der Kirche', *Geist und Leben* 39 (1966), pp. 4–24, esp. pp. 7–11; cf. 'The new image of the Church', *Theological Investigations*, X; cf. the *Commentary on the Documents of Vatican II* (cf. note 4); also *Lebendiges Zeugnis*, Nos. 2–4 (October, 1966), pp. 32–45, cf. 'On the presence of Christ in the Diaspora Community', *Theological Investigations* X; B. Neunhäuser OSB, 'Gesamtkirche und Einzelkirche', *De Ecclesia*, ed. G. Baraúna, vol. 1 (Freiburg, 1966), pp. 547–573. Cf. also 'The presence of the Lord in the Christian Community at worship', *Theological Investigations* X.

[28] cf. *The Episcopate and the Primacy* by the author (together with J. Ratzinger) (Freiburg and London, 1962), the author's commentary on the third chapter of the Constitution on the Church referred to on p. 5 note 4, and a study of the question of the bearer of full authority in the Church in the *Festschrift für Erzbischof P. Parente* (special issue of the Roman periodical *Euntes Docete*), cf. 'On the relationship between the Pope and the College of Bishops', *Theological Investigations* X.

the magisterium;[29] the relationship of scripture and tradition;[30] the place of law in the Church as the sacramental gift of the Holy Spirit; charismatic roles in the Church;[31] the theology of the diaconate;[32] the eschatological character of the Church;[33] the non-Christian's possibility of salvation;[34] the ecclesiological aspect of Penance[35] (and of all the sacraments); the nature of revelation and salvation-history;[36] the general application of the synodical principle in the Church's constitution; the ecclesiological significance of the Evangelical Counsels and of the religious Orders in the Church; the meaning and importance of what is called the hierarchy of revealed truths;[37] the theology of mission;[38] the possibility of a *communicatio in sacris* among separated Christians;[39] the theology of the function of the non-Christian religions in collective and individual

[29] For this problem in the light of the decisions of the Council cf. *Commentary on the Documents of Vatican II* (cf. note 4).

[30] cf. K. Rahner, 'Scripture and Tradition', *Theological Investigations* VI (London and Baltimore, 1969), pp. 98–112; K. Rahner/J. Ratzinger, *Revelation and Tradition* = *Quaest. disp.* (Freiburg and London, 1966); K. Rahner, 'Tradition', *LThK* X (Freiburg,[2] 1965), cols. 293–299.

[31] cf. K. Rahner, 'The Theology of the Restoration of the Diaconate', *Theological Investigations* V (London and Baltimore, 1966), pp. 268–314; also 'Die Lehre des II. Vatikanischen Konzils über den Diakonat', *Der Seelsorger* 36 (1966), pp. 193–200, cf. 'The teaching of the Second Vatican Council on the diaconate', *Theological Investigations* X.

[32] cf. K. Rahner, *The Dynamic Element in the Church* = *Quaest. disp.* (Freiburg and London, 1964); *Handbuch der Pastoraltheologie* I (Freiburg, 1964), pp. 154–160; II/1 (Freiburg, 1966), pp. 76 ff., 274 ff. (literature); *Vom Sinn des kirchlichen Amtes* (Freiburg, 1966), pp. 33 ff.

[33] cf. *Theological Investigations* VI (London and Baltimore, 1969), pp. 253–312.

[34] cf. K. Rahner, 'Anonymous Christians', *Theological Investigations* VI (London and Baltimore, 1969), pp. 390–398; also 'Atheism and implicit Christianity' in this volume, pp. 145 ff.

[35] For further details cf. the studies referred to in notes 2 and 3.

[36] cf. K. Rahner, 'History of the World and Salvation-history', *Theological Investigations* V (London and Baltimore, 1966), pp. 97–114; K. Rahner/J. Ratzinger, *Revelation and Tradition* = *Quaest. disp.* (Freiburg and London, 1966); in greater detail A. Darlap, *Mysterium Salutis* I, pp. 3–156.

[37] cf. the Decree on Ecumenism, No. 11, and the question of the simplicity of faith in the *Handbuch der Pastoraltheologie* II/1, pp. 142–145.

[38] For the fundamentally new aspects of the Decree on the Church's Missionary Activity cf. J. Ratzinger, *Die letzte Sitzungsperiode des Konzils* (Cologne, 1966), pp. 59–63; K. Rahner, *Handbuch der Pastoraltheologie* II/2, pp. 46–80.

[39] cf. the Decree on Eastern Catholic Churches, Nos. 26–27; the Decree on Ecumenism, Nos. 9 and 15. Cf. the commentary by Abbot M. Höck, *Commentary on the Documents of Vatican II* (New York and London, 1967).

salvation-history;[40] the Pope's obligation to avail himself of the Church's collegial organs (even if this obligation cannot juridically be standardised any further); the theology of the local community and altar-congregation as the Church;[41] the possibility of a historical development of the *jus divinum* in apostolic times;[42] the theology of the Word[43] and theological hermeneutics; the Church as *sacramentum salutis mundi*;[44] the theology of sin in the Church;[45] the theology of the Church's historically determined knowledge of truth;[46] and of the equally possible fallibility of this knowledge; these and many other broadly speaking ecclesiological themes have been broached by the Council. In addition to the work of directly commentating the Council's theological texts, systematic theology will doubtless have to concern itself considerably with these matters, and it will certainly have to do and say more than the traditional maxims current in theology before the Council. After this explicit programme on the part of the Council it can really no longer be said that present systematic theology – apart from the retrospective study of the history of dogma – can only conquer new territory in peripheral areas or special fields like that of Mariology, as everything else is already clear and cannot be better expressed.

[40] cf. K. Rahner, 'Christianity and the non-Christian Religions', *Theological Investigations* V (London and Baltimore, 1966), pp. 115–134; H. R. Schlette, *Towards a Theology of Religions = Quaest. disp.* (Freiburg and London, 1966); also 'Die Kirche und die Religionen', *Umkehr und Erneuerung*, ed. Th. Filthaut (Mainz, 1966), pp. 292–311; J. Ratzinger, 'Der christliche Glaube und die Weltreligionen', *Gott in Welt. Festschrift für K. Rahner* (Freiburg, 1964) II, pp. 287–305; H. Fries, 'Das Christentum und die Religionen der Welt', *Das Christentum und die Weltreligionen = Studien und Berichte der Katholischen Akademie in Bayern* 27 (Würzburg, 1965), pp. 13–37; H. Küng, *Christenheit als Minderheit = Theol. Meditationen* 12 (Einsiedeln, 1965); J. Feiner, 'Kirche und Heilsgeschichte', *Mysterium Salutis* I, pp. 324–336.

[41] cf. the literature referred to in note 27.

[42] cf. K. Rahner, 'Reflection on the Concept of "ius divinum" in Catholic Thought', *Theological Investigations* V (London and Baltimore, 1966), pp. 219–243.

[43] cf. the various works by L. Scheffczyk, O. Semmelroth, H. U. von Balthasar, J. Betz, W. Breuning, H. Fries, K. Rahner et al.

[44] cf. the Dogmatic Constitution on the Church, Nos. 1, 9, 48, 59; the Pastoral Constitution on the Church in the Modern World, Nos. 42 and 45; the Decree on the Church's Missionary Activity, No. 15; P. Smulders, 'Die Kirche als Sakrament des Heils', *De Ecclesia*, ed. G. Baraúna (Freiburg, 1966) I, pp. 289–312 (literature); K. Rahner, 'Das neue Bild der Kirche' (cf. note 27), cf. 'The new image of the Church', *Theological Investigations* X.

[45] cf. K. Rahner, *Theological Investigations* VI (London and Baltimore, 1969), pp. 253–294.

[46] cf. K. Rahner/K. Lehmann, *Mysterium Salutis* I, pp. 727–787 (literature); K. Rahner, 'Zur Geschichtlichkeit der Theologie', *Integritas. Festschrift für K. Holzamer*, ed. D. Stolte/R. Wisser (Tübingen, 1966), pp. 75–95, in this volume, pp. 64 ff.

I may be mistaken, but the description of future moral theology in the Decree on Priestly Formation[47] strikes me as a biting but just criticism of the sort of moral theology generally widespread in seminaries. The Decree conceives the tasks and methods of moral theology quite differently from actual practice to date. For it demands a moral *and biblical* theology, a moral theology positively orientated towards love, the abandonment of a constricted concern merely for the individual's salvation, a morality of service to the world; these are all things which are so far not to be found in the average text-book.[48]

VI

There is a very understandable and attractive temptation, but one which would carry with it dire consequences for the future, and that is to think of the main task of systematic theology in the next few decades as the writing of commentaries on the Council's documents, and justifying historically and deepening systematically the themes explicitly discussed by the Council. Such a development in the theology of the next few years, however, would contradict the spirit and the intention of the Council. The Council did not intend to invite theology to be the means of the Church becoming turned in on itself.[49] It was the Council's intention to confront the Church of its own time with determination and courage. That was the Council's real aim. But in this situation of a Church which wishes to seek and find modern man and does not intend to be a historical relic of sociologically earlier times, the Church has to face quite different and more radical questions than those like the question of a more refined ecclesiology, for instance, which were explicitly posed by the Council. The latest questions are at the same time the oldest and most fundamental for Christianity. First of all the question of God, which requires in answer a theology of all forms of atheism[50] and agnosticism.[51] This question must ask, within a unified transcendental framework that

[47] cf. Nos. 11 and 16.

[48] Details in the extensive study by J. Fuchs, 'Theologia Moralis Perficienda. Votum Concilii Vaticani II', *Periodica de re morali, canonica, liturgica* 55 (1966), pp. 499–548 (literature).

[49] For the diverse results of an ecclesiological self-reflection cf. K. Rahner, *Das neue Bild der Kirche*, pp. 4–7; cf. 'The new image of the Church', *Theological Investigations* X.

[50] Apart from the paper referred to on p. 15 note 34 cf. the whole issue of *Concilium* 3 (1967) (March).

[51] cf. J. B. Metz, 'Unbelief as a Theological Problem', *Concilium* 1 (1965) (June); also, 'Kirche für die Ungläubigen?', *Umkehr und Erneuerung* (cf. p. 16 note 40), pp. 312–329.

yet gives full scope for man's whole essence, about God himself and about the possibility and the 'practice' of a genuine experience of God for modern man,[52] for whom God does not 'exist' 'in' the world.[53] This God-seeking theology must not deny the classical distinction between a metaphysical knowledge of God and the theology of the revelation of God, but must comprehend both and unite them in a new perspective.[54] It must take modern man's distress seriously with his experience – perhaps wrongly interpreted – of the 'absence of God', and must suffer this experience together with him.[55] Theology must not merely demonstrate in the abstract that the contingent character of finite being and the formal transcendence of the intellect imply God, such that experience of this contingence and transcendence implies experience of God.[56] It must inquire more precisely *where* and *how* modern man can so *experience* this that he is enabled to realise genuinely and confidently the objective nature of its implications, without desperately having the impression that he ought to be *silent* about what ultimately eludes language, leaving 'God' – though unexpressed – to the field of the love of one's neighbour, the courage of personal committal to one's own future, or the honest and willing acceptance of a bitter and absurd existence.

Then there is the question of Christ within an evolutionist world view[57] and within the perspective of a salvation-history which embraces the whole of humanity from the very outset, understanding Christ really as the apex of this general history of salvation and revelation.[58] There is the question of a framework of Christological concepts avoiding any under-

[52] cf. K. Rahner, 'Christian living formerly and today', *Theological Investigations* VII (London and New York, 1971), pp. 3 ff.

[53] In detail cf. K. Rahner, 'Science as a "Confession"?', *Theological Investigations* III (London and Baltimore, 1967), pp. 385–400; also, 'The man of today and religion', *Theological Investigations* VI (London and Baltimore, 1969), pp. 3–20; 'Being open to God as ever greater', *Theological Investigations* VII (London and New York, 1971), pp. 25–46.

[54] cf. K. Rahner, 'Bemerkungen zur Gotteslehre in der kath. Dogmatik', *Catholica* 20 (1966), pp. 1–18; cf. in this volume, pp. 127–144.

[55] Besides the papers referred to in note 53, cf. the author's *Im Heute glauben* (Einsiedeln,[3] 1966), pp. 24–31.

[56] For the new shape of such a philosophy of religion cf. B. Welte, *Heilsverständnis* (Freiburg, 1966); also his *Auf der Spur des Ewigen* (Freiburg, 1965), pp. 315–336.

[57] cf. K. Rahner, 'Christology within an evolutionary view of the world', *Theological Investigations* V (London and Baltimore, 1966), pp. 157–192.

[58] cf. the studies referred to on p. 15 note 40. Also E. Schillebeeckx, 'The Church and Mankind', *Concilium* 1 (1965) (January).

tones likely to seem mythological to the ears of modern man,[59] and the search for a method of retracing the progress of the earliest pre-Pauline Christology from the Historical Jesus to the Christ of Faith.

Further, the question arises of an anthropology[60] which should interpret modern man to himself *as he actually experiences himself* in an existence embracing more than the 'animal rationale' of an abstract metaphysics; the question of a Christian anthropology which grasps the original unity of nature and grace[61] and does not banish what we in Christian terms call 'grace' to some region beyond concrete existence,[62] an anthropology which does not simply abandon factors like intercommunication,[63] love, the experience of the absurd,[64] of death,[65] to moral theology or the realm of pious literature.

Finally we must include everything which can come under the heading of dogmatic eschatology. We lack a real hermeneutics[66] of eschatological statements; there must be much more radical thought about the relationship between individual and collective eschatology if our proclamation of the 'last things' is to be really worthy of belief today. The fundamental tenor of modern man's existence by no means exempts him from the danger of falling back into an Old Testament attitude towards the 'beyond'; the hope and postulate of an eternal life for the individual are not common assumptions forming a basis for discussion, as in the time of the

[59] For further details cf. the studies referred to on p. 13 note 24. Cf. K. Rahner, 'I believe in Jesus Christ', this volume, pp. 165–8.

[60] cf. K. Rahner, 'Theologie und Anthropologie', *Wahrheit und Verkündigung. Festschrift für M. Schmaus*, ed. L. Scheffczyk/W. R. Dettloff/R. Heinzmann (Munich, 1967) I, pp. 1389–1407, cf. in this volume pp. 28–45.

[61] A more exhaustive treatment in K. Rahner, *Handbuch der Pastoraltheologie* II/2, pp. 208–228.

[62] cf. K. Rahner, 'Reflections on the experience of Grace', *Theological Investigations* III (London and Baltimore, 1967), pp. 86–90; also his *Alltägliche Dinge* (Einsiedeln, 1966).

[63] Details in the *Handbuch der Pastoraltheologie* II/1, pp. 31 f., 271 f.; 'Reflections on the unity of the love of neighbour and the love of God', *Theological Investigations* VI (London and Baltimore, 1969), pp. 231–249.

[64] cf. *Handbuch der Pastoraltheologie* II/1, pp. 34 ff.; K. Rahner, 'Christlicher Humanismus', *Orientierung* 30 (1966), pp. 116–121, esp. 119 ff., cf. in this volume pp. 187 ff.

[65] Ibid., K. Rahner, 'On Christian dying', *Theological Investigations* VII (London and New York, 1971), pp. 285 ff., cf. also pp. 25–144.

[66] For a first attempt cf. the essay 'The Hermeneutics of Eschatological Assertions', *Theological Investigations* IV (London and Baltimore, 1966), pp. 323–346, cf. also pp. 347–354 and *Theological Investigations* VII (London and New York, 1971), pp. 159–168.

rationalistic Enlightenment, but attitudes into which men of today and tomorrow must first be carefully 'initiated'. Christian eschatology has not yet been obliged to face up sufficiently to the secular and utopian 'eschatology' of the age beginning now, with its view of a single humanity,[67] its 'hominisation' of environment,[68] and man's manipulation of himself[69] – a period in which man's *practice*, as opposed to what was previously his *theory*, appears in a totally new way as his highest and as his specific characteristic. A theology of hope[70] has yet to be developed out of the dry attempts text-books have made concerning the theological Virtue of Hope. We have as yet no theological ontology of hope, showing man as essentially one who exists *in hope*, and whose hope springs from an independent and original source which cannot be explained adequately simply in terms of a knowledge of the organic and evolutionary character of being and its possibilities. Only such a theology of hope as this could really come to grips competently with the Marxist conception of man.

The dialogue desired by the Pastoral Constitution of Vatican II between the world's hope and the hope of Christianity[71] has yet to take place. In short, the subject-matter which the Council has delivered to tomorrow's theology is not the same subject-matter as discussed explicitly by the Council itself (if we exclude the remarks concerning 'the Church in the Modern World'), but the fundamental themes of the

[67] Initial starting-points in K. Rahner, 'Marxist Utopia and the Christian Future of Man', *Theological Investigations* VI (London and Baltimore, 1969), pp. 59–68, cf. also pp. 43–58; *Theological Investigations* V (London and Baltimore, 1966), pp. 135–153; *Handbuch der Pastoraltheologie* II/1, pp. 32 f., 33 f., 254 f.; II/2, pp. 40 ff., 42 ff., 109–202, 275 ff., cf. also supra, note 64.

[68] cf. J. B. Metz, 'Die Zukunft des Glaubens in einer hominisierten Welt', *Weltverständnis im Glauben*, ed. J. B. Metz/J. Splett (Mainz, 1965), pp. 45–62.

[69] For the issues involved cf. K. Rahner, 'Experiment Mensch. Theologisches zur Selbstmanipulation des Menschen', *Die Frage nach dem Menschen. Aufriß einer philosophischen Anthropologie. Festschrift für Max Müller*, ed. H. Rombach (Freiburg, 1966), pp. 45–69, cf. in this volume pp. 205–224 and 225–252.

[70] cf. J. B. Metz, *Verantwortung der Hoffnung* (Mainz, 1968); cf. the author's 'On the theology of hope', *Theological Investigations* X.

[71] cf. p. 7 note 7 and the Pastoral Constitution on the Church in the Modern World, Nos. 85, 90, 92, 43, 3, 25, 21, 19, 56, 40, 23, 28; the Decree on the Church's Missionary Activity, Nos. 20, 16, 41, 11, 38; the Decree on Ecumenism, Nos. 4, 9, 11, 19, 21, 23, 14, 18; the Decree on the Apostolate of the Laity, Nos. 12, 14, 29, 31; the Decree on the Bishops' Pastoral Office in the Church, No. 13; the Declaration on Religious Freedom, No. 3; the Declaration in the Relationship of the Church to Non-Christian Religions, Nos. 2 and 4; the Decree on Priestly Formation, No. 19; the Decree on the Ministry and Life of Priests, No. 19; the Declaration on Christian Education, Nos. 1 and 11.

Christian message upon which rests the whole hierarchically structured edifice of Catholic dogma: i.e., ultimate things concerning man's deepest need and his most exalted vocation. This is what tomorrow's theology must ponder if it is to be a theology worthy of the Council. It must carry this out with a faith which is prepared to be vulnerable,[72] which is continually breaking through the clear definitions of formulas into the incomprehensibility of God,[73] a faith which compels theology to realise that this incomprehensibility is something quite simple and natural.[74]

It would also be good for theologians to consider how one might tell a modern man briefly what it is that Christianity proclaims and offers, yet at the same time in a comprehensible way and in a dynamic formula capable of driving him deeper into the fulness of faith.[75] There is no need for us to wish to replace or lay aside Apostolic Tradition. But practically no-one is taking the considerable pains necessary to correct the present tendency, where, on account of the widely different forms of theology and preaching, modern man cannot see the wood for the trees and thus does not penetrate to the 'fundamentals' of the faith which bear the 'hierarchy of truths',[76] which in turn give meaning and credibility to the whole complex structure of Christian doctrine. There are, or were, such 'short formulas'; they need not necessarily consist of only one sentence or of very few. Probably the earliest authoritative extant examples are 1 Cor 15: 3–5 and 1 Thess 1:9 f.;[77] the most recent can be found in the Decree on the Church's Missionary Activity, No. 13.[78] But much more could be done in this direction, all the more since one must not be in a hurry to regard the formula 'the Word (the Son) of God became man' as being very meaningful or as commending itself to faith nowadays. As a bare formula, devoid of any further explanation, it can be very easily misunderstood, or so abbreviated that it is rejected almost instinctively as

[72] cf. K. Rahner, *Im Heute glauben*, pp. 24–31.

[73] cf. K. Rahner/K. Lehmann, *Mysterium Salutis* I, pp. 689 f., 691 f., 696 ff., 768 f.

[74] cf. the papers referred to on p. 18 notes 52 and 53.

[75] For the need and the point of this kind of short formula, together with a sketch of the essence of faith cf. K. Rahner, *Concilium* 3 (1967) (March), cf. in this volume, pp. 117–126.

[76] cf. the Decree on Ecumenism, No. 11.

[77] For the exegetical import of these credal formulas cf. K. Lehmann, *Auferstanden am dritten Tag* (Freiburg, 1968) (incl. exhaustive literature).

[78] The text runs: '[Yet it is sufficient] that a man realize that he has been snatched away from sin and led into the mystery of the love of God, who has called him to enter into a personal relationship with Him in Christ.' (*The Documents of Vatican II*, ed. Walter M. Abbott, S.J. (London, 1967), p. 600.)

myth. Furthermore it is not safe to assume, in undertaking such a task, that people understand what is really meant when one uses the word 'God'.

VII

It is my opinion that these particular tasks of 'systematic' theology will also result at last in a correct and promising understanding of '*ecumenical* theology'. Of course there must be *direct* ecumenical theology, controversial dialogue,[79] discussing the differences of doctrine between the Christian communions, clearing away misunderstanding, slowly learning to translate the various languages of the disparate theologies into each other, a theological controversy seeking unity and not more and more subtle justification for the disunity of the Churches. Certainly much has already been successfully achieved in this field in the last few decades.

It must be clearly emphasised that we have much to learn, not only from Protestant exegesis and biblical theology, but also from Protestant systematic theology. The task of learning does not only imply that, as far as the traditionally controversial themes are concerned, we must first of all discover *exactly what* the Fathers of Protestantism, its confessions of faith and its present theology precisely mean in all their various nuances; not only must we go beyond the often frighteningly over-simplified representations of Protestant doctrine found too frequently in our textbooks;[80] above and beyond this there is an almost inconceivable wealth of theological questions and studies in Protestant theology concerning subjects which are not directly and explicitly matters of controversy, but which are all the same of greatest importance for theology on both sides. The relationship of word and sacrament or of institution and the occurrence (of grace), or the questions of theological hermeneutics, for instance, are not only, or even primarily, controversial matters on which the churches are divided, but rather themes of mutual concern, where Catholic theology can learn a great deal from Protestant theology and where in certain circumstances the lines of division of opinion cut right across confessional boundaries. In short, Catholic theology must in

[79] Here it is impossible to deal in detail with the change of style of previous controversial theology. Cf. R. Köster's *Luthers These 'Gerecht und Sünder zugleich' in der Interpretation Rudolf Hermanns* (Diss. theol., Innsbruck, 1965), pp. 1–62; also R. Köster, *Zeitschrift für kathol. Theologie* 88 (1966), pp. 121–162 (a revised version of the cited introduction to the dissertation).

[80] Of course the same is true of the other side, as far as Catholic doctrine is concerned.

future be willing to learn from Protestant theology in the area of systematics also. It is obliged to do so by the Council's Ecumenical Decree. In future the names of Protestant theologians should not only occur in our text-books at the point where 'adversarii' and their 'errores' are cited.

All this, if properly understood, is important and must be strongly emphasised here. But if ecumenism in general is only to have a real chance of uniting Christendom by the progress towards one future Church (which a Catholic too may say, who believes in the enduring and obligatory character of his Church's defined dogma and is convinced that the true Church of Christ 'subsists' in the Roman Catholic Church),[81] the same thing applies all the more to ecumenical theology. All churches and Christian communions will only find the same language and a common confession of faith, not in the first place by discussing present doctrinal differences as they have emerged from the past, but by all taking pains to learn the new language of the future which is to serve to proclaim the Gospel of Christ – without over-simplifying superficialities of Robinson's kind[82] – so that tomorrow's man can understand it. Christian theology for today's 'heathen' is also the best ecumenical theology.[83] Naturally efforts are being made in this direction on both sides. But they are insufficient in quantity and quality, at least on the Catholic side. We do not have the 1,000 volumes on 'atheism' which would be needed if we were to justify the innumerable books of Mariology which we do have.

Given all this, we may make a similar observation with regard to the Protestant side. It is precisely the 'orthodox' theology, with which we are most closely concerned, which is in danger of remaining a theology for an ever-diminishing circle of pious believers, and of being preoccupied with the discussion between the various theological alignments within Protestantism and with the ecumenical dialogue, to the neglect of tomorrow's theology for the 'heathen' with whom we in the *diaspora* live. But if *this* theology is pursued by both sides it will be the most hopeful and important branch of an ecumenical theology. Might it not come about, for instance, that when Protestants manage to present the doctrine of

[81] cf. the Dogmatic Constitution on the Church, No. 8, cf. the commentary by Alois Grillmeier, *Commentary on the Documents of Vatican II* (New York and London, 1967) I, pp. 170 f., 199 f., and note 33 (literature). Further K. Rahner, 'Kirche, Kirchen und Religionen', *Theologische Akademie* 3, ed. K. Rahner/O. Semmelroth (Frankfurt, 1966), pp. 70–87, esp. 79 ff., cf. 'Church, churches and religions', *Theological Investigations* X.

[82] For a correct Catholic understanding of the simplicity of faith cf. K. Rahner, *Im Heuteglauben*, pp. 32–42; *Handbuch der Pastoraltheologie* II/1, pp. 142 ff.; II/2, pp. 164 ff.

[83] In more detail cf. K. Lehmann, *Concilium* 3 (1967).

Justification in a form which modern man can really find credible – and I am not denying the burden and difficulty of such a new task – Catholic theologians might be able to give their assent to it? If we Catholics can see more clearly, through a theology in dialogue with modern man, that the question of 'morality' and 'works' is ultimately the question of God, his grace and thus the question of faith, might it not be that the Protestant Christian could come to understand that we Catholics do not after all subscribe to a theology of self-justification, but that for us too 'faith' may be the key word for our relationship with God? If then, instead of justifying the differences and divisions in the Church, conditioned as they are by history, society, psychology and race, by means of increasingly subtle theological distinctions and theories, we determined to strive for a possible common confession of faith, sufficient (though not ignoring the remaining deep differences between the 'schools') for the Church's unity in the matters of Baptism and the Supper of the Lord, and sufficient for a social unity as far as is necessary according to the will of Christ; if the Catholic Christian asked nothing more of the separated brethren than what *genuine* dogma[84] and *ius divinum*[85] demand (and we still await a clear decision in this direction); then one can hope against hope for a unity in the Church embracing all who expressly acknowledge Jesus Christ as Lord.

VIII

We must speak of yet another theology and its future tasks: *practical* theology, usually known to us as 'pastoral theology'. Pastoral theology can no longer be merely a collection of pious recommendations for the simple parish clergy in the holy and effective execution of their office, especially after a Council which intended to be essentially 'pastoral',[86] in which the Church reflected specifically on the novel future she is going forward to meet, and in which there was discussion of the college of bishops, the office of a bishop, bishops' conferences, of the responsibility of the whole Church for mission and of each part of the Church for the whole. Practical theology today must concern itself with the Church's *total* sphere of action, with the help of theological reflection on the

[84] cf. the remarks on p. 4 note 1.

[85] cf. the study mentioned on p. 16 note 42.

[86] For the problems involved in this concept cf. K. Rahner, 'Zur theologischen Problematik einer "Pastoralkonstitution"' (cf. p. 7 note 8) and the author's introduction in K. Rahner/H. Vorgrimler (ed.), *Kleines Konzilskompendium* (Freiburg,[2] 1967), pp. 13–33; also K. Rahner, *Das Konzil – ein neuer Beginn* (Freiburg, 1966).

Church's present situation.[87] If a Council discusses 'the Church in the Modern World' in a special Constitution, theology too must deal with the subject with the greatest thoroughness and clarity and in a truly theological way. So far, however, we do not find this particular theme treated as an explicit topic of theology; the Council of the Church has left its usual theology far behind in this matter. One cannot fail to be aware of this, however critical one may be as to the details of the Pastoral Constitution.

Where else should this theme of the Council's be expressed and where should the questions be brought together, if not in pastoral theology? Indeed, the Constitution's title itself declares this to be the case, and it is also emphasized by the Decree on Priestly Formation, which demands an independent discipline of pastoral theology and also that the latter should permeate and fertilize all other disciplines.[88] Canon *law* alone cannot carry out this task. Not only because its business is more the history and interpretation of *existing* law than the question 'de lege *condenda*', but chiefly because the total activity of the Church is not commensurate with the observation of explicit legal norms, neither with those in force nor with those which should be.[89] In an age of cybernetics, of the great social organizations with their self-regulating controls, questions such as how the Church as a whole is to live and act, how the central authorities in Rome should be constructed, how we should have a strategy of mission and not merely 'tactics', how a diocese should be administered, how we should be influencing the 'politics' of learning and culture with its wide sphere of penetration; all these issues can no longer be entrusted in a paternalistic manner to the wisdom, *savoir faire* and experience of the leading men of the Church.[90] Of course, the decision must be theirs. But the consideration and study necessary *before* the decision, in all questions of the Church's present commission, require nowadays scientific method and systematic execution. We need a pastoral theology which, as far as the scope mentioned here is concerned, does not yet exist. The pastoral Council calls for a new pastoral theology, broader in its compass and deeper in its methods, which, within the enduring statements of

[87] cf. the study referred to on p. 7 note 8 and the author's remarks in the *Handbuch der Pastoraltheologie* II/1, pp. 178–276.

[88] cf. the Decree on Priestly Formation, Chapter VI, Nos. 19–21.

[89] cf. K. Rahner, *Handbuch der Pastoraltheologie* I (Freiburg, 1965), pp. 333–343.

[90] cf. the author's studies: 'Kirchliches Lehramt und Theologie nach dem Konzil', *Stimmen der Zeit* 178 (1966), pp. 404–420; 'Vom Dialog in der Kirche', ibid. 179 (1967), pp. 81–95, both in this volume, pp. 83 ff. and 'Dialogue in the Church', *Theological Investigations* X.

ecclesiology concerning the Church's permanent essence, and enlightened by a theological view of the present situation, seeks to discover at least approximately what are the imperatives which must determine the Church's concrete action as a whole. Practically everything remains yet to be done in this kind of scientific 'practical theology' with its own formal object and its own method.

IX

The Council's 'challenge' to theology is great; greater, no doubt, than the Council fathers themselves realised. This renewal of theology, its *aggiornamento*,[91] should be encouraged by those in authority in the Church as well. Not only by the regional bishops' conferences carrying out the task committed to them by the Council thoroughly and with all speed, and finding and issuing a new *ratio studiorum* for the training of the clergy; not only by the bishops being magnanimous and courageous in providing enough priests for the work of study in spite of the shortage of clergy, which is to some extent real and to some extent imaginary;[92] not only by the bishops encouraging lay theologians above and beyond the requirements for schoolteachers of religion, giving them aims and opportunities for their own theological study, since there is by no means any need for the διδάσκαλοι and the πρεσβύτεροι in the Church to be always the same people;[93] not only by the bishops in their home dioceses maintaining – as far as conditions allow, and in their own interest and in the interest of theology itself – the kind of contact with theologians which they found in Rome (much to the surprise and joy of the theologians and themselves); not only because the Papal Secretariats for Ecumenism, Non-Christian Religions and Modern Atheism can only fulfil their functions as a result of a renewed theology and they should thus help to encourage it; but in a world which has now become a world of science, of 'egg-heads' and specialists, the Church could and ought officially to accept the responsibility of furthering theology in many other ways and institutions of theological study, beyond what has been said here. There is still very

[91] cf. p. 24 note 86.

[92] For this problem cf. the author's indications in N. Greinacher/H. T. Risse (ed.), *Bilanz des deutschen Katholizismus* (Mainz, 1966), pp. 506–508.

[93] For instance, why should there not also be laymen among the professors of the Catholic faculties? Can one debar laymen from exercising functions not necessarily connected with priesthood without betraying the spirit of the Council? Cf. the composite volume referred to in note 92, esp. pp. 504–506.

considerable progress to be made to make Catholic theology international.[94] Since no-one can do everything, why could there not be internationally agreed and arranged centres of special study in theology to the advantage and with the co-operation of the whole of Catholic theology? Could there not be a collection of funds from the whole Church for Catholic theology as for Catholic missions, though on a more modest scale? Could not the contact between Church administration and Church study be closer and institutionally more regulated? Could not the Congregation for the Propagation of the Faith, which arose out of the old Holy Office, *positively* encourage theology by creating 'study commissions' on the more important questions which concern it, and by entrusting them to theologians outside Rome as well, working ideally in a team project?[95] In brief we must ask whether the whole business of theological study in the Church could and must not adopt, in its own way, with less self-consciousness and to a greater degree than hitherto, the sociologically and technically determined organizational forms which have become essential and hence usual in modern science and society.[96]

Programmes and institutions cannot replace men of creativity, least of all in theology. It follows that in the future too, theology will remain the gift of the Spirit to the Church. But he will summon and empower it out of the longings and needs of the times. There must be theology, so that 'the Word of the Lord may speed on and be glorified' (2 Thess 3:1). If theology trusts in the Grace of God and is really one with its mission to tomorrow's world, it will become good theology, achieving what the Council has empowered it to do.

[94] The first-fruits of this kind of concrete co-operation are the international theological journal *Concilium* (1965 ff.) and the lexicon *Sacramentum Mundi* (English edition 1968 ff.).

[95] For instance, when one studies the Council's Constitution on the Sacred Liturgy one may doubt whether the decision of the Holy Office (now the Congregation for the Propagation of the Faith) in 1957 concerning concelebration (*DS* 3928) would have been exactly the same if an *international* commission of expert theologians and liturgists had studied the question seriously *beforehand*.

[96] cf. p. 25 note 90.

2

THEOLOGY AND ANTHROPOLOGY

THIS short paper[1] is intended to show that dogmatic theology today must be theological anthropology and that such an 'anthropocentric' view is necessary and fruitful. The question of man and its answering may not be regarded, therefore, as an area of study separate from other theological areas as to its scope and subject-matter, but as the whole of dogmatic theology itself. This statement does not contradict the 'theocentricity' of all theology as expressed, for instance, in St Thomas' doctrine that God is as such the formal object of revelation theology. As soon as man is understood as the being who is absolutely transcendent in respect of God, 'anthropocentricity' and 'theocentricity' in theology are not opposites but strictly one and the same thing, seen from two sides. Neither of the two aspects can be comprehended at all without the other. Thus, although anthropocentricity in theology is not the opposite of the strictest theocentricity, it *is* opposed to the idea that in theology man is one particular theme among others, e.g. angels, the material world; or that it is possible to say something about God theologically without thereby automatically saying something about man and vice versa; or that these two kinds of statements are connected with one another in respect of their object, but not in the process of knowing itself.

Similarly, this anthropological focus in theology is not opposed to or in competition with a Christological focus. It is not possible to demonstrate this in more detail here; we merely observe that anthropology and Christology mutually determine each other within Christian dogmatics if they are both correctly understood. Christian anthropology is only able to fulfil its whole purpose if it understands man as the *potentia obœdientalis* for the 'Hypostatic Union'. And Christology can only be undertaken from the point of view of this kind of transcendental anthropology; for in order to say today what the 'Hypostatic Union' is without being suspected of merely reproducing no longer feasible 'mythologies', the idea of the God-man needs proof of a transcendental orientation in

[1] cf. the list of sources for the occasion of this paper.

man's being and history under grace.[2] A purely *a posteriori* Christology, unable to integrate Christology correctly into an evolutionary total view of the world,[3] would not find it easy to dismiss the suspicion of propounding mythology.

I

This anthropology is naturally to be understood as a transcendental anthropology. A *transcendental investigation* examines an issue according to the necessary conditions given by the possibility of knowledge and action on the part of the subject himself. Such an investigation presupposes that the subject of the act of knowing is not simply a 'thing' among others which can be made at will the object of a statement including other objects, but which is not present at all – even implicitly – in statements purely about other objects. If I speak of Australia I have not said anything, not even implicitly, about Java. But in such a statement (from the point of view of its content and import) I have said something implicitly about man as its subject (in so far as the statement, in order to be possible at all, necessarily presupposes various things about man). I have expressed and affirmed this by means of subjective implication. Therefore, if one wishes to pursue dogmatics as transcendental anthropology, it means that whenever one is confronted with an object of dogma, one inquires as to the conditions necessary for it to be known by the theological subject, ascertaining that the *a priori* conditions for knowledge of the object are satisfied, and showing that they imply and express something about the object, the mode, method and limits of knowing it.

In general, transcendental investigation does not assume that the material content of the object in question can be adequately deduced from the transcendental conditions whereby it is known by the subject, nor that this content, known *a posteriori*, is unimportant for the subject's existence (his 'salvation') and for the truth of his knowledge. It does not regard this content as in itself merely indifferent material whereby the subject experiences his own *a priori* and necessary being. This applies fundamentally and decisively to a theological transcendental investigation and method as well. For instance, not only is it important for a true Christology to understand man as the being who is orientated towards an 'absolute Saviour' both *a priori* and in actuality (his essence having been

[2] cf. 'On the Theology of the Incarnation', *Theological Investigations* IV (London and Baltimore, 1966), pp. 105–120.

[3] cf. 'Christology within an Evolutionary view of the World', *Theological Investigations* V (London and Baltimore, 1966), pp. 157–192.

elevated and set in this direction supernaturally by grace), but it is equally important for his salvation that he is confronted with Jesus of Nazareth as this Saviour – which cannot, of course, be transcendentally 'deduced'.

On the other hand, to interpret the whole of dogmatic theology as transcendental anthropology means that every dogmatic treatment must also be considered from its transcendental angle, and that one must therefore face the question, what measure of actual material content subsists in the theological subject's *a priori* 'structures' implicit in a particular theological statement? In other words it means that the transcendental side of knowledge must not be overlooked but taken seriously. The problem we mentioned of the relationship between transcendental, *a priori* theology and descriptive, historical and *a posteriori* theology is not solved, of course, by what we have just said. The problem only reveals its depth and acuteness when one is aware of the fact that in theology the final *a priori* precondition for the subject's theological knowledge, i.e. grace (ultimately the self-communicating God, acting freely in history) is the real content, or rather, the objective foundation of what is known and experienced *a posteriori* in history. One finds that in theology the *a priori* character of the subject and the *a posteriori* quality of the historical object enjoy an exclusive and unique relationship. But we must return to this matter later.

Let us illustrate what we have outlined in the abstract with a few small examples chosen at random.

Theology discusses angels. In this it bases itself on the Old and New Testaments. Traditional academic theology speaks of these angels as of any other objects and phenomena. Certain things are said about them in the scriptural revelation; therefore there are angels. By collating and systematizing the data of scripture an angelology can be developed in the same way that one speaks of anything else of which one has somehow acquired knowledge. If it had so happened that God had not revealed it, then there would be no angelology; but since it has pleased him to reveal it, as he might have revealed innumerable other facts which remain hidden from us (e.g. whether there are body-soul creatures, possessed of 'sanctifying' grace, on other stars), we do have an angelology (but no theology of extra-terrestrial embodied intelligences). A modern man will ask first of all what this utterly strange angel-lore has to do with him, since angels do not occur in his scientific sphere of experience; for what purpose God is supposed to have communicated this knowledge, and whether it is credible at all. Scandalized, he will be driven to examine the course of history of this so-called revelation, and will be tempted to conclude that the remarks about angels in the Old Testament (upon which the New Testament depends) do not give the impression of having been communicated from heaven, but of having drifted into the minds of the Old Testament theologians from their cultural and religious environment. Now into this situation of tension between traditional angelology and scepticism of it, a transcendental theological anthropology is to be introduced. I.e. the question must be asked: where in man's theological understanding of himself is there an area which might be occupied by such a thing as an angelology? What kind of theological self-understanding on the part of man finds expression in angelology? In other words: if we assume heuristically that revelation tells man whence he comes and what he is in the present and future, and *only* this, can it be made intelligible from this that an angelology belongs within such a revelation? Perhaps what is really expressed in revelation is not the existence and nature of angels as such at all, but man's relationship with them. Angels are assumed as given (and for the moment we may leave it as an open question whether this assumption is affirmed as a proposition or propounded as a hypothesis in anthropological revelation as such). We are not concerned here to show how and within what limits an angelology can be developed from such a starting-point.[4] It is only our intention to demonstrate by means of an essentially small and recondite example what is the significance of this kind of anthropological emphasis and focus in dogmatic theology.

Let us take another example. The doctrine of the Trinity cannot easily be elicited from scripture if one is precise in one's biblical theology.[5] When the doctrine is presented in pure objectivity, the listener often wonders what it means, how he can understand any of it at all, and why it has been revealed for the purpose of his salvation; for it seems to him like a subtle, dialectical game with concepts, in which each proposition appears to eliminate every other one, and in which one can scarcely gather what is left intact in any proposition apart from various words (provided that, in attending to one proposition, one does not forget a large part of what the others contained, and thus understand it in what is from the point of view of controversial dialectic an inadmissible way). Simply to claim that one is concerned here with a mystery, and that the doctrine

[4] For a starting-point for an angelology cf. the article 'Angelologie' in *LThK* I (Freiburg,[2] 1957) cols. 533–538.

[5] cf. recently the comprehensive work of F. J. Schierse, 'Die neutestamentliche Trinitätsoffenbarung', *Mysterium Salutis* II (Einsiedeln, 1967), pp. 85–131.

of the Trinity is necessary in order to be able to make any Christological statement, is on its own insufficient to help us out of the situation. For even in the case of a mystery one must understand *why* there is *more* to it than merely an occasion for a *sacrificium intellectus* in the face of a formula of apparently unintelligible verbalisms.[6] Nor is it convincing to appeal to Christology if one considers that since Augustine academic theology has assumed unhesitatingly that any divine person can exercise a hypostatic function in a human nature; consequently we are saying very little if, when speaking of *God's* incarnation, we emphasise that it takes place through the *Logos*, whose hypostatic function *per se*, under these presuppositions, cannot be distinguished in any way from any other divine person's possible function.[7]

However, if the anthropocentric perspective is applied to the doctrine of the Trinity, many things become more intelligible without at the same time destroying the mystery. We need only make the quite legitimate assumption that, on account of God's absolute *self*-communication in 'uncreated' Grace, the immanent Trinity is strictly identical with the economic Trinity and vice versa,[8] and we are then able to read the doctrine of the Trinity 'anthropologically' without falsifying it. In other words if we presuppose that our relationship with God, formed by grace (including its concrete appearance in salvation history), has a directly trinitarian structure; that it is always a relationship with the inconceivable God; that it is communicated by the appearance in history of God's absolute self-committal in Jesus; that this self-committal 'comes home' to us as Love at the innermost centre of our being, without losing its strictly divine character; that the consequent trinitarian structure of our direct relationship with God through grace is also proper to God because of his actual self-communication – if we assume this, then the *permanent* mystery of the '*immanent*' Trinity is made possible.[9] This frees us from the impression of a dialectic of mere conceptual subtleties and renders it intelligible to us why that mystery had to be revealed at that particular moment in the history of revelation, when revelation had progressed to

[6] For a correct conception of mystery cf. 'The Concept of Mystery in Catholic Theology', *Theological Investigations* IV (London and Baltimore, 1966), pp. 36–73.

[7] For more details cf. K. Rahner, 'Current Problems in Christology', *Theological Investigations* I, pp. 149–200, but especially the article mentioned in note 2.

[8] In more detail cf. 'Remarks on the Dogmatic Treatise "De Trinitate" ', *Theological Investigations* IV (London and Baltimore, 1966), pp. 77–102.

[9] For a deeper foundation for a starting-point for speculative trinitarian doctrine the author refers to his more extensive contribution in *Mysterium Salutis* II (Einsiedeln, 1967), pp. 317–401.

the express awareness that the perfect gift of salvation is not only a gift from God by God, but is God himself. It is also no bad thing that according to this sort of understanding of the Trinity our relation in grace to the three divine Persons does not mean merely an 'appropriation'[10]; incarnation and man's divinisation through grace are more closely related than academic theology usually teaches. It is a further recommendation for this approach to the doctrine of the Trinity that it excludes right from the beginning the impression (which persists in spite of its explicit rejection in academic doctrine) that each divine 'Person' has a distinct centre of consciousness in respect of knowledge and freedom and that this is the real meaning of the word 'Person' in trinitarian doctrine as well.[11] It is not our intention here to develop a doctrine of the Trinity. The example merely illustrates what significance a transcendental anthropological approach can have in all topics of dogma, even in areas where one might perhaps least suspect its fruitfulness.

II

We must be content with these two examples and now turn to ask *why* this anthropological change of direction in theology is *necessary*. There are fundamental reasons from the nature of the case, i.e. from theology and its object. Besides this there are reasons from the contemporary situation and reasons of basic theology and apologetics.

1. First of all the *reasons* or reason from the nature of the case. As a consequence of the nature of every occurrence of intellectual (and hence also theological) knowledge, the question of the object of such knowledge raises at the same time the question as to the nature of the knowing subject. This inextricable interrelation of the 'objective' and 'subjective' side of knowledge does not need, of course, to be discussed or to be equally explicit in every sphere of study. A concrete discipline in natural science does not have to investigate its philosophical foundation as well: the latter is concerned with the mode of being and structure of the subject who is concretely engaged in science. But where the study of a particular field becomes really 'philosophical' in a specific sense – and theology must

[10] For the basic problems cf. 'Some Implications of the Scholastic Concept of Uncreated Grace', *Theological Investigations* I, pp. 319–346.

[11] For the issues involved in the concept of *person* cf. *Theological Investigations* I, pp. 156 ff.; but in the first instance the contribution to *Mysterium Salutis* II to which we have already referred, esp. pp. 385 ff.

do this of its very essence – every question concerning any object whatever also formally implies the question of the knowing subject.

A question is first stated philosophically by being put formally as the question concerning a particular object as such in the *totality* of reality and truth, for it is only in this way that the highest reasons, the philosophical ones, are sought out. If this is done, the subject is also investigated, not only because it is a 'material' part of the totality, but because the totality (as that to which man is transcendentally orientated) can only exist in the subject as such according to the latter's own subjective uniqueness. The philosophical question as to a particular object is necessarily the question as to the knowing subject, because *a priori* the subject must carry with it the limits of the possibility of such knowledge. Thus the 'transcendental' structures of the object are already determined *a priori*. A really *theological* question can only be put, however, if it is understood as being simultaneously a philosophical one in the sense we have shown. For it is only a theological question as long as it sees the individual object with its origin in and orientation towards God.

But God is not one object among others in the realm of man's *a posteriori* knowledge but the fundamental ground and the absolute future[12] of all reality.

As such he can only be understood as the absolute point of man's transcendental orientation. Thus every theology of this kind is necessarily transcendental anthropology; every *onto*logy is onto*logy*.

If one wishes to avoid falling into a heretical and positivistic fideism, what has been said must be applied also to revealed theology. Revealed theology has the human spirit's transcendental and limitless horizon as its inner motive and as the precondition of its existence. It is only because of this transcendental horizon that something like 'God' can be understood at all. 'Natural', 'philosophical' theology is first and last not one sphere of study side by side with revealed theology, as if both could be pursued quite independently of each other, but an internal factor of revealed theology itself;[13] if philosophical theology, however, is transcendental anthropology, so is revealed theology too.

However, the thesis in question can be given a still more direct theo-

[12] For the concept of the absolute future cf. *Theological Investigations* VI (London and Baltimore, 1969), pp. 59 ff.

[13] cf. K. Rahner, 'Philosophy and Theology', *Theological Investigations* VI (London and Baltimore, 1969), pp. 71–81; for this question the studies by H. Bouillard are also of importance. In addition to his great work on Barth and his introduction to Blondel, cf. his *Logik des Glaubens* (Freiburg, 1966).

logical basis. Firstly, revelation is revelation of salvation and therefore theology is essentially salvation theology. What is revealed and then pondered upon in theology is not an arbitrary matter, but something which is intended for man's salvation. By this statement we do not imply the sort of principle (as in the case of a 'fundamentalism') according to which certain objects can be excluded at the outset from the sphere of possible revelation, for what salvation really is is determined materially for the first time in the event of revelation. But the statement must be taken seriously. Only those things can belong to man's salvation which, when lacking, injure his 'being' and wholeness. Otherwise he could eschew salvation without thereby being in danger of losing it. This does not entail a rationalistic and unhistorical reduction of man to the status of an abstract transcendental being in his merely formal structure as such, as if what is historical and not deducible and what is experienced concretely *a posteriori* had no significance for salvation. It means that everything of significance for salvation is to be illuminated by referring it back to this transcendental being (which is not the same as *deducing* the significance *from* the transcendental being). In this sense, 'reduction' does not mean diminution but the process of establishing by reflex investigation. A comparison may clarify what is meant: the concrete beloved person who is the object of my love and in whom it is realized (and without whom it does not exist) cannot be deduced *a priori* from human possibilities, but is rather a historical occurrence, an indissoluble fact which has to be accepted. But in spite of this, such love for this concrete person can only be understood when one comprehends man as the being who must of necessity fulfil himself in love in order to be true to his nature. Even the most unpredictable, concrete love, occurring in history, must therefore be understood transcendentally in this way, in order that it may be what it should be. And this applies above all in the case of salvation. For even if this is a historical event, what it concerns is precisely man's actual nature; it is his nature which is to be consummated in salvation or the loss of it. If revelation and theology are essentially concerned with salvation as such, theology's structure when confronted with any object whatsoever is bound to imply the question as to man's nature, in so far as this nature is susceptible to 'saving' influence from the object involved. In other words, a theological object's significance for salvation (which is a necessary factor in any theological object) can only be investigated by inquiring at the same time as to man's *saving receptivity for* this object. However, this receptivity must not be investigated only 'in the abstract' nor merely presupposed in its most general aspects. It must be reflected upon with reference to the concrete object concerned, which is only *theologically relevant* as a result of and for the purpose of this receptiveness for salvation. Thereby the object also to some extent lays down the conditions for such receptiveness.

In addition to these more formal considerations there is a decisive and clearly outlined issue. The Council's Decree on Ecumenism emphasises that not all articles of faith in the 'hierarchy' of truths are equally close to the 'fundamentals' of the Christian Faith.[14] Thus according to the Council there is a foundation, an inner core in the reality of faith, to which all other realities (and articles of faith) are related. In the nature of the case this 'foundation' can only be God himself in so far as he is our salvation through his absolute self-communication, i.e. what we in theology usually call 'uncreated grace'. Salvation is mediated exclusively in and through this grace. Grace must therefore belong at least to the core of the salvation/revelation reality. If grace and the Trinity are understood, the reality of the triune God as such is given as well. For a full understanding of this grace another important condition must be presupposed: this grace is the grace of *Christ* (and he is not merely external to it as the reason for its being conferred), even in the case of prelapsarian grace. At the same time this means that, within the history of grace (as the self-communication of God acting freely in history), the history of humanity has come *in Christ* to its own historical and eschatological apogee, irreversibly manifested. If Trinity and Incarnation are implicit in the mystery of grace, it becomes intelligible that grace not only *belongs to* the core of the salvation/revelation reality, but *is* this core. (Of course the same could be said of the Trinity, especially *qua* 'economic' Trinity, and also of Christ as the apogee of God's self-communication to the world, precisely because these three realities mutually imply each other.)

Now it is only possible to speak of this grace in a meaningful way at all within a transcendental anthropological context. For, without destroying the fact that grace is God himself in self-communication, grace is not a 'thing' but – as communicated grace – a conditioning of the spiritual and intellectual subject as such to a direct relationship with God. The most objective reality of salvation is at the same time necessarily the most subjective: the direct relationship of the subject with God through God himself. If what 'grace' is must not merely be expressed in a mythological-sounding verbalism which communicates no experience, it can only be understood from the point of view of the subject, with his transcendental

[14] The Decree on Ecumenism, No. 11.

nature, experienced as a being-in-reference-to the reality of absolute truth and free-ranging, infinite, absolutely valid love. It can only be understood in one's innermost regions as an immediacy before the absolute mystery of God, i.e. as the absolute realisation of man's transcendental nature itself, made possible by God in his self-communication.[15]

Without an ontology of the transcendental subject a theology of grace (and hence all theology whatsoever) remains fixed in a pre-theological picture-language and cannot give evidence of a starting-point for transcendental experience. This transcendental experience is indispensable today if theology is to do justice to modern man's question as to whether all the talk of 'Divinization', 'Sonship', 'God's Indwelling' etc. is not merely poetic concepts and indemonstrable mythology. Let us emphasise once more that this transcendental direction in the theology of grace means a similar direction for the whole of theology. For today even ontic Christology itself (in spite of its abiding validity) urgently needs translating into an onto-logical Christology, i.e. one which at the outset understands the 'nature' to be assumed not as a thing but as a transcendental spiritual quality. Since nature and being not only 'has', but *is* actuality and transcendence, the substantial unity with the Logos must be basically expressible in the terms of actuality and transcendence. It must be translated into these terms in order that what is meant by the 'Hypostatic Union' is said really clearly enough and is sufficiently protected from being misunderstood as mythology. All theology stands in need of this transcendental and anthropological change of direction because all theology is dependent upon the mutually determining doctrines of the Trinity, Grace and Incarnation, and these three basic doctrines today fundamentally require a transcendental approach.

2. A considerable objection could be made against what has been said: if it really is so necessary for all theology, surely there must always have been this kind of transcendental anthropological programme and method of investigation? – for good theology has not emerged today for the first time. Since, however, there has clearly been no such investigation, the demand for it cannot be legitimate.

First of all we must draw attention to the very basic difference between proclamation and theology, although in practice proclamation always contains an element of theological reflection,[16] and conversely theology

[15] cf. the article 'Gnade', *LThK* IV (Freiburg,[2] 1964), cols. 991–1000; also 'Selbstmitteilung Gottes', *LThK* IX (Freiburg,[2] 1964), col. 627.

[16] cf. K. Rahner/K. Lehmann, *Mysterium Salutis* I (Einsiedeln, 1965), pp. 634 ff., 661 ff.; K. Rahner, *Handbuch der Pastoraltheologie* II/1 (Freiburg, 1966), pp. 135–142.

can never adequately transmute the proclamation into theological reflection.[17] Modern theological eschatology for instance has been left behind almost totally in a pre-theological stage of proclamation. By and large the ecclesiology of Vatican II has still not progressed beyond a certain systematization of biblical picture-language, apart from particular sections on Constitutional Law. Seen from this point of view it is by no means *a priori* impossible that there is as yet no really scientific, i.e. transcendentally reflected theology in many areas and topics. Why should it be impossible? The fact that there is a lot of thinking, talking, writing and 'systematizing' in some way or other in theology (and this is all good and laudable in itself) is no proof that theology has reached that stage of conceptualisation and reflection which must differentiate it from proclamation. This qualitative difference only really occurs, however, where and in so far as there is expressly transcendental thought, i.e. where the *a priori* presuppositions for knowledge and realisation of the particular realities of faith are explicitly included in one's reflections, determining the choice of terms for theological objects.

At the same time we by no means wish to imply that this transcendental anthropological method has been utterly absent from theology until now. There can be no question of that. We cannot give detailed examples here to show how this transcendental method has been at work everywhere in theology (even if in different intensities), at least since St Thomas, even if it had not yet become completely aware of itself nor comprehended itself explicitly in formal principles.[18]

But in the end, whatever the historical facts may have been, we must say that today's *contemporary situation* demands a transcendental anthropological programme and method. Plato, Aristotle and Thomas will remain immortal philosophers from whom we must learn. But this does not alter the fact (even if the kind of philosophy studied in the Church has only taken notice of it in the last forty years or so) that philosophy today and hence theology too *cannot* and must not return to the stage before modern philosophy's transcendental anthropological change of direction since Descartes, Kant, German Idealism (including its opponents), up to modern Phenomenology, Existentialism and Fundamental Ontology. With few exceptions, e.g. Blondel, it can be said that this whole philosophy is most profoundly un-Christian in so far as it pursues a transcendental philosophy of the autonomous subject, who stands aloof from the tran-

[17] For the concept of *kerygma* cf. *Mysterium Salutis* I, pp. 622 ff.

[18] For Thomas Aquinas cf. the outline by J. B. Metz, *Christliche Anthropozentrik* (Munich, 1962), my introduction, pp. 9–20.

scendental experience in which he experiences himself as continually dependent, with his origin in and orientation towards God. But this same philosophy is also most profoundly Christian (more than its traditional critics in modern scholastic professional theology have grasped), for according to a radically Christian understanding man is not ultimately one factor in a cosmos of things, subservient to a system of co-ordinate ontic concepts drawn from it, but the subject on whose freedom as subject hangs the fate of the whole cosmos: otherwise salvation-history and profane history could have no cosmological significance, and Christological cosmology would be infantile concept-poetry. This inner dividedness is, however, not only a symptom of modern philosophy but of all man's works, and hence a symptom of philosophy in all ages; we must not let it hinder us from seeing what is Christian in this significant epoch of modern culture. We must accept the situation in all its fundamental essence, as a factor henceforward indispensable in a modern Christian philosophy, and so too in modern Christian theology.

Perhaps it might be said that the 'modern period' to which this transcendental anthropology is especially adapted is already a thing of the past or in process of decline together with its philosophy.[19] There may be a little or a great deal of truth in that. But philosophies do not change like fashions; each philosophy disappears into the succeeding philosophy of a new period of history and thus retains what is most characteristic of it.[20] If it is the case that Christian Neo-Scholastic Philosophy, together with theology, have been mostly asleep during the modern period, they cannot be spared the task set by modern philosophy on the grounds that perhaps this philosophy is declining in its contemporary form: the lost ground must be at least made up if theology is really to do justice to the spirit of the age which is to *follow* the 'modern period'. This is particularly applicable since a conjectured future philosophy corresponding with the constitution of tomorrow's society will have its roots in a part of German Idealism, perhaps in the Hegelianism of the Left and its critique of ideology. If the topics treated in the coming philosophy are hope, society, the critique of ideology, a new form of freedom within a new social bond, the experience of God in man's experience of planning himself etc., philosophy's theme will have become once again man and his being which he has submitted to planning and thus also to the

[19] Naturally this thesis of R. Guardini's *Ende der Neuzeit* (Würzburg, 1950) cannot be discussed here.

[20] H. Rombach demonstrates well that this series of events is a true characteristic of modern philosophy, *Die Gegenwart der Philosophie* (Freiburg,[2] 1964).

unpredictable future.[21] Therefore, seen from tomorrow's particular and local form of philosophy, the change to a transcendental anthropology constitutes a challenge for today's and tomorrow's theology.

3. Finally we must try to find a basis for this challenge from the point of view of apologetics and theological fundamentals. The tendency towards 'demythologisation' in Protestant theology and elsewhere stems from a serious concern, and with all its premature, heretical and unacceptable characteristics it is aiming at a theology which we shall need in the future (and of which we have an insufficient amount up to now), if the ancient and abiding Gospel is to be preached in a form sufficiently worthy of belief.[22] It can be said (and in part justly) that demythologisation theology is a new edition of the old theological Liberalism and Rationalism. But have we applied ourselves enough to the genuine topics and concerns of this rationalistic, liberal theology? That is the real question. Both we and orthodox Protestant theology have been satisfied too readily with the idea that the Barthian school has despatched the liberal school in Protestant theology. Although a great many individual themes of Barth's great work will remain, it is Bultmann who has triumphed over Barth on the whole in European Protestant theology.[23] And that is not merely an unjust and tragic accident in the history of ideas.

Modern man feels that thousands of statements in theology are just forms of mythology and that he is no longer able to believe them in all seriousness. Of course this is ultimately false, but there are real reasons behind the impression. It is due not merely to pride and stupidity on the subjective side, and objectively to the mysterious quality of the truth and reality of faith. Let us look dispassionately at today's real cultural situation: if a modern man who has not been brought up as a Christian hears the words 'Jesus is God made man' he will straight away reject this explanation as mythology which he cannot begin to take seriously nor to discuss, just as we do when we hear that the Dalai Lama regards himself as a reincarnation of Buddha. If this modern man hears of two people

[21] I have dealt in more detail with the problem raised here in 'Experiment Mensch. Theologisches zur Selbstmanipulation des Menschen', *Die Frage nach dem Menschen. Festschrift für Max Müller zum 60. Geburtstag*, ed. H. Rombach (Freiburg, 1966), pp. 45–69, cf. in this volume, pp. 205 ff.

[22] For this simplicity of faith cf. K. Rahner, *Im Heute glauben* (Einsiedeln,[3] 1966), pp. 32 ff.

[23] This over-simplification is intended only as a rough observation of what has happened: consequently it by no means excludes the possibility of attempts at a rapprochement of both theologies, especially if they are both progressing towards a larger totality. (Cf. the works of E. Jüngel and others, for instance.)

dying in similar state and condition, and one is said to go straight to heaven because he happens to be the recipient of a Papal Indulgence, whereas the other spends many years in Purgatory because the Pope, as Keeper of the Keys of Heaven, has not opened up straight away; he will regard Indulgences, represented in this way, as a clerical invention against which his own idea of God radically protests. It will not be easy to convince him that God desires the salvation of all men, including children dying while not responsible for themselves, even *after* the Fall, and yet is unable to allow children dying unbaptised to approach his face because he cannot dispense with his own rule of the necessity of Baptism.

One could multiply these examples at length. There ought not to be so many. Furthermore, it does not seem to me that theology has dealt with these countless difficulties in a sufficiently intellectual way; above all, not in a way which holds out much promise for the practice of religious education. Let us repeat that in apologetics it is little or no use appealing in a positivistic manner to the 'mystery' actually revealed by God. If the *fact* of a verbal revelation were psychologically so absolutely compelling that doubts were utterly impossible, one could impose acceptance of its content in this positivistic manner as a mystery beyond all discussion. But if modern man finds the *content* of revelation unworthy of belief through the fault of theology, he will think himself justified, not illogically, in further doubting the *fact* of revelation. Incidentally these remarks show that we need to strive for a much larger area of mobility for fundamental theology and dogmatics than is usually the case.[24] All these difficulties of modern man can be traced to a common formal structure: theological statements are not formulated in such a way that man can see how what is meant by them is connected with his understanding of himself, as witnessed to in his own experience.

Of course one cannot demand (and it would be heretical Modernism to do so) that the attempt must be made simply to deduce strictly all theological statements *from* man's experience of himself as if they were the latter's objectifying conceptualisation and articulation. That is not what is meant, although this problem is more difficult than the traditional opponents of Modernism mostly think,[25] for there *is* also an *experience* of grace,[26] and this is the real, fundamental reality of Christianity itself.

[24] cf. esp. K. Rahner, *Theological Investigations* VI (London and Baltimore, 1969), pp. 123–131, 132 ff.; *Im Heute glauben*, pp. 39 ff.; 'Intellectual honesty and Christian faith', *Theological Investigations* VII (London and New York, 1971), pp. 47–71.

[25] cf. K. Rahner/K. Lehmann, *Mysterium Salutis* I, pp. 657 ff.

[26] cf. *Theological Investigations* III (London and Baltimore, 1967), pp. 86–90.

If we leave this question here, it must be remembered that the connections between man's experience of himself and the content of the statements of dogma must be conceived otherwise than simply as logical connections of deduction or explication.[27] There are correspondences, above all by virtue of the fact that 'nature' – understood as personal, intellectual and transcendental – is an inner and necessary constituent not abstractly of grace *per se*, but of the actuality and process by which grace can be conferred. If these connections were uncovered and thought about as the subject-matter required by dogma, rightly understood, dogmatic statements would not only appear more worthy of belief from the point of view of religious education and doctrine; rather, thorough reflection on these correspondences would enable one to penetrate deeper and more effectively to the significance of particular statements and would lead to the elimination of latent misunderstandings, unsuitable schemes of presentation and unjustified conclusions. The discovery of such connections between the content of dogma and man's experience of himself is, in actual fact however, nothing else but the required change to a transcendental anthropological method in theology. Thus today's demand for it is founded on reasons of fundamental theology and apologetics.[28]

III

What are the consequences for theology which will result from the fulfilment of the demand for a theology along transcendental anthropological lines? In conclusion we shall answer this question by reference to a few examples. Above all, by using this method it would be at last more possible to arrive at a credible idea of the process of revelation in its recipient. For it is a very strange thing that the kind of fundamental theology common today has such an indefinite idea of the nature of the process of revelation in the prophet himself, except in so far as it represents the process as a 'miracle' instead of a 'sign' and thereby renders it unintelligible why there should be so many parallels to it in analogous phenomena in the history of religion. The method we are recommending could do much in this field: the transcendental deduction of man as the one who listens to God in history;[29] insight into the fact (and the reason

[27] For a factual account cf. K. Rahner/K. Lehmann, *Mysterium Salutis* I, pp. 756 ff.

[28] cf. 'The Second Vatican Council's Challenge to Theology', in this volume, pp. 3 ff.

[29] In more detail, K. Rahner, *Hörer des Wortes* (Munich,[2] 1963).

behind it) that the Word of God can always appear only as a heard and believed word and yet can remain the Word of *God.*[30] Another significant theme, which we shall refer to in a moment, is the understanding of salvation-history with reference to man. It is also worth mentioning in particular the understanding and the correct appraisal of the true nature of the 'sign' (including its distinctness from the 'miracle'). If *salvation-history* is necessary for salvation, theology must discuss the theme of man's *a priori* transcendental character as being within and subject to salvation-history, in the same way that history determines the philosophy of history and the latter is even an element of the former. But so far there is as good as no theology of man's 'salvation-historicity' in professional theology: salvation-history is recounted, but there is no reflection upon its formal structures and, above all, upon its transcendental necessity.[31]

We alluded previously to the significance of this method for the doctrine of the Trinity and for Christology, so we shall not go into it in any more detail here. Because there is in professional theology still largely a lack of a theology of salvation-history and of man's transcendental salvation-historicity, the necessary presuppositions for an *ecclesiology* adequate for today are also lacking. The foundation of the Church in its formal authority and structure is usually treated almost as if God could have founded this Church at any time at all, had he wanted to. In academic ecclesiology the eschatological and salvation-historical position and function of the Church, so essential to its whole character, is scarcely considered. There is no understanding of such an eschatological phase of salvation-history, however, because there is to a large extent no transcendental reflection upon salvation-historicity and the resultant phases of salvation-history. For instance, how can one make it credible that we now have an infallible Pope, if humanity and God together in their common concern for the good of all men were able to manage successfully without such an infallible source of truth for perhaps two million years? Historical changes which are of importance for salvation are only credible if it can expressly be made intelligible that man must have a salvation-history as a result of his very nature, i.e. that, as in other respects, it is not only a matter of the permanently valid essential structures alone as such, but that also in respect of salvation man is connected with concrete history and its succeeding phases. From this point of view it might be possible to distinguish more clearly the true nature of this kind of

[30] cf. 'Wort Gottes', *LThK* X (Freiburg,[2] 1965), cols. 1235–1238

[31] cf. the sketch by A. Darlap, *Mysterium Salutis* I, pp. 3–153.

ecclesiastical infallibility from its perverted form which, like all reality in the human sphere, inevitably and perpetually accompanies it.

No further explanation is needed to make it clear that a good ecclesiology needs all those concepts which can only be acquired suitably as a result of a transcendental analysis of the essence and necessity of human intercommunication. The method we suggest has a large and important field of application in the doctrine of the sacraments too. How else is one to investigate adequately the nature of the symbol, the ability to act as symbol, the necessity of symbols, the basic concept of sign-causality, the nature of the symbol's function in intercommunication, in order thereby to create important principles for the doctrine of the sacraments and for understanding it? If it were clear in the doctrine of grace that grace does not have a character as 'thing' but an onto-logical character – as the condition of willed personal acts in relation to the immediacy of God – it would be more clearly grasped than is commonly the case in the doctrine of the sacraments that infant Baptism should not be taken as the basic model of a sacrament. It would emerge that a sacrament is God's enduring offer to man's transcendental nature, mediated through the historical and symbolical categories of intercommunication, of participation in his (God's) freedom in the concrete decision-making of his existence. Then it would be clear that sacraments really do have nothing to do with magic. Meaningful principles for the frequency of receiving the sacraments could be developed, the number seven could be more easily justified – which cannot really be demonstrated easily in a purely positivistic and historical way. It could also be made clear for instance that Indulgences cannot be thought of as taking effect in any other way but by a more intensive and radical love of man, slowly integrating man's whole being into itself.

If we set aside Faith, Hope and Love on the one hand and the positive commands of the Church on the other, we see that the major part of *moral theology* is obliged to concern itself with what we are accustomed to call 'natural law'. Irrespective of how we are to determine the precise relationship between this natural law and grace, in any case it is only possible to justify natural law from within, by means of a transcendental deduction of the nature of man and – furthermore – of his fundamental setting in a historical situation with its unique claims on him. It cannot be done by a purely *a posteriori* collating of factual particulars and conditions of man's individual and social existance, even if they are ascertained to be of 'general' occurrence. For not everything that *is*, nor even everything that is or seems to be *general*, is automatically what *must be.*[32] Particularly in moral theology a transcendental anthropological theology would be able to gain insights of considerable practical importance, especially (though not exclusively!) in the matter of eliminating claims which pose illegitimately as natural law.

In order to be equal to today's demands *eschatology* needs the foundation provided by a transcendental anthropology, in which man is comprehended as the being who plans himself, looking forward to an open future, as the being who *hopes*, empowered by God to embrace an absolute future. It is only this kind of transcendental anthropological and formal futurology which can provide explicit hermeneutic principles which are needed today to interpret eschatological assertions,[33] if the latter are to appear worthy of belief. It seems to me that academic eschatology is still not far enough beyond the mentality of the professor of dogmatics who says he never maintained that the Archangel Michael's judgment-trumpet was a 'tuba materialis' but he would certainly defend the view that the sound of this trumpet was a 'tonus materialis'. Instead of really being theology, which always essentially involves criticism of images and models, academic eschatology is often a sort of puzzle in which one tries to unite into a single picture the images of scripture, which cannot be so fitted together in a plastic form, neither do they claim as much. A transcendental foundation of eschatology would reveal that eschatology is not an anticipatory report of the phenomenal aspects of future events, revealed by a God who already witnesses them, but the necessary interpretation, inescapably integral to man's nature, of his present existence – eschatologically subject to grace – within the perspective of its absolute future.

There is no need to add to these observations. They were meant only to open up the view of those tasks which are automatically set by the demand for an anthropological perspective in theology. At the same time we eliminated the possible and manifest misunderstanding that this anthropological transcendental understanding of theology implies a *material* reducing of theological doctrine generally. The theology we have described surrenders no really obligatory assertions. But it becomes a little more modest in the face of its own commission. In spite of all the hard thought which may be involved in it, it will ultimately become 'simpler' again. Only thus will it enter into the correct relationship with the constantly valid kerygma. What is essential remains.

[32] cf. the essay referred to on p. 41 note 24, esp. pp. 56 ff.

[33] cf. 'The Hermeneutics of Eschatological Assertions', *Theological Investigations* IV (London and Baltimore, 1966), pp. 323–346.

3

PHILOSOPHY AND PHILOSOPHISING IN THEOLOGY

THE subject under discussion is so difficult and extends over such a wide area that it is not possible to do justice to it and produce a well-rounded discussion in this small compass.[1] We can only take up certain points; whether what is said here is particularly important and relevant must remain a matter capable of question.

We shall not therefore concern ourselves with the old questions, e.g. the fundamental relationship of philosophy and theology, their distinctness and interrelation;[2] the meaning and the limits of an autonomous philosophy and a 'Christian Philosophy';[3] the possibility and obligation of being a believing theologian and at the same time a philosopher; the historical origins of modern philosophy (seen as man's transcendental and existential-ontological interpretation of himself) in Christianity, etc. All these individual questions would lead back, in theology, to the wider question of the relationship of nature and grace (including of course the further question whether this traditional way of setting the problem is the basic one and one which is appropriate today),[5] and this implies the question of the liberation of the secular in its secular autonomy,[5] i.e. the fundamental constitution of the relation of nature and grace by God, who not merely gives, but *is* grace. In reducing the problem to these

[1] cf. the list of sources at the end of this volume.

[2] cf. the author's 'Philosophy and Theology', *Theological Investigations* VI (London and Baltimore, 1969), pp. 71–81. Also cf. principally G. Ebeling, 'Theologie und Philosophie' I–III, *RGG* VI (Tübingen,[3] 1962), 782–830 (literature).

[3] For this concept cf. J. B. Metz, *LThK* II (Freiburg,[2] 1958), cols. 1141–1147 (literature).

[4] cf. K. Rahner, 'Concerning the relationship between Nature and Grace', *Theological Investigations* I, pp. 297–317; 'Nature and Grace', *Theological Investigations* IV, pp. 165–188.

[5] cf. the presentation by K. Rahner and J. B. Metz in the *Handbuch der Pastoraltheologie* II/1 (Freiburg, 1966), pp. 222 ff., 242 ff., 267 ff.; II/2 (Freiburg, 1966), pp. 35 ff., 40 ff., 42 ff., 203–267.

terms it must be kept in mind that 'theology' – as opposed to revelation, kerygma and faith – is itself not a primary quantity,[6] but must first arise out of the relation of nature and grace, secular experience and faith. Thus it contains within itself a profane element which is related to theology's whole essence in a different way from the 'nature' which, *qua* reality and knowledge, is an inner constituent of revelation and faith. So we shall not discuss all these things here.

This whole contribution therefore cannot be anything more than a relatively loosely connected series of observations.

I

There must be 'philosophising' within theology if by 'philosophising' here one understands the activity of thinking about the revelation of God in Christ in the Church's proclamation, implemented with the support of all the means and methods of the intellect and by relating the act and content of faith to everything which man experiences, questions and knows. In the last analysis it is not so important whether this sort of activity should be called 'philosophising' or not.[7] On the one hand one might say for instance that what is meant thereby is precisely what is meant by the business of theology; on the other hand it can also be asked whether, even if one considers the secular material in such theology, it can still be called 'philosophy' today or whether something else has assumed the position previously held by philosophy as constituting the secular element and function within theology. This something else would not have to be called 'philosophy' if the word were to retain its historically given meaning.[8]

We shall need to speak of this later on. But if we exclude these questions, I think that the statement '*Within theology there must be philosophising*' retains an intelligible and important sense which is not as common an

[6] For this distinction cf. K. Rahner, 'Theology in the New Testament', *Theological Investigations* V (London and Baltimore, 1966), pp. 23–41; also (together with J. Ratzinger), *Revelation and Tradition* (Freiburg and London, 1966).

[7] A purely semantic and historical study will have little result. On the other hand there are even many areas of modern science where people really 'philosophise' in a positive sense, although one would prefer not to use this word for various reasons.

[8] Here we merely refer to the phenomenon that, especially after Hegel, modern philosophy has assumed a different form (compare Marx, Nietzsche, Heidegger and Sartre for instance). One is clearly aware in any case of a certain reticence with regard to the term 'philosophy' or 'philosophise'.

assumption as one might imagine, at least in the practice of theology. According to the statement, this 'philosophising' must take place *within* theology. This ought really to be discussed explicitly, since it can be questioned whether theology today can assume the existence of a ready-made and thought-out 'philosophy' – as maintained in the theory and practice of Neo-Scholasticism – which needs only to be kept in view and 'applied' in theology, or whether this is to a large extent no longer practicable today, even if one has no wish to proclaim the 'demise of metaphysics'. To this question we merely reply as follows: *in actual fact* and thus for the purposes of instruction *there no longer exists today any philosophy which can be assumed as ready-made and already adapted to the needs of theology. This applies equally to the Catholic Christian.* In this sense there is no longer a Neo-Scholastic philosophy as a (relatively) complete 'system', since Neo-Scholasticism has in actual fact dissolved into a wealth of philosophies which, while maintaining a more or less conscious and productive contact with the Scholastic philosophy of the Middle Ages and the Baroque, have taken up such a profusion of modern themes and complexes of problems (even though in very differing degrees) that it is scarcely possible today to speak any longer of a *single* circumscribable Neo-Scholasticism, able to function as *the* given instrument and *the* given partner-in-dialogue of theology.[9] And the reverse is true as well: as a result of its own approaches, methods and needs, theology itself puts so many questions and demands before philosophy as far as concepts and the possibilities of systematisation go, that traditional Neo-Scholasticism, as it was until recently and still is, is simply inadequate to meet these needs. Therefore there remains no alternative but to 'philosophise' within theology itself. We need only observe, on the one hand, that this is in accord with the essence of theology, and on the other hand that it implies no prior judgment with regard to an autonomous secular philosophy nor to questions of the present theological teaching curriculum.

Apart from this question, our first thesis contains a certain protest against a dogmatic positivism and a biblicism, two dangers which seem to me imminent today. There is certainly still a dogmatic positivism today. If *confines* dogmatics to the ordering and structuring of official

[9] Thus it is obvious that, in spite of the tendency towards a *philosophia perennis*, Neo-Scholasticism itself since the seventeenth century has not been immune from clearly modern philosophical influences in its approach and method, and bears all kinds of traces reminiscent of Descartes and Kant and of the Critical Method. It was not until P. Scheuer, P. Rousselot, J. Maréchal and others that the step was taken towards an *explicit* engagement with modern philosophy.

doctrinal statements and – ultimately – to rendering the latter intelligible by means of the retrospective history of dogma. It does all this *only* within the terms, conceptual models and horizon of understanding provided by these official pronouncements. This positivism will not have been overcome as long as this kind of dogmatics works with the concepts and perspectives of a calmly academic Neo-Scholasticism and so cultivates a certain rational and conceptual skill. Of course, this dogmatic positivism exists nowhere concretely in chemical purity. But it exists. If one is correct to regard the manipulating of Neo-Scholastic conceptual forms, in which official doctrinal pronouncements of recent times have been formulated, as still not free from dogmatic positivism, then it must even be said that this positivism is very widespread indeed. It is false because it signifies an unjustifiable and in practice impossible limitation of the true task of theology. It is unaware of the historically determined nature of concepts, even of those used in doctrinal declarations,[10] by absolutising them as being 'natural', intelligible to all, and perpetually adequate for the expression of dogma. It is not aware that the man who is engaged in theology, while retaining the unity of his own consciousness, must be in an open dialogue with the totality of his intellectual and spiritual existence, and that in actual fact this totality is today no longer identical with the secular thought-forms in which the official doctrines have until now expressed the faith and the kerygma. This kind of dogmatic positivism must therefore be exploded; there must be more 'philosophising' in theology in the sense already outlined.

Perhaps the biblicism against which the same demand is directed is only another form of positivism. However, it must be mentioned separately. Of course it is practically possible to carry on the tasks of exegesis and biblical theology in such a way as to be 'philosophising' in our sense to a more or less satisfactory degree. But if this happens, i.e. if what is aimed at is an understanding of the biblical statements, charged and confronted with the whole of the modern secular understanding of existence and the world, then biblical theology is obliged to burst the bounds of its own nature; not only because in this case official doctrine and the Church's historical development of dogma must be explicitly applied, thereby clearly going beyond the nature and capabilities of biblical theology, but chiefly because the secular understanding of existence and of the world must be the object of critical theological reflection. And this is plainly

[10] cf. K. Rahner, 'Zur Geschichtlichkeit der Theologie', *Integritas, Festschrift für K. Holzamer*, ed. D. Stolte/R. Wisser (Tübingen, 1966), pp. 75–95, cf. also in this volume pp. 64 ff.

more that biblical theology can do, if it is to be more than simply a poor name for theology in general, precisely because its 'soul' must be scripture, as Vatican II rightly says (though without wishing thus to encourage a biblicism). In addition, if biblical theology is to remain aware of its natural limits, it cannot consequently undertake of itself the task of reducing the plurality of individual, categorised scriptural statements to the single, original salvation/revelation-event which lies 'behind' scripture. Scripture itself lives from the event, and relative to this event scripture is *already* 'theology' and must always be expressed *anew*, although this by no means implies that the original uncategorized salvation/revelation-event can ever be attained as such in 'transcendental' purity in isolation, without the mediation of the process of categorizing and objectifying.[11] It cannot be solely the business of biblical theology itself to go back to this original event by means of reflection, nor to go forward into the single and yet perpetually pluralistic totality of man's understanding of existence and of the world. For this reason biblicism represents a misunderstanding of the true essence of theology as a whole, for within it there cannot be as much 'philosophising' as is necessary. It is also un-Catholic, since in the Catholic understanding of faith theology does not begin with an unquestioning and blind acceptance of scripture as the *norma non normata* of every expression of faith and theology,[12] and since Catholic theology is not faced with the dilemma, on the one hand of dissolving scripture by historical and exegetical study into a collection of disparate historical documents of religion, nor on the other hand, of elevating scripture in this theology to a position of absolute authority, involving a boundless *sacrificium intellectus*. All this must be said not ultimately so much because there is a 'light of natural reason' but because the salvation/revelation-event of faith does not begin in the first place in the express meeting with scripture but precedes it by God's gracious self-communication. On account of God's desire for the salvation of all men this self-communication takes place (at least in the form of an appeal to man's freedom) everywhere and at all times, even *before* the explicit confrontation with the pronouncements of the Church's apostolic kerygma.[13]

[11] Besides the literature mentioned on p. 47 note 6, cf. K. Rahner/K. Lehmann, *Mysterium Salutis* I, ed. J. Feiner/M. Löhrer (Einsiedeln, 1965), pp. 686–689; 698 ff., 700 ff.

[12] For a correct understanding cf. K. Rahner, 'Scripture and Tradition', *Theological Investigations* VI (London and Baltimore, 1969), pp. 98–112.

[13] Besides the studies mentioned on p. 47 note 6, cf. the author's writings on

Within theology itself, therefore, there must be philosophising, or, more simply, there must be radical thought, radical questioning and radical confrontation. That is at bottom the most edifying theology. For a theology of this kind needs to keep in mind its task of serving the Gospel of Christ; consequently it must not become an 'academic' curiosity, using the data of faith as objects of speculation without being existentially involved. On the contrary. 'Philosophising' goes on in theology as long as man radically confronts the message of the faith with his understanding of existence and of the world, for it is only in this way that the saving message can speak to the whole man as a free person. It is not possible here to give concrete practical examples of what this demand implies and how it would bring about change in dogmatics and moral theology. Our critical demand does not mean that we think that this kind of philosophising theology does not exist at all, but that even today there is not enough of it, as far as average teaching and, dependent on this, the possibilities of official Church pronouncements are concerned. For instance, where can one find a doctrine of the Trinity or a Christology which goes further than the mere repetition of the traditional formulas, making possible a really kerygmatic proclamation, genuinely orthodox and suitable for teaching, so that what is meant in these doctrinal treatises really *adequately* comes home to modern man without avoidable difficulties? Can our text-book theology generally talk of 'Angels', 'Sin', 'Penance', 'Purgatory', 'Indulgences', the 'Virgin Birth', 'Sacraments' in such a way that the 'hierarchy of truths'[14] – i.e. the rootedness of all these separate affirmations in the central foundation of the faith – is in each case made clear to modern man and is capable of being assimilated sufficiently by him? Is it not too often the case today that a text-book of dogmatics looks like an expanded version of the *index systematicus* of Denzinger? Does it become apparent that dogmatics is aware of the present crisis of faith? – without thereby falling into a pious sentimentality? Not, that is, by lamenting the situation, but by making efforts to *think*, not taking the easy way out, not trying to talk merely to the person who believes in any case, but to the doubter, to the person who is earnestly questioning and to him who does not believe; not by quoting the formal authority of

'anonymous Christians'; in particular also the relevant conciliar texts. An analysis of these texts is attempted by K. Rahner, 'Atheismus und implizites Christentum', *L'Athéisme contemporain* (ed. J. Girardi, in several languages), cf. also in this volume, 'Atheism and Implicit Christianity'.

[14] cf. the Council's Decree on Ecumenism, No. 11.

scripture and the *magisterium* in particular questions of dogma, but by trying to render the matter intrinsically worthy of belief.

II

A second thesis may perhaps be formulated as follows: *as opposed to earlier times, a 'philosophising' theology is confronted today with a pluralism of philosophies. It must take up its stand vis-à-vis them and work with them, but they cannot be adequately synthesised by each other nor by theology.* Theology today is experiencing perforce what we may be permitted to call its 'gnoseological concupiscence'.

What we have just said by no means implies the relativistic or agnostic thesis that there is quite legitimately a pluralism of mutually contradictory philosophies, fundamentally irreconcilable '*per se*', or that man may well abandon at the outset the effort of trying to overcome his gnoseologically concupiscent situation by seeking to approach asymptotically an integration of the philosophies and thus a gnoseological integration. But while rejecting this kind of sceptical relativism we must not draw a veil over the unavoidable fact of the contemporary intellectual scene, that today the individual has to exist in an actual pluralism of philosophies, unintegrated and yet mutually coexistent, not separated by a cultural no-man's-land; this pluralism is present and will remain so.[15] Secondary reflection on the matter has produced a new situation and the resultant knowledge has become, in turn, a further factor of the situation. There was certainly a pluralism of philosophies before. But they were either historically separated by the no-man's-land dividing different cultures from each other, or else they came face to face within a common and readily-assumed perspective of understanding as mutually contradictory philosophies, automatically rejecting and excluding each other, or else capable of being integrated and 'transcended' in a wider synthesis. Even when confronted with many philosophies, *one* man could develop *one* philosophy, 'his' philosophy, consciously proclaiming it as 'Philosophy'. If one does *not* have the idea that philosophies are intended for storage in computers and if one remembers that philosophy can only exist concretely in the individual's mind – a fact which no dialogue can change – one is obliged to say that there is today an irreducible pluralism of philosophies,

[15] cf. K. Rahner, 'Reflections on Dialogue within a Pluralistic Society', *Theological Investigations* VI (London and Baltimore, 1969), pp. 31–42; cf. ibid., pp. 21–30 ;*Handbuch der Pastoraltheologie* II/1, pp. 208 ff., 245 ff., 261 ff.; II/2, pp. 203 ff.

that we are aware of it, and that the fact and the awareness of it are contributory determinants of the theologian's situation and therefore constitute a question for theology.

Therefore our reason for proposing the thesis is not that these philosophies are *per se* irreconcilable. In so far as they *are* irreconcilable they show themselves as false; that creates no new, previously nonexistent problem. Rather, the thesis holds because these philosophies, quite apart from the consideration of their truth-value, can no longer all be appropriated and known by the individual and consequently by the theologian, and because at the same time we know this fact as though in a *philosophia negativa* which is now not merely the consciousness of a materially empty field of awareness, but the consciousness of a historically present reality which has not, however, been mastered and which is in fact intractable. Later on we shall discuss how this 'concupiscent' pluralism of philosophies has arisen; not only from the actual mutual confrontation of the plurality of cultures in a world which has become one and which yet remains unintegrated, not only from the growing differentiation and complexity of the individual philosophies, but at bottom it originates in a pluralism of the human sources of experience, which can never be adequately comprehended. In the plurality of non-philosophical disciplines these sources of experience are ranged, as a matter of historical fact, in a variety of methods, problems and results which it is beyond the individual's capacity to grasp. This means that a comprehensive system of knowledge and education is no longer possible, even if one were to look upon the 'system' as an 'open' one.

Of course there are today *new* ways of arriving at a certain synthesis of man's diverse kinds of knowledge. For example, there exist now formal homologies between the problems and methods of the particular sciences. These homologies enable even the individual scientist (and the philosopher) in a particular field to gain a certain understanding of those disciplines with which he is not professionally concerned and conversant. However, such new methods of synthesising particular aspects of knowledge do nothing to modify the basic fact that concerns us here: more is known and questioned in the modern philosophies than can be dealt with by the individual alone, and the realisation of this inability is itself one factor in our intellectual existence today.

Whatever the more particular reasons may be, therefore, the known and experienced fact is incontrovertible: we know that there is a pluralism of understandings of the world and of existence, no longer capable of being integrated adequately by anyone, whether we call them 'philosophies' or not. We do not need to admit this in a spirit of resignation, for it remains our task and duty to avail ourselves of as much of this pluralism as possible. But the fact remains: every man and every theologian, although he must philosophise in theology, knows less and less of 'Philosophy', since there are continually more and more philosophies, which no single person can assimilate.

At this point too one ought to produce concrete examples, but it is impossible here. Would not a modern philosophy of language be of the greatest importance for theological hermeneutics? But can I understand anything of it, if I must first know something of philosophy and theology? Is it *a priori* impossible for logistics to be of value for theology too? How shall I make any judgments about it if I understand none of it, and *could* only grasp it by first having understood the subject *completely* and as a specialist? How many theologians could say in all seriousness that they really understand something of German Idealism, and that they could deal with its problems and concepts and think within its perspectives? Is such a thing a 'luxury' for the theologian, considering that this German Idealism has been a contributory factor of the cultural and intellectual world we live in, even if we never hear more of it than we find in a newspaper supplement? Is it possible to pursue theology seriously today without knowing anything of the philosophies which have sprung from Marxism and the modern sociologies? Are we theologians justified and excused simply because all 'educated' people are in the same position in their want of education, and because it is considered proper only to speak when those who know differently are not present? Can it really be denied that the relationship of theology's intellectual level to that of other spheres of intellectual life was previously better than today? It is assuredly not that theology's level has dropped but because the other level has risen relatively quicker and more vigorously. But can we take comfort from that? What are the consequences to be drawn for theology from this pluralistic situation? I would like to mention especially two consequences in what follows: in a totally new way there is today inevitably a multiplicity of theologies, or they are in the process of growing slowly. The Church's teaching office with its particular function has been placed in a totally new situation.

III

Let us look at our first proposition: *today there is inevitably a multiplicity of theologies*. There have always been many schools of theology. This fact was not only tolerated but acknowledged by the Church as an expression of the richness of its life and of the development of the faith within the Church. This recognition is still important today for a right attitude towards the new phenomenon to which we are drawing attention. But the former situation – of the many different schools and approaches in theology – is not the same as what is meant here. The 'schools' of old were either largely separated by a cultural no-man's-land, e.g. the theologies of the West and of the East, or else they existed *within* a milieu which was to a large extent historically, culturally and philosophically homogeneous, common and available to everyone. Or, on the other hand, the 'schools' opposed each other in clear controversy and contradiction, so that one had to *and was able to* decide in favour of one and against another; or else they could be comprehended and marshalled from a common standpoint of the kind we have mentioned, and thus to a large extent could be positively integrated into a higher unity. These former schools and approaches with their demarcated historical outlines do not really exist any longer today.[16]

If we are correct in what we have said about the practical impossibility of integrating the pluralism of philosophies in our historical situation – which we have seen as 'gnoseologically concupiscent' – then there exists today a pluralism of theologies in a much more radical sense, presupposing that we must always 'philosophise' in theology. What present-day theologian seriously has a simultaneous, accurate and sufficiently deep understanding of Scholastic Philosophy and its origins; Transcendental Philosophy in all its profoundly different forms; Existential Philosophy; the various impulses, issues, tendencies, new analyses and perspectives legitimately contributed by Marxist Philosophy; modern Philosophy of Language and hermeneutics; the philosophy which seeks to elucidate theoretically the relation between the plurality of modern sciences; and the philosophies of the East, now appearing on the scene of world civilisation as known but as yet uncomprehended quantities? Above all, who has any knowledge which is at all reliable concerning those particular modes of understanding of the world and of existence which are produced directly by the sciences as such without the mediation of a philosophy, and which are lived out eminently practically and 'unphilosophically', refusing to accept any self-reflection mediated by philosophical theory? No-one. We may say that one must nonetheless know something about

[16] In so far as they are still actually present, compared with the whole modern cultural situation they lead an esoteric existence which today no longer directly affects the concrete social and sociological position of theology as such.

all these things. That may be true. But to follow this imperative means in practice that the individual merely acquires a denatured and second-hand version of what really needs to be lived and known. We may say that even today theology together with faith must reflect upon its sphere of origin, which lies deeper and more fundamentally in human existence, *prior* to this plurality of understanding of the world and of existence. Thus theology can and must be seen as the study of faith at a level prior to that of the profane sciences, speaking to man before he 'goes out' into the unintegrable pluralism which is his existence and his world. That may be equally correct, and it may provide the impetus to a new and more original self-interpretation of theology. Theology is then no longer understood primarily as a revealed synthesis and amplification of the profane view of existence, which it surpasses, but as its deeper source and thus also as the slender root which alone makes possible such pluralistic and unintegrable interpretations of existence. The result of this theology is not a synthesis of the pluralistic experiences of existence, but a transferring of them to the intractable mystery of God in humility and hope. It may even be that, starting from this sort of consideration, we may be able to grasp the nature of what is called the 'basic theological course' which is the subject of much discussion, but which is hardly understood at all.[17]

However, all this does not change the fact that, on account of the unintegrable plurality of modern experiences of existence, side by side with each other, mutually acknowledged and yet not really *known*, there are or will be many theologies. It will no longer be possible to apply oneself to clearing up their differences and dissolving them in another synthesis. For ultimately it is in practice impossible to distinguish adequately between what is common to all men's understanding of existence – and there certainly is such a thing – and its plurality of historical appearances. Therefore there cannot be a theology which *only* works with this common material. Every theologian will bring to his theology the particular form, the historical and fragmentary nature of his own given understanding of existence. He will no longer entertain the innocent naïveté of earlier times in thinking that his contribution alone is what is important and decisive, truly metaphysical and supra-historical, and that further distinctions are peripheral and matters of small moment.

In speaking of many theologies we emphatically do not mean that they

[17] For some preliminary observations cf. K. Rahner, 'Reflections on the Contemporary Intellectual Formation of future Priests', *Theological Investigations* VI (London and Baltimore, 1969), pp. 113–138, esp. 123 ff.

exist as mutually delimited and separable. In that case they would resemble the old theological schools: one theology is acquainted with the other; they are mutually distinct and contradictory. The modern pluralism of philosophies and theologies consists rather in the fact that no clear, coherent, individual pictures can be formed any longer. Each theology and philosophy knows too much to be merely itself, and too little to become the only Theology or Philosophy.

A second-order situation has arisen in this cultural 'concupiscence': previously what constituted a situation's promise was that there was something in it which remained unreflected, not amenable to objective presentation; today it is precisely what has been once objectified and the subject of reflection which eludes us. Previously it was the as yet unconquered future – nowadays it is the uncontrollable past. If one wishes to say anything 'new' in this field, one does so with the fear that it merely *seems* new because one does not know enough and therefore cannot know that it has already been said somewhere at some time, or because it is unimportant and second-hand erudition. Like in a big city: there are *too many* neighbours for any *one* to be a real neighbour. We have a completely new kind of Alexandrinism: in earlier times it was possible to reach the end of a circumscribed culture; thereafter it could only be kept in order; beyond it were only barbarians (i.e. an unfruitful land, its promise as yet only dimly sensed). Nowadays we know that we have come to the limit of all possible kinds of old-style civilization.

Of course there is still a new future in spite of all this. But it will come from a different direction. It will come from dialogue with the sciences. But we shall speak of this later. In the future, man will not objectify himself in his art and philosophy as the rational and theorising being, offering himself in this role as theology's dialogue-partner; he will appear as practical man in the works of his hands, which change him in a way he cannot clearly express.

But if we turn aside from this hoped-for new land, we see philosophy and theology too (even if the latter's history is not exclusively dependent on that of philosophy) like a wide plain full of nothing but allotments: it is impossible to walk through them all or to plant them all oneself; in every one there is something which the garden next door does not contain. Neighbours good-naturedly exchange a few onions over the garden hedge, or mischievously throw their weeds over; but there is no longer any large, grandly-conceived and well-planned garden in which every kind of plant can be found growing. Compared with the Neo-Scholasticism of nineteenth-century theology and the situation before the first World

War, Catholic theology and other theologies in the last forty years give the impression of a great new departure. This is indeed the case; it is a most laudable phenomenon; but it sprang, primarily at least, from the fact that there was an almost inconceivable amount of progress to be made in dialogue in order to *catch up with* modern philosophy and the historical sciences. The real situation, therefore, will not be revealed until this task has been completed. Will it take a very long time? Will the work change imperceptibly as if of its own accord, and become a dialogue with the new partner of whom we have yet to speak? Or will theology become as Alexandrine as philosophy, in so far as it tries to live only from its own resources? In fearing this danger we are not transgressing against our faith in the power and dignity of theology. The Gospel message comes from the Ever-living God. But theology as such, however important it certainly is for evangelism and for faith, always remains a *human* piece of work, and hence not necessarily more creative and vibrant than philosophy.

IV

We now turn to our second proposition, which draws the practical consequences from the situation we have just described: *the Church's teaching office has been put into a totally new situation as a result of the plurality of theologies.*

First of all we must say something more about the pluralism of theologies. As we have said, there are going to be many theologies, even if no Catholic theology will subscribe to the kind of premature agnosticism which characterises authoritative pronouncements of earlier times as mere 'interpretations' of the actual content of faith, no longer necessarily 'relevant' today. For the irreversible plurality of theologies does not mean that we must deny their ability to act in dialogue, nor that they can learn nothing intelligible and compelling from the Church's ancient doctrinal pronouncements. But today it is to the plural theologies that these official pronouncements are addressed. It is already becoming obvious: how could there be a system of dogmatics today able to function equally intensively from the points of view of biblical theology, history of dogma, scholastic metaphysics, existentialist ontology, salvation-history, aesthetics, politics, comparative religion? The attempt – laudable in itself – to leave out none of these aspects can only result in practice in none of one's aims being achieved to any satisfactory degree. This remains true even in the case of a team project. A book produced in this way is to be read by one individual who cannot bring to it all the preconditions necessary to understand completely what all the team members together have written. Besides this a workable 'team' would no longer be able to cope with the rate of production of modern theology. One might say that this is only impossible in practice, not in theory. But the practical impossibility remains.

It may be asked, therefore, whether there may not have to be in the long run two forms of theology running parallel: one trying to do what it can to undercut today's cultural pluralism, making use only of that side of existence which is still common to all and which will remain so. It would work with this common experience and 'redeem' it by responding with the answers of faith, even if only able to do this in an approximate way. In this way it would develop a kind of higher Catechism, or perhaps the 'basic theological course' we have already referred to. On the other hand there would be the other kind of theology, with the courage to let itself disintegrate into many theologies. All of these in their own way would confront the individual pluralist views of existence, no longer communicable to each other, and, assimilating them and criticising them more closely, would become established in particular spheres of mutual comprehension. There are of course limits to this kind of pluralism. It does not mean that theology in the Church can say whatever it likes. The Church's teaching office, the common confession of faith and the possibility of anathematising certain propositions remain. Possibly in the rather more distant future the teaching office will have an easier task in one particular respect: the pluralism of theologies and the unimaginable possibilities of conceptual forms, language and fine shades of signification mean (if I may put it thus) that a theologian who has been censured on account of a particular statement has many more 'ways out' than at present without endangering his honesty and obedience. He will have more opportunity to keep saying what he means in different ways; whereas before a particular formula could seem to be the only possible way of objectifying the particular, apparently indispensable experience of religious faith. In the past, censure struck the censured person at an existentially deeper level than will be the case in the future; it is to be hoped that tomorrow we shall be more aware of the inadequacy of our own language and its unintelligibility to others in such a pluralistic situation than most of our modern Western-style intellectuals seem to be.

However, out of this pluralism of theologies arises a new situation for the Church's teaching office, which we shall mention in brief; we cannot deal with its whole range of problems here.[18] It seems to me that the

[18] cf. an introduction in K. Rahner, 'Kirchliches Lehramt und Theologie nach

position can be clearly seen if one compares, for instance, 'Humani generis' with Ottaviani's letter of July 1966. In the Encyclical we can sense the confident awareness that it is able to formulate the opposing position unequivocally and to demarcate its own official doctrine by positive statements; in the Cardinal's letter we are aware of a certain embarrassment in the face of theological trends which are scarcely tangible and not commonly available or intelligible. Consequently it manages only to ask questions and to give general warnings instead of making doctrinal pronouncements. If we put the matter at its most acute: how is the bearer of teaching authority in the Church to give his verdict on a particular theology if he is *not* and *cannot* really be acquainted with it? – if he cannot really understand it except by knowing the profane presuppositions on which it is based and which he does not share? One may ask whether in the future there should not be ideally as many 'teaching authorities' as there are theologies. To give a very small example, are there in Rome the kind of consultant theologians, fully conversant with the ontological and existential presuppositions which have led to the translation of 'Transubstantiation' into 'Trans-signification' or 'Transfinalisation'? Can such specialised knowledge be expected and required?

We have indicated a problem, but no solution. If the problem does not seem a very urgent matter, it is chiefly because the theologies constituting this new situation for the teaching office are not yet as clearly formed and differentiated as will probably be the case in future.

V

We have already referred to a further important factor in the present relationship between philosophy and theology, and we now turn to consider it especially. *In future, theology's key partner-in-dialogue*, to which it will have to relate its 'philosophising' in the sense we have adumbrated, *will no longer be philosophy in the traditional sense at all, but the 'unphilosophical' pluralistic sciences and the kind of understanding of existence which they promote either directly or indirectly.*

This is in many ways a platitude, since it is plain that the historical sciences have already stirred up and changed theology more than modern philosophy has done. The natural and social sciences, too, by creating

dem Konzil', *Stimmen der Zeit* 178 (1966), pp. 404–420; also 'Vom Dialog in der Kirche', *Stimmen der Zeit* 179 (1967), pp. 81–95, cf. in this volume pp. 83 ff. and 'Dialogue in the Church', *Theological Investigations* X.

modern technological man, by their world-picture and the many questions resulting from it, have changed theology's situation to a profound degree.[19] If we observe very little of this in our text-books as yet, it indicates a failure, not a legitimate detachment of theology from science. In spite of this we must inspect our proposition more closely, for it is not as natural and innocent as it at first seems. We do not intend to debate the question of the 'demise of metaphysics'. This 'demise' is indeed proclaimed on the most varied quarters, but in itself it is not a clear thesis at all. What is quite clear is the concrete pluralism of the sciences, which, with all their topics, *a posteriori* methods and wide-open field of activity, do *not* consider themselves as dependent branches of philosophy, however much they may have arisen out of Western metaphysics.[20] These sciences do not acknowledge philosophy as the prescriber of their fields of operation, but rather as one of the factors involved in actual practice and as the necessary spur of criticism. Thus they take their decision about their understanding of existence *before* philosophy is able to have its say. At most it is accepted as reflection on the pluralism of these sciences and their methods, and it is only regarded by them as valid in the role of a formal theory of science.

Even if one submits modern science's understanding of itself to critical examination, questioning the transcendental *a priori* conditions of all science whatsoever, considering the ontological implications of a formal theory of science and thus drawing up an ontology of a particular kind, the fact remains that *earlier theology had as its only standard partner-in-dialogue a* SINGLE *philosophy, united in spite of all its internal tensions and controversies*. Although this was in fact the product of history, its historical conditioning had not yet become the subject of reflection by a positive historical science; philosophy had a history, but its history was not something which called philosophy itself in question. To the extent that there already were sciences in the mediaeval 'Universitas litterarum', they had scarcely any theological relevance. Today things are different: there are sciences which consider themselves no longer as tools and handmaids of philosophy, but they are relevant to theology; most important of all, theology no longer lives in the context of a *single* philosophy, established

[19] cf. K. Rahner, 'Experiment Mensch', *Die Frage nach dem Menschen. Festschrift für Max Müller*, ed. H. Rombach (Freiburg, 1966), pp. 45–69, cf. in this volume pp. 205 ff.

[20] Naturally we cannot enter into detail historically regarding the different theses as to the origins of modern science in Western thought and philosophising. Cf. M. Müller's systematic treatment, 'Wissenschaft', *LThK* X (Freiburg,[2] 1965), cols. 1189–1193 (literature).

as the primary and autonomous standard. Philosophy may not conceive itself as a 'complete system'; it must be aware that it cannot adequately reproduce man's total potential and therefore cannot be his absolute lord and master. This applies *today* chiefly because the sciences are fellow-contributors to man's understanding of himself without having been empowered to be so by philosophy. They perform this function by *doing things*, reaching out in power and grasping the future, and consequently they exhibit a very problematical relation to the abiding 'essence' of man.[21] How far this view of science is justified, how far it can be called in question by criticism – in turn implying philosophy, which thus enters into a new stage of self-understanding – these matters need not concern us at the moment, for in any case theology must pursue its task in its *actual* situation and can do nothing to alter it immediately. At least in the concrete situation determined by the cultural, intellectual, social and natural sciences, it is science, no longer mediated by philosophy, which constitutes theology's partner-in-dialogue. If this is only visible to a very modest and limited degree in theology as it appears at present – and then mainly in isolated particulars, not in a confrontation with the 'spirit', the 'ethos' of these sciences with their 'openness' towards what cannot be predicted in the world – it says nothing against our thesis but against theology as it actually is in practice. By nature theology ought to be more suited to *this* partner than to philosophy. For theology is primarily concerned with history and the future. Whereas philosophy can really only consider the facts of historicity and orientation towards a future in a *formal* manner, the sciences represent history and future; especially if one remembers that history and future are not *things* but are created by man and his practical awareness, and thus bear 'science' within themselves as an essential factor.

It would only be possible, of course, to give a clear content and colour to this latter thesis if one could describe in concrete terms a theology which had developed within the situation of the modern scientific world-view right from the very beginning, not merely by the process of supplementary and concessionary apologetics, and which was conditioned in part by the unsynthesised pluralism of mutually alien sciences, thereby constituting the plurality of theologies such as we have mentioned earlier. It need imply no detraction from the autonomy of the theology of the

[21] cf. esp. J. B. Metz, *Verantwortung der Hoffnung* (Mainz, 1968), K. Rahner, 'Christian living formerly and today', *Theological Investigations* VII (London and New York, 1971), pp. 3–24, esp. pp. 16 ff.; also *Theological Investigations* X, 'On the theology of hope'.

Christian Revelation if it were to take up its place deliberately in the open context of modern science. It is certain that if it did so, a different form of theology or theologies would emerge. To sense this one only needs to imagine what a dogmatics would look like which had grown out of a context of a whole-heartedly embraced and experienced unity of spirit and matter, a context of a dynamic open world of the future, to be seized in hope and action, a world constituting the sphere of man's battle against his self-alienation for the hominisation of his environment, the context of a single history of religion, a single political world.

We cannot say anything further about all this here. But I hope it has become clear that traditional philosophy's loss of function in modern society and science must not lead simply to an 'unphilosophical' mode of study in theology. Pure positivism does most harm in theology, although the latter remains a 'positive' study and although its particular opportunities lie in that direction today too. Theology must not merely be aware of the change in philosophy: it must plan out its own intrinsic relation to philosophical thought and other forms of man's interpretation of existence. If this task is really taken seriously, 'thought' will retain its great importance for theology. One might even say that the future of theology as a human endeavour for the presentation of the Gospel depends not least on the courage to pursue this 'thought'.

4

THE HISTORICITY OF THEOLOGY

THE Society of St Paul (*Paulusgesellschaft*) in Germany and Spain desires to be a place where dialogue is carried on between theology and modern science;[1] the partners in such a dialogue, if it is to be real, must presume a readiness to learn on both sides. Otherwise there will be a one-sided harangue instead of a dialogue. The desire to learn through dialogue presupposes – perhaps in a different manner than is the case in one-way instruction – that each dialogue-partner takes into account the possibility of a mistake on his own part. We do not need to examine here whether, in what way, and with what reservations this presupposition can be adopted in a dialogue in which an authoritative Church discusses its own dogma with modern science. However this difficult question is to be answered in greater detail – and the Council's Decree on Ecumenism contains some important points on this matter – theology can and must make this presupposition on entering into dialogue with modern science. It is possible for theology to appear capable of error, threatened by error, and often indeed actually to err. This is not only because theology has to discuss many things with present-day arts and sciences which are not matters of defined Church dogma and for which, therefore, no irrevocable concurrence can be demanded on the part of the faithful. In cases like these the theological partner must consequently presuppose the fundamental possibility of error on his own side as well. But the assumption is chiefly valid because even when presenting and defending Church dogma the theologian cannot simply repeat the defined precepts of Councils and Popes alone. For them to be the object of a dialogue he must rather explain them, explicate their concepts, locate their propositions in a wider frame-

[1] The scope of this lecture was determined by its origin and location (see the list of sources); this also explains the lack of footnotes. For a comprehensive documentation and reference to other literature cf. K. Rahner/K. Lehmann, 'Kerygma und Dogma: Geschichtlichkeit der Offenbarungsvermittlung', J. Feiner/M. Löhrer (ed.), *Mysterium Salutis* I (Einsiedeln, 1965), pp. 704–707 and 783–787.

work of understanding; he must continually try to eliminate possible misunderstandings, demonstrate consonance with other assertions of faith and truths of reason, and translate them so that they correspond to the partner's given perspective of understanding (for the latter is never a mere *tabula rasa*, but always understands according to previously established preconditions, which are fundamentally incapable of being the object of adequate reflection and thus cannot be tested). In this difficult undertaking the individual theologian – and only a concrete person can be a partner-in-dialogue – is of course supported by the whole of theology which is guided by the Church's official authority and the Spirit, but he takes on this task on his own account and risk. Since he must say what is especially *his*, even when discussing defined truths of the faith; since he only possesses infallible dogma in his own individual, subjective and conditioned understanding; since he cannot adequately separate these two elements; since in the case of dogmatic concepts there can be no adequate definitions, utterly transparent to reflection (as perhaps in the case of the axioms of mathematics and geometry), the individual theologian can and must quite candidly take into account the possibility of error on his side and the consequent necessity of himself changing, even when in dialogue concerning Church dogma.

This possibility of error in theology, the readiness to undergo change intellectually, not only as a passive object of a process of change, but as a subject by a free decision (which is at the same time the most difficult, bitter and yet most felicitous form of change and 'evolution') finds its ultimate justification in the historicity of theology. A Society concerned with dialogue between Christian theology and modern science, therefore, does well at its inception to think about the historicity of theology. In this it is considering one of the most important presuppositions of its own being. Of course, the present discussion must necessarily and inevitably remain fragmentary and incomplete. For behind the problem of truth and history lies in fact the whole problem of the metaphysics of all knowledge whatsoever, from its beginnings right up to the present day. The possibility of uniting absolute truth and the historicity of truth is one of philosophy's most fundamental questions. It is clearly impossible to say anything really sufficient on this score in one short hour.

So we shall only attempt to show according to theological considerations that theology must take account of its historicity, and what practical consequences arise from this for the Christian who is also a man of science.

I

The experience of a history of revelation, i.e. a history of the saving truth imparted to us by the free personal act of God, is one of the most fundamental data of theology and of Christian dogma itself. No Christian can doubt this assertion. It can be found explicit at the beginning of the Epistle to the Hebrews (1:1). It is an astonishing and mysterious statement. It is an everyday experience of individuals and humanity as a whole that no-one can ever know everything knowable, that everyone is made aware of new knowledge of which he was previously ignorant, that man discovers what is useful to him only slowly and as a result changes his everyday life very significantly. It causes us little surprise. But that truth should have a history, truth which is ultimate, constituting its own very essence, which is itself an analogous, many-layered reality, truth which is decisive for man's ultimate salvation, speaking to man's most inner and immortal centre at the point where he borders on the eternal God – that is an astonishing assertion, by no means self-evident. Throughout the course of Christian history there have been plenty of theories which did not wish to recognise the truth of this, or at least tried to water it down.

Indeed it is strange: for the ultimate, the eternal is surely that to which man must stand in a relation of freedom, able to say Yes or No, if he is to work out his own salvation and not merely be saved passively, or be rewarded for one kind of salvation with a totally different kind. But if one says that man is always and everywhere concerned with this most inner peculiarity of his, this transcendence in respect of God and its existence in grace; that this dark brightness at the centre of his being is always present, either for his salvation or for the reverse, and is thus outside the history of his truth – like an immovable star above the restless ocean of time – there seems to be no longer any history of saving truth, or else the existing history of revelation seems not to be a history of the truth decisive for salvation. But it is to be maintained, however, that there *is* a history of the revelation of saving truth. That is why our assertion is so surprising. If such a thing does exist, then there is also a history and a historicity of theology, and it remains problematical how and why a history of revelation can come to a close, bearing in mind the *continuing* history of civilisation and the immeasurableness of God; how it can be complete (at the death of the Apostles, as we are accustomed to say) and only pursued further in the form of a mere history of the development of dogma and theology.

Whatever the result of the fundamental theological question with regard to the truth of salvation, i.e. how it can both be decisive for salvation and at the same time have become historical, one thing needs to be clear in any case (and it is of the greatest importance for the understanding of the historicity of theology too): the history of revelation may not be watered down to a succession of individual propositions, communicated one by one by God to the bearer of revelation, and by addition causing the 'deposit of faith' to grow gradually, until in the revelation in Christ it has reached its final extent and now only requires to be administered and tapped by the Church.

This kind of quantifying model for the history of revelation is no doubt unsatisfactory. Not only because in this case it remains actually obscure why the Incarnation of the Divine Logos, of Truth, in the flesh of history is not the beginning and the centre of this quantitative *summa*, but – from a temporal view – the final addition to a body of saving truth which had sufficed to create man's saving immediacy before God *without* this addition for thousands and thousands of years. (No wonder that mediaeval theology, afraid of the historicity of revelation, always postulated an explicit belief in the coming Saviour at least on the part of the 'Patriarchs'.) Such a merely quantitative growth of revelation is insufficient as a model for its history for many other reasons as well. An individual truth exists only within a totality of truths, in a wider perspective of understanding. This may not always be very clear in each case because this totality of meaning, the perspective of understanding, the intellectual system of co-ordinates and references within which and by means of which any particular statement can alone be understood, may be felt as utterly self-evident and hence inaccessible to reflection. But all the same it is so. What is apparently a quantitative additional growth to a previous totality of knowledge in fact changes the totality, introduces new perspectives and puts new questions to previous insights. Answering these questions again modifies previous knowledge.

What has been said could be illustrated with particular examples in the history of revelation. For instance, the advent of the belief in angels in the field of revealed faith makes clearer God's transcendence (and vice versa); insight into the possibility of a positive fulfilment of life in the beyond changes the whole moral evaluation of life (and vice versa); it is only the New Testament doctrine of participation in the holy God's divine life through his 'pneuma' which first implies the doctrine of Original Sin. In the New Testament a real theology can be seen, i.e. it is apparent that God does not effect revelation by simply adding new 'propositions' 'from outside' to the basic substance of the Christian Faith (Jesus as the Risen eschatological Bringer of Salvation), but that the total basic Christian message unfolds and develops from an inner dialectic and a dynamic source. Each factor of this totality is always dependent upon every other factor, and grows and develops – however much it may remain the same – together with the others.

In this process, the cultural, religious and secular environment in which the history of the revelation-event takes place acts as a spur to the latter's growth itself, as a precondition without which this history is not even conceivable. For revelation is not revelation of concepts, not the creation of new fundamental axioms, introduced in a final and fixed form into man's consciousness 'from outside' by some supra-historical transcendent cause. It is revelation by means of concepts taken from the history of human civilisation (although, of course, the latter stands continually in the light of the grace of the self-revealing God). Thus these concepts always have a prehistory, they are connected by thousands of root-fibres with the whole of man's historically developed understanding of himself. For example one only needs to investigate the words 'pneuma', 'logos', 'flesh', 'blood', 'righteousness', 'redeemer', 'sinner', etc. in the New Testament as to their precise and actual meanings with all their aspects, nuances, differences of usage and accompanying undertones; also the closer and more distant environment, the 'field' of meaning, of the terms. If this is all taken seriously one finds oneself in the midst of the vast, labyrinthine history of these terms, which can be by no means adequately 'defined' (and thus disposed of) by a mere 'definition of terms'. This is especially the case since such a definition would again have to use terms which could not be laid down by means of simple, indivisible and yet unequivocally 'clear' elements.

This is not the place to examine how, under these presuppositions, the Divine Revelation can and must be conceived to happen. At all events the idea found in academic theologies is impossible or at most acceptable only as a very formal pattern. This idea assumes tacitly and without reflection (and by and large without any further consideration at all) that the transcendent God inseminates fixed and final propositions into the consciousness of the bearer of revelation (albeit by using a given human terminology not susceptible to historical change). This kind of idea would almost eliminate the possibility of a real history of revelation.

II

In a word, if there is a history of revelation, then and only then is there a real history of theology, recognising a real historicity as one of its essential elements. Of course this assertion can be proved directly by reference to historical empirical fact. If it were not true, the theologian would not need to write and to study the history of dogma and of theology. But he does. And yet our assertion can only be proved, in the sense in which it is meant, provided that existing history of dogma and theology itself is not misinterpreted by the theologian.

Here too there is among theologians an unreflected 'model' of the history of dogma and theology beneath the surface which denies its true historicity. It is understood as a system of logical relations and consequences of the basic data of faith (*articuli fidel*), projected separately and in succession on to the stream of time although in reality they are timeless and supra-historical, capable of being reunited as a system. It is certainly the case, if this 'system' exists, that the concrete logical relations and origins of individual statements can be viewed and justified in a deductive theology of this sort. But this applies only if the system exists, only if the particular statement, the new or metamorphosed concept, the new dogmatic formulation already exists. (This is of course always the case in this king of logical, 'timeless' operation, but it does not thereby become automatically 'real'.) One only needs to ask the naïve proponent of such an unhistorical view of the history of civilisation to anticipate the future of theology in the next few millennia by means of his method – which he ought to be able to do if he is right, and yet cannot do to see the inadequacy of this kind of rationalistic interpretation of the history of dogma and theology.

The real and effectual logic of this history takes place only within it. The logical deductions of a theologian coming afterwards and distilling later dogma from the original data of revelation are only possible, however, because this process of distillation has already occurred in history. They are only conceivable as the realisation of what has already happened in history, and the theologian remains dependent upon this actual history notwithstanding all possible logic. If the 'syllogism' (in the broadest sense of the word) is already there, its context can be understood. But it must be there already. Understanding it does not mean that it therefore *is*. Today it is possible to speed up the solution of problems which are quantifiable by calculating machines and thus to hasten what one might call the 'history' of these calculations. But I do not think that computers could be built for theology to any significant degree, chiefly because no-one would know how to programme them. Theology must work fundamentally with analogical concepts, and these are not suitable for quantifying thought-processing. The first and characteristic event of theological logic is and remains this history itself which has a completely logical energy and structure, but one which can only really take place within this actual history. The historical situation, as the concrete context in which the 'logical' occurrence first takes place, is indispensable to the occurrence. And since the total historical context of subsequent events of this kind in the progress of dogma cannot be foreseen, the future history of theology cannot be predicted or calculated in advance, in spite of the utmost rational discernment.

The following simple example may serve to illustrate what is meant with regard to theology's genuine historicity (and hence its fundamental openness to the future at all times and in all matters): one has the impression that many not insignificant theologians admit the growth of many important theological concepts (how could anyone still deny the fact today?), and ultimately also that these concepts are not merely different words for a terminology which was already present beforehand. The concrete – and unreflected – interpretation of these theologians, however, runs as follows: once these concepts are there, they acquire a fixed and final character, by virtue of which they are removed from the situation of perpetual openness to the future in history, and stand like fixed stars, immobile and unquestionable, shining down on the future history of theology. Then these same theologians declare in all goodwill and innocence that one must naturally explain these terms, make them intelligible and continually think them out anew etc. For they too assume and know that it is not enough simply to say 'person', 'nature', 'hypostasis', 'Hypostatic Union', 'substance', 'accidence', 'Transubstantiation' etc. in order to understand what is really meant and also what is not meant thereby. In any case it is only too evident in the history of theology that these individual explanations turn out very differently, and cannot in reality be reduced to such a formula as could be generally accepted, and which was also at the same time so clear as to appear to need no further explanation at all. But in listening to these theologians one becomes aware of the following: this explanation of 'perennial' concepts must surely apply necessarily to other terms: but the latter have in fact a continuing history of their own. Thus the concept which was previously assumed to be 'perennial' is once more submerged in the fluid stream of the history of theology. There is a further objection: under certain circumstances at any rate the explanation ought to be better and more intelligible, with a wider range of aspects, and it ought to be more careful and lucid in its guarding against misunderstanding than the concept it is explaining. Otherwise the 'explanation' becomes a confusion. Why should not new concepts be formed from these explanations in the course of their historical evolution, to overtake and replace the concepts explained in former times, not declaring their meaning to have been false but transcending this meaning in the new concept by a more comprehensive, sensitive treatment and more effective protection against misunderstanding? This is what happened before: pre-Chalcedon Christology – at least in the East – did not possess the concepts used by us today and yet had to express the Hypostatic Union. Our meaning is the same as this ancient Christology, but we cannot use its ways and means of expression as formerly, for we have different concepts, not merely different vocables, from those of Cyril of Alexandria. In these concepts much is clear to us (and much is perhaps less clear) which was not so at that time. What happened in the past will be the case in the future as well. The slow pace of this historical progression in the history of theology may be justifiable in a particular field in the very nature of the case; in many areas a retarded or stagnating development in theology will be an unhealthy sign for this theology itself. Basically, however, one cannot simultaneously look forward to a future history of the development of dogma in particular themes, and yet regard it as closed in other areas and declare all further history to be forbidden.

Our place is in history and it is only in its forward-moving course that we possess the eternal truth of God, which is our salvation. This saving truth is the same within history, but, while remaining the same, it has had and still has a history of its own. This 'sameness' communicates itself to us continually, but never in such a way that we could detach it adequately from its historical forms, in order thus to step out of the constant movement of the flow of history on to the bank of eternity, at least in the matter of our knowledge of truth. We possess this eternal quality of truth in history, and hence we can only appropriate it by entrusting ourselves to its further course. If we refuse to take this risk, the formulations of dogma wrongly claimed to be 'perennial' will become unintelligible, like opaque glass which God's light can no longer penetrate.

In addition, theology must not ignore the fact that on the one hand it must employ already given concepts which it has not itself subjected to exhaustive reflection, but on the other hand these concepts of pre-theological origin continue their history in the extra-theological realm. The content of meaning of the terms used continues to change and thus can lead to deeper insight or to misunderstanding when these concepts and words are employed in theological formulas. Nowadays, for example, on hearing the word 'person' we are bound by an almost inevitable historical conditioning to imagine something which is by no means safely allowable when used in the context of trinitarian and Christological dogma. This is the case even with simple words like 'marriage', 'bread', 'wine'. The subtle theologian may be able to look after himself to some extent in these cases. But what about the ordinary theological 'consumer'? All, however, have to bear the burden of history, which is laid on theology too.

III

What are the implications for a theology which is aware of its historicity?

1. Theology must take into account changes determined by the total historical situation in which it exists. The history of theology must not be imagined as the unfolding of a complete system which, though taking place in time, unfolds solely according to the conditions of the system itself and its structure and can be predicted – assuming that the system is transparent from the beginning. This is not the case, even if the presupposition has to be made that what is developing in history (the *depositum fidei*) cannot itself grow any more. Here, too, history takes place within and springing from a real, cultural and sociologically conditioned total situation, which cannot be adequately reflected upon and which is thus not completely foreseeable in all its implications and consequences. Faith itself (as *fides qua* and *quae*) is the ultimate, comprehensive interpretation of human existence, involving its real concreteness in which the whole salvation of existence is to be effected. And so even if it were possible to express an abstract assertion about the nature of man, devoid of any historical reference, it would be insufficient as a statement of faith, confronting man in the concrete flesh of his history.

It is precisely expressions of faith (and thus theology) in respect of man which must by their very nature involve themselves above all in man's historical situation. This means dialogue with and within this situation in so far as the latter has itself been the object of scientific and theoretical reflection; it also means courage to become involved with the unreflected situation, accepting it and speaking from within it in the Christian hope that the truth of God, which must needs be expressed, will not – by the Spirit of God – be substantially corrupted (either objectively or subjectively) by being expressed from within the particular historical situation, even when unaccompanied by a final and transparent confirmation as to the legitimacy of the historical situation. It is obvious from this point of view that a complete, self-enclosed theological system is an absurdity. Seen in this way theology is and has always been eclectic theology. A truly living theology is free from the fear of not being sufficiently pure and systematic; the fear that it must not draw concepts, complexes of problems and perspectives from simply any quarters. This anxiety is unfounded in any case, because, when seen from the point of view of the history of ideas, the only material source for theology – scripture and tradition – has itself been involved in 'eclecticism' and in consequence has always gone without a material and adequately transparent synthesis of its plurality of data. It has never been able to ascertain positively and adequately whether and in what manner everything fits together.

2. If we exclude the fundamental change in the modern world from the cosmocentricity of the Classical and Mediaeval times to our modern anthropocentricity (i.e. the explicitly transcendental perspective of modern times), we see that the situation in which and to which theology's assertions must be spoken is characterised by three things:

(a) Firstly, by the rational world-view of the natural sciences, according to which every factor is explained by its antecedent factor and points to a subsequent factor – at least as far as methodology is concerned – and in which the world is a dynamic and developing system (though not capable of being adequately translated by us into our system in any positive and material way). Theology has not yet come to the end of this matter in its open and critical dialogue with today's situation; in its dialogue with a 'methodological atheism' (and its consequences for man's basic constitution) which inheres immanently in the presuppositions of this world-view, theology has not yet concluded its examination of the legitimacy and the limits of such methodological atheism; nor in respect of the possibility and the essence of the 'sign' (*Wunder*); nor with regard to the meaning of the idea of the 'abiding', unchangeable nature of man, and of the moral and juridical aspects of natural law; nor as regards the meaning, the implications and limits of an evolutionist world-view in general and the possibility of integrating Christian salvation-history into such a world-view.

(b) Today's situation is determined by the processed experiences of human historicity and the connection between all the individual elements and phases of history both in the time-continuum and in the interdependence of the various human dimensions (biological, social, cultural, etc.). Since it is nowadays interpreted almost inevitably after the manner of the natural sciences, this experience is sealed off from experience of what is absolutely new and simply unpredictable in new historical phenomena. Irrespective of whether and how far this mentality is correct or incorrect, one can only deal with it effectively provided that one has expressly understood in a theological manner that man's whole history, from its very first origins, has been knit together with divine grace, that one of the constituents of man's historical existence is always inevitably his *supernatural existentiale*. Consequently theology cannot expect salvation-history as officially expressed to appear without any real continuity with the history before and around it. As this dynamic relationship of grace and revelation in the whole of history has not yet been sufficiently pondered upon by theology, the latter's dialogue with the modern situation with regard to historicity has not been developed enough.

(c) The situation of the modern world is that of a world which has become dynamic, in which man consciously plans and creates himself and his environment with a view to the future. This is another aspect of the modern situation with which theology has not been sufficiently concerned. It is true that since Leo XIII it has asserted more clearly the principles of human social organisation according to natural law, but it has regarded them chiefly as being contained in assertions concerning society's permanent essence, and thus as factors instrumental in conserving order and stability. But theology has neither given close enough examination to the historically conditioned 'models' behind this kind of vague 'principles', nor has it sufficiently developed – out of the dynamic quality of the times and of the Christian message – the imperatives and prototypes needed for the this-worldly future which is to be actively created. The dialogue with this aspect of the situation was actually not declared necessary until the Second Vatican Council. As far as the future of theology itself is concerned, all depends on the task being begun now in earnest. A Christian eschatology must also develop a theology of the relationship between Christian existence and projected this-worldly utopias. Just as Christianity, as a result of its unique understanding of the world, has emancipated from itself a secular world so that the latter may grasp its freedom and its own significance, so too, from the position of its own eschatological view of the future, Christianity must allow a this-worldly vision of the future to emerge legitimately from within. If it does this, theology will change.

3. The situation in which theology carries on its dialogue with the world is conditioned in part by sin. It is strange how little the Christian

teaching about sin is explicitly applied to the field of knowledge. Of course sin in this field, where it basically takes the form of an *actus intellectualis* as such, is radical error, personally committed. And Christian theology has a lot to say about truth and error. But quite apart from the fact that theology only deals in a very defective way with man's achievement of truth or falsehood from the point of view of its moral character as 'decision', guilt (as concretely objectified in e.g. the cultural, social situation of a particular time) in the field of knowledge can be incurred in quite different ways besides merely through propositions which, taken by themselves, must be described as 'falsehood'. Prejudice, bias, deafness to other aspects of reality, obstinate conservatism isolating itself from new knowledge, premature emphasis, heresies which come to light in a way of life but which consequently or instinctively withdraw from theoretical expression, the failure to take other opinions seriously, the impatient haste or obstructive lethargy which can miss truth's real *kairos* as that which brings salvation (in ecclesial jargon termed misunderstanding the 'opportuneness' of a truth), an unbalanced urgency in presenting a particular truth – these and many other possibilities of sin exist apart from the falsehood of a proposition even in the realm of the most rarefied and pure theoretical knowledge.

If man's concrete situation is determined therefore (whether he himself deals righteously or sinfully) in part by sin as a general 'existentiale' of human existence, this applies also in the ways we have mentioned, and in other ways, to man's situation in respect of his knowledge. Man's situation in knowing is not only historically finite (contingent, bound to a particular perspective), but it is also always partially conditioned by man's sin in the matter of objectification. Human reflection is quite unable to 'rid itself' adequately of sin prior to any thought within the situation (for to do so it would again require to think 'in a situation'). Theology's historicity is therefore also determined in part by sin. It could be said that even the situation in which truth is found is determined in part by 'concupiscence', and this conditioning factor can never be adequately eliminated. Consequently even the concrete attaining of truth itself, which is always more than the mere 'possessing' of the truth of a true statement, is subject to the question as to whether one has dealt righteously or sinfully, a question which can ultimately only be answered by the judgment of God.

What has been said however, implies two things for theology and its historicity:

(a) Theology's dialogue with and within the present situation neither can nor need be pursued with the idea that theology's partner-in-dialogue is the bearer of a knowledge which does justice in all things to the truth and to the present hour. Within and in spite of its own historicity theology has a thoroughly critical function to exercise with regard to the 'spirit of the age'. Theology changes the concepts it adopts for its own communications, and must have the courage to contradict and to contest ideology's absolutising of insights which may be in themselves correct. At the same time theology must always retain the self-critical awareness that it will by no means always recognise the sinfulness of the spirit of the age easily and as a matter of course wherever it crops up and in its most decisive instances; it must be aware that it is itself always in danger of unwittingly protesting against a coming situation merely in the name of an earlier historical situation. It must realise that the very act of contradicting a time-bound ideology demonstrates the historicity of theology, for the latter cannot choose its opponent for itself, and in a strange way it falls beneath its opponent's law in contradicting it.

(b) But theology must also know about the sinfulness of its own historicity, not only the sinfulness of the situation in which it finds itself. Setting aside for the moment the error which always clings to it, we may observe in theology that very concrete form taken by man's sinfulness in the field of knowledge. Theology itself can be tedious, complacent; it can be narrow-minded in not taking the questions of the times seriously and not being open to bear the full weight of them, with the result that they are not really brought to mind. Theology may imagine that a formal framework can be a substitute for a concrete answer to a genuine problem. It may think it has the answer already before it has taken account of the new questions; it may think that the proof must be correct because the conclusion (perhaps taken as settled from another quarter) is correct. It can imagine too easily that it has uncovered a contradiction when it is in reality only too weak and comfortable to find a synthesis. It can be tempted to regard Church orthodoxy as automatically demonstrating scholarly competence. It can imagine that the great questions of God and the world have been discussed enough and that all that is required is to pass on the sacred formulas like an inheritance of ancient and precious jewels; it can harden its heart and not see behind the opponent's false assertions the deep distress of a fellow man; it can forget that not all talk about truth is automatically done in love, although this ought to be the case. It is possible for theology to be carried on in a sinful manner. This is because the theologians are themselves sinners. Theology's dialogue with the spirit of the age can only be pursued correctly if theologians always tacitly reckon with the historicity of their own theology, in which their own sinfulness is objectified.

4. As is apparent from what has just been said, the historicity of theology implies the possibility and the effects of error even in theology not officially condemned (at least at a particular time) by Church authority. Theology must take account of this in its dialogue. It is unfortunate that although this fact is not denied *in thesi*, and is also admitted as a historical fact, it has not been recognised as a subject-matter for theology as such. Thus it happens, for instance, that the kinds of theological error are distinguished by the so-called 'theological qualifications' according to their occurrence in particular propositions; but error is not distinguished in its inner essence itself. However, it is by no means easy to say where and what an 'error' is, where it is only 'ignorance', where the *abstractio* which is not yet a *mendacium* begins and ends, where a particular individual perspective, within which a particular reality is seen, claims such absolute validity (in actual fact, even if it is not claimed in theory) that it becomes effectively an error. The question hardly ever arises as to the significance of the presence of two propositions, which seen objectively are mutually exclusive, within a single consciousness – though, indeed, in different degrees of clarity and agreement. When does a distinction introduced into a statement make it clearer, when does it reveal it as previously wrongly understood, i.e. as error? At the same time it must be remembered that, because of its concrete actuality as the object of our thought, even a statement which must be designated simply as true (e.g. a definition) can enter into a field of meaning and frame of reference which latter, since they are themselves not proof against error in their construction, again make the question of the truth of the relevant proposition much more difficult than it at first seemed. And if even the truest statement does not say everything about the reality it intends, but selects its material, it is only too easy to draw consequences from it which are unwittingly and tacitly based on the assumption that the whole of intentional reality is hidden within the proposition in question.

One ought to demonstrate all this with examples in greater detail than is possible here, in order to communicate the importance of the questions raised. It is not easy to distinguish error from ignorance in theology. If, since the Council of Trent at least, the celebrant's special function at the Mass was so one-sidedly uppermost in the average awareness of theologians and the faithful that all that remained for the Christian was mere attendance at Mass, was that ignorance or error? If someone maintains the dogma of Original Sin but is simply unaware that this sin and personal habitual sin are united in an analogous and not in a univocal concept, has he then made a true statement and merely been ignorant of a second and different one, or has he misunderstood a dogma and committed error? Why is the dogma of 'Transubstantiation' true (which no-one will doubt), although the *substantia panis* does not exist in the sense in which it was conceived at the time when the dogma was formulated? Now we can make 'distinctions' in these cases, but precisely that was impossible in earlier historical situations. Why and in which cases does this kind of inability to make distinctions not constitute an error in the earlier understanding of the particular assertion?

However these questions are to be answered, there are errors in theology, even in the theology not officially condemned. This is proved by the history of theology, and not only the history of times long past, e.g. when the Immaculate Conception was not only not known, but was a matter of admitted dispute. It has also been so in our most recent past. The changes which have appeared during the last hundred years up until the most recent time cannot all be included under the heading of 'the transition from the implicit to the explicit', from the less to the more precise, or as the simple addition of new supplementary insights. There has also been the transition from error to true insight, not without struggle, pain and bitter personal sacrifice. Much of what is and what must be taught today – this applies even to Vatican II – with regard to questions of biblical studies, questions of the nature of marriage, freedom of conscience, sociological questions, questions on the borderland between science and theology, problems in the history of dogma – much of this was at an earlier time disputed, fought over and highly suspect in theology; opposed to it was the *sententiae communis* protected and propagated by the *magisterium*, even though not, of course, in a definitive and obligatory form. The generally accepted academic theory that there are *sententiae per se reformabiles* in the theology and in official teaching as well, is not merely a theory but also – if we are honest – a theory confirmed by fact.

It is not fortuitous that Vatican II (against considerable opposition from conservative theologians on the Council's Theological Commission) asserted that the Church's *magisterium* is infallible not when propounding a doctrine in a merely general way, but when it declares one as commanding the absolute assent of faith. Of course that does not mean that where this is not the case one can think and teach whatever one wishes, as if there were no such thing as the obligation of theological assent (even if the latter is itself capable of reform). But the facts and the Church's doctrine oblige the theologian to be modest and self-critical, taking the possibility of error into account even when presenting a traditional doctrine and one which is favoured by the Church's teaching office. Theology must be aware of this since it does not only *live* its historicity, as it did almost exclusively in the past, but nowadays is also consciously *aware* of it. It must ponder the matter and always seriously include it anew in its calculations. In one respect, therefore, it will move more slowly and hesitantly (it may be symptomatic that not a single new definition was produced at Vatican II), but on the other hand it will often more easily find the courage to give up an obsolete position without each time having to apply too much skill in interpreting traditional formulas. In this new situation, where theology has become capable of reflecting upon its own historicity, it is indeed hard to have to become conversant right from the start with a genuine synthesis comprising a correctly understood obligation to the past and the courage to commit oneself to the present and the future; but it is also quite clear and does not dispense one from the necessity of giving up theological positions which are no longer tenable. This courage is a better act of faith than the anxious conservatism which only gives up such a position when development has far outrun the mental framework of the thesis in question, so that the latter can only be found haunting text-books; and the damage done by this time is very great as regards the readiness to believe and the confidence in the Church's teaching authority on the part of intellectuals and also of ordinary people.

In theory and practice the most important form taken by such a possible error in theology (irrespective of whether anyone does or does not want to call it an 'error') is when a really important, indispensable (and possibly also defined) affirmation reveals certain 'impurities', standing within a field of meanings and problems which cannot make the same claims as the affirmation itself, or being illustrated by a model which is not timeless but itself subject to the process of historical change. What is decisive is that this 'impurity' cannot be observed automatically at all times and in all cultural periods; thus it is not so easy to decide later on whether this 'impurity' (the model, or, in short, that which is implicitly and unconsciously understood in addition to the true theological propositions) was originally put forward with the same absolute claims as the particular affirmation itself, and hence whether it shares the latter's theologically obligatory character or not. In the end one can show historically that the formulation of the indispensable theological statement originally included the implicit, unconscious content which justly appears to us today in such a problematical light, and which we eliminate from our understanding of the indispensable affirmation. Once we have this 'distinction', once it is accepted and current everywhere, the problem is over. And even the most conservative theologian will then say that the affirmation in question was always understood within the context of this distinction – which is of course by and large a somewhat unhistorical interpretation of the history of theology. But a long struggle is required before this 'distinction' becomes accepted, and the immediate impression is that the 'distinction' is actually destroying the true affirmation itself and is arbitrary. Indeed it may be that the 'progressive' opponent of the 'impurity' is actually of the opinion that his denial of the impurity is also a denial of the affirmation itself, because he too is incapable of envisaging such a distinction. The historicity even of theological truth is revealed most clearly by this rejection of a particular model. And it is not a rejection in favour of a metaphysical affirmation which is now 'pure', but a rejection in the transition to a new model which is not amenable to adequate reflection at all. (Every concept needs a *conversio ad phantasma.*)

Plenty of examples could be found for what is meant. Only a few can be indicated here. The statement 'There must be private property' is correct. But now much was thought to follow from this in practice from the middle of the nineteenth century on! How much that by no means follows, and yet which was thought to be justified by this affirmation. Augustine was correct in saying that Original Sin was passed on *generatione*. But as yet he was unable to distinguish this concept from the *libido generandi*. And that was wrong. Viewed historically, did he intend something incorrect by this statement? 'God inspired the Bible' is an indispensable affirmation. But it was previously thought to mean all manner of things which have had to be given up. 'The Gospels are historical accounts' – a true statement. But what does that mean precisely, and what does it no longer mean, although it was thought to do so in earlier times? 'Original Sin as such incurs damnation' – a correct statement. But how am I to imagine this 'damnation' in greater detail? May I, must I immediately imagine it (like Augustine) as the damnation which results from personal sin? Does this statement oblige me to maintain that there really is this kind of damnation resulting merely from Original Sin, or is it only a question of a hypothetical statement? 'Marriage is an institution orientated towards procreation' is a true statement. But does this 'definition' exhaust the nature of marriage? Or has not the affirmation often been taken unconsciously – and wrongly – as an adequate definition of marriage? 'In a society all have not the same function' – a true statement. But has it not been unconsciously understood as sanctioning an undemocratic, paternalistic society? 'Error has no rights' – a true statement. But have not false consequences long been drawn from this? Has it been made clear that it was itself wrongly understood, and that hence an error has been propounded?

Error exists, therefore, in theology. It cannot easily be separated from defined dogma straight away. Theology's possibility of error is the most radical indication of its historicity, in so far as the latter is related to the knowledge of truth as such.

IV

This historicity is accepted and realised by the dialogue continually maintained with the spirit of a particular period, expressed in its sciences. Inasmuch as in this dialogue theology is the representative of God's Revelation and the Church's Faith, it need not regard the other partner-in-dialogue as of equal status with itself. This question too is not so easy, however, because even on the secular and non-ecclesial side, viewed objectively, it is not merely human intellect and worldly experience at work, but most decidedly the effects (perhaps hidden and anonymous) of the illumination of supernatural grace and faith and the impulses of the Holy Spirit.

But however this may be, the Church speaks (at different levels, and hence also through the mouth of its theology) as the historical and social representative of a truth from which she cannot fall, as a result of the eschatological promise of God and his grace. The 'world' does not possess this promise (or rather, possesses it only through the Church). Although, however, the dialogue between the Church's theology and the world is not simply a dialogue between two equal partners seeking truth in the same way, it is still a real and open dialogue. This is simply because the Church, on account of the historicity of her theology, is a learning Church, because her pilgrim's course through history also follows the path of truth. For she is guided into all truth by the succouring Spirit of God himself. But this same Spirit leads her ever anew into the truth which she always possesses, through confrontation with her constantly new situation. And since this same mystagogy of the Spirit challenges man's free endeavour and his responsible decision-making to enter into the truth of the Church, the Church today is pledged to carry on the dialogue with the world as a way of perpetual self-realisation and reappropriation of her truth. For there has never before in history been so much 'raw material' for the Church's faith to confront. The Church is faced with an inconceivably immense task. The course of history, especially the history of science, is accelerating at a previous unimaginable rate. Consequently this applies also to the course of the history of theology.

5

THEOLOGY AND THE CHURCH'S TEACHING AUTHORITY AFTER THE COUNCIL

On the 24th of July Cardinal Ottaviani as Pro-prefect of the Congregation for the Propagation of the Faith sent a letter to the chairmen of the bishops' conferences. This letter, which was originally intended to be confidential, was concerned with certain tendencies and dangers in modern Catholic theology and in the Church's theological mentality. Evidently the confidential nature of the letter could not be preserved. Very soon larger or smaller reports or excerpts appeared in the press. Consequently it was decided at Rome to publish the letter in the *Acta Apostolicae Sedis*.[1] As a result it is available to everyone and has thus also become an object of public reflection and discussion.

The content of Ottaviani's letter to the bishops is as follows:

The letter begins with the assertion that it is the task of the whole people of God now to really translate into action what has been decided at the Second Vatican Council in matters of doctrine or discipline.[2] The letter continues that it is the task of the episcopate to watch over, to lead and to further this 'movement of renewal' begun by the Council (one may add that all three tasks are to be attended to equally). This must happen in such a way that the genuine unfalsified content and intention of the Vatican documents and decrees is respected in every detail. It is the task of the bishops themselves to protect this doctrine since they are held to have a real commission of authoritative teaching under Peter as their head. However, it is to be regretted that news has come to Rome from various parts of the Church concerning abuses in the interpretation of the Council's doctrine and irresponsible opinions, appearing here and there and causing not a little confusion in the minds of many of the faithful.

[1] cf. *AAS* 58 (1966), pp. 659–661.

[2] We would commend this statement – issued by such high Church authority and by a man who is entirely above the suspicion of indiscretely craving for novelty – above all to those circles in the Catholic Church in Germany (e.g. certain of the 'Una voce' groups) who apparently regard it as their privilege to defend ancient truth and hallowed tradition, and who under certain circumstances are not afraid to attack representatives of the Episcopate with most ridiculous suspicions.

Of course it is imperative to distinguish properly between the deposit of faith and any other opinions; consequently all attempts to understand the doctrines of faith better are to be encouraged. But from the reports of learned theologians and from the study of published theological works the Congregation has become aware of not a few theories which 'to a certain extent' affect dogma and the fundamentals of the faith itself and are no longer keeping within the limits of a legitimate freedom of opinion and hypothesis.

The letter then gives instances to support this observation, emphasising explicitly that it is quoting *examples* of these 'errors', not giving a balanced and exhaustive description of these theological dangers. *Ten* of them are enumerated. 1. Concerning revelation: recourse to scripture with an intentional exclusion of tradition, including the restriction of biblical inspiration and the infallibility of scripture, and the false evaluation of historical texts. 2. Concerning the doctrines of the faith: here and there people are of the opinion that dogmatic formulas of faith are so much involved in the flux of historical development that even their objective import can change. 3. Concerning the teaching office, especially the Pope: it is often so neglected or slightly regarded that it is almost seen as a matter of opinion. 4. Concerning the existence of an objective, absolute, firm and unchangeable truth: certain people practically refuse to acknowledge such a thing and subject truth to a kind of relativism, asserting that truth must necessarily follow the rhythm of the development of consciousness and history. 5. Concerning Christology: certain concepts are used in the re-examination of Christology which are hardly compatible with defined dogma; a 'Christological humanism' is spreading (*serpit*), reducing Christ to the level of an ordinary human being who only gradually became aware of his divine sonship; the virgin birth, miracles and even the resurrection are only held verbally, and in actual fact are made into purely natural matters. 6. Concerning sacramental theology: quite apart from the other sacraments, in the case of the Eucharist certain facts are overlooked or not sufficiently attended to; certain people, pursuing an exaggerated symbolism, proceed as though there were no transubstantiation but only a kind of 'trans-signification'; the truth of the sacrificial aspect is unjustifiably neglected. 7. Concerning the sacrament of Penance: besides the neglect or denial of the personal confession of sin, some people conceive this sacrament as a 'reconciliation with the Church' without emphasising sufficiently that it is also a reconciliation with God. 8. Concerning Original Sin: there are those (*nec desunt qui*) who attach little value to the teaching of the Council of Trent or interpret it so that Adam's original sin and the transmission of the guilt of sin itself become obscured. 9. Concerning moral theology: not a few are spreading error concerning the objective nature of morality, denying natural law, advocating a situation ethics and corrupt opinions on the morals of sex and marriage and human responsibility in this field. 10. Concerning ecumenism: however much all the work done in this area is to be praised in its encouragement of love and unity with the separated brethren, the Apostolic See (!) regrets that there are people who wrongly interpret the conciliar Decree on

Ecumenism and understand ecumenical work in a way which detracts from the truth of the unity of the faith and the Church in a dangerous indifferentism and irenism.

Finally the letter observes that the errors and dangers which are propounded and incurred in individual instances here and there have been set before the bishops in this short summary so that each bishop can concern himself with overcoming or preventing them in accordance with the duties of his office.

As one can see, there is no mention of particular countries where these errors and dangers can be observed particularly. Although the ten points quoted are said to be examples, their theological compass is so wide (more or less explicitly) that practically the whole of theology can be subsumed under their headings except the question of God and modern atheism. Ostensibly the letter is concerned only with dangers and errors of Catholic Christians[3] and theologians, but one may wonder here and there whether in fact it was not also aimed beyond this sphere at Protestant theology or bore in mind the echo which the latter has had among us, which, though not in a tangible written form, is revealed in many people's attitude of mind and in oral theological discussion. The text scarcely discloses whether the extent and urgency of the errors and dangers are regarded as greater in particular topics or whether they are all roughly equal in this respect.

It is the intention of this essay to set forth a number of theological observations which arise or are at least possible from reading this letter. They can only be discussed very generally here as it is clearly impossible in a short essay to deal with the themes raised by the ten errors and dangers referred to.

I

First of all let us make one or two observations concerning the spiritual and intellectual climate within which Ottaviani's letter is to be read. It is one of a certain insecurity and perplexity. To admit this is not unworthy of a Christian nor of authority in the Church. There are questions which are of great import and yet for which no immediate answer is forthcoming. A situation can be opaque; it can have many levels; it can be difficult to weigh up the individual tendencies, currents and opinions or to know when a particular thing is perhaps loudly proclaimed in the Church and yet remains peripheral and uncharacteristic of the majority

[3] The Protestant Church is itself suffering even more from the issues raised here, as is clearly shown, for instance, in Bishop Hanns Lilje's Pastoral Letter: 'Hirtenbrief über den Kirchentag', *Lutherische Monatshefte* 5 (1966), pp. 462–470 (cf. in the same issue of the journal Bishop H. Meyer, 'Theologie und Gemeinde', pp. 470 ff.). Naturally, however, we cannot discuss this different situation here.

of theologians and Church people. It can be hard to recognise what is a short-lived fashion, due to disappear of its own accord, and what is the beginning of a more serious danger to come; or what is only theology making up for lost time with rather a lot of noise because it was previously dominated by a stagnant theological conservatism, which stubbornly and in fear isolated itself from the real questions. Consequently it remains difficult to say where tendencies appear which really threaten the faith of the Church. The letter does not attempt to draw a veil over this situation of uncertainty. It draws attention to complexes of problems and questions, gives warnings, but does not reach any really doctrinal decisions, not even of a preliminary kind. That is quite within the rights of the Congregation for the Propagation of the Faith. Indeed, it is its duty.

In addition there is this: today it is in the first place never merely a question of repeating the ancient truth, presenting it authoritatively and saying No to deviations from it. We are concerned with presenting this truth in such a way that it really 'speaks to' men and is accepted willingly as being intrinsically true. Whatever the formal doctrinal position may be, it is not sufficient in actual fact to refer back to the formal juridical authority of the Pope and the bishops. Whether we wish it or not, we are subject to the necessity of finding a way between, on the one hand, a 'monolithism'[4] to which everything was clear and where at least anything of any importance could be decided on easily, unambiguously and, above all, quickly and was in fact so decided in a papal declaration of some kind (Encyclical, papal address, declaration from the Holy Office etc.), and on the other hand the tangled chaos in which theologians and laymen feel that in matters of faith they can think and say anything and everything they wish.

The first way is no longer possible as it was pursued previously. It is clear that Vatican II preferred a different method, was more careful and reticent in dogmatic pronouncements, gave more scope to 'dialogue' within the Church, and allowed the different theological currents to be expressed in a less inhibited manner. It has been shown that in many

[4] The reader is asked to excuse our using a word from the realm of politics in this context. But it seems briefly and clearly to characterise a particular way in which Church authority (which is not simply identical with the rights and duties of the *magisterium* itself) used to react before John XXIII and the Second Vatican Council. This attitude, which prevailed since Pius IX and above all since the fight against Modernism, may have been justified in its time, but it is nowadays no longer appropriate to the situation and must change, precisely so that the *magisterium* can exercise its function effectively.

questions an unequivocal and obligatory doctrine can be less easily formulated than was thought to be the case twenty years ago. Complexes of questions, theological terminology and methods have become so diverse in recent decades that it has become much more difficult to say exactly what a theological idea really means when it is 'translated' into another theological language – a task which is necessary, however, in the modern theological pluralism.

The second way, for a Catholic understanding of the faith and the Church, is a false path: there must be a confession of faith in the Church; it is not the case that there are merely equally valid 'interpretations' of the most diverse, disparate or even contradictory kinds in the Church, behind which the common 'meaning' is found only as what is unutterable and inexpressible. There is an authoritative teaching office which is able to express the Church's faith in genuine human conceptuality as true and binding on everyone. It can reject a contrary affirmation and can command assent in saying that such an affirmation is contrary to the truth, however much all the Church's expressions of faith on the one hand point in the direction of the incomprehensibility of God, and on the other hand include the element of congruity within a community of language which could be otherwise.[5] Naturally it cannot be our task in this short essay to provide a foundation for this 'inbetween' situation in a theological theory of knowledge or even to give practical rules for following this 'via media'. In this area much remains to be done.

The tendencies and views mentioned by Ottaviani do exist. They exist in the German-speaking world too, although not all in the same degree of clarity. Of course these views do not exist as a complete system. Nor can all the dangers and errors be found to the same extent in German theological literature. It is rather that many of these things are present in the form of a particular mentality, or only come to light in private oral discussion. Naturally these tendencies are clearly expressed in Protestant theology except in the case of specifically Catholic themes likes transubstantiation for example. So it would be very remarkable if they were absent from Catholic theology in the German-speaking world (especially today when both theologies influence each other much more than ever before). We have these tendencies too. We shall not illustrate this with individual references, since in the first place it by no means depends on how far the tendencies and attitudes mentioned have found expression in actual theological literature. But we must observe (1) that, as we have

[5] cf. K. Rahner/K. Lehmann, *Mysterium Salutis* I, ed. J. Feiner/M. Löhrer (Einsiedeln, 1965), pp. 686–703, esp. 693 ff.; cf. ibid., pp. 727–782 (literature).

said, these tendencies have certainly not been formulated as a 'complete system'; and (2) that there are also questions not mentioned in the letter, although they are just as important (if not more so), which must be attended to. The question of God, of the possibility of experiencing him, the question of atheism and all that is connected with atheism as its foundation – these too belong among the problems which find themselves in a situation of insecurity.

The individual spheres of problems referred to in the letter are also (though not exclusively) concerned almost always with genuine questions and obscurities, with the difficulty of finding a genuine synthesis of the inheritance of faith with what constitutes the modern mentality and with the new questions and insights of the theological and profane sciences. Consequently nothing is effected by giving a simple 'No' to all this and by repeating traditional doctrine of which even the very formulation is monotonous to the ear. This was often stressed by the Council too. But Ottaviani's letter makes rather too little mention of this. In addition the letter's treatment of the issues is unfortunately marked by a vagueness, inevitable to a certain extent, but which is not very helpful. One is obliged to say this in all modesty and openness, even while bearing in mind that this letter was a request to the bishops and did not intend to be a long exposition of theological doctrines.

For instance, when is the *vis inerrantiae et inspirationis* incorrectly 'constricted' (*coarctant*)? For there *is* a legitimate and necessary drawing of boundaries. When is the objective meaning of a dogmatic formula wrongly altered? For there *is* a movement of change in theology which, for instance, purifies the enduring meaning of a dogmatic formula of accompanying misunderstandings which were previously almost inevitable, or which separates it from interpretations which were previously not so clearly distinguishable and now may be freely discussed.[6] When has the doctrine of the Church's teaching authority been under-valued? For there has been progress in theological knowledge (in the last century too) which has caused reformable doctrines of the teaching office to be recognised as being also *de facto* to be reformed.[7] When has there been a false relativism? There exists a development and a history of doctrine, which cannot be interpreted merely as the result of new supplementary

[6] cf. K. Rahner, 'Zur Geschichtlichkeit der Theologie', *Integritas*. 'Geistige Wandlung und menschliche Wirklichkeit', ed. D. Stolte/R. Wisser, *Festschrift für K. Holzamer* (Tübingen, 1966), pp. 75–95, in this volume, pp. 64 ff.

[7] One only needs to consider the concrete example of evolution (in relation to the concept of Creation, etc.).

items of knowledge but which understands the ancient, 'enduring' truths in a new way. Which new concepts are being tried out in Christology which are incompatible with the Christological definitions? For there is in Catholic theology a process of rethinking of Christology, which is clearly necessary and must work with a modern conceptuality without incurring theological censure. When has the definition of 'transubstantiation' been damaged, when is the concept of 'Agape' *plus aequo* emphasised at the expense of 'sacrifice'? There are certainly many obscurities in the doctrine of original sin, but when can one speak of 'obscuring' the doctrine if biblical aspects are stressed which are not clearly visible enough in the traditional doctrine? If we are right in rejecting a 'situation ethics' (which?; and what does it imply?), what is the sound core which it does have and which is not sufficiently clear in traditional moral theology? What are the *perniciosae opiniones* in modern sexual morality and how can they be distinguished from the good elements of progress beyond the teachings of Pius XI and XII, which have doubtlessly been accepted or at least prepared for by the Council? When and by what means is a correct ecumenism perverted by a false irenism and indifferentism?

One cannot deny that the tendencies and dangers mentioned in the letter actually exist. Nor can one say that a letter of this sort, or the Church's teaching office in Rome, could do much more than giving this kind of very general warning. But it is precisely this which reveals the situation: modern theology inevitably deals with a mass of problems and methods of conceptual expression and is so weighed down by the awareness of the ambiguity of all statements that it is not so easy as previously to replace a real or suspected error with another, positive and unequivocal statement in which men of goodwill recognise that not only something correct is said but also something which is equal to their 'concern'.

The situation must be looked at and appreciated soberly; for only then can one ask how the Church and her teaching authority relate in the most correct and effective way within this situation. It is a situation of a pluralism of scholarly theological methods and terminologies, an inconceivable breadth of scope of theological problems, in the face of which no individual theologian can be an adequate specialist at all. For this reason the theologians' theses are no longer simple Yes or No answers to a doctrine which has been traditionally handed on and is fixed and formulated, equally familiar to all, but they are often related to the particular doctrine in a uniquely disparate way. These theses are mostly formulated in a 'dialogue' with philosophies, profane theorems, world-views, which are themselves ranged quite disparately beside one another and are not known and understood in their plurality by any one individual. However much one must always strive to speak with *one* language, to understand each other mutually, these attempts have material limits today. The attempt to produce an absolutely homogeneous theology from the point of view of terminology and the questions it deals with, accessible to all theologians, if it could succeed at all, would end up as the theology of a small sect, unable to address itself to its environment any more. In addition, this situation is characterised and made more difficult by the fact that not a few contemporary Christians maintain in themselves a strange 'unity' of two attitudes: on the one hand the tendency towards 'reinterpreting' doctrine, often with little respect for authoritative Church doctrine, whereby the desire for novelty easily dominates over the preservation of what is permanently valid in ancient doctrine, and on the other hand the desire to stay in the Church and to make room within it for one's own understanding of the faith. If one may put it crudely: before, one simply said No to an affirmation of authoritative Church doctrine and left the Church; now one tries to interpret this doctrine in one's own way and desires it to become commonly held in the Church. By this over-simplified but not insignificant description of the situation we do not mean that authoritative doctrine needs no interpretation but only to be simply repeated, precisely in order that it shall remain and be believed. But the question is, what are the limits of such an interpretation? What are the limits which cannot be exceeded, so that the Church may have the definite courage to say No when they are exceeded, and that the proposer of the interpretation may have the courage and honesty to leave the Church, whose confession of faith he can maintain only verbally and not according to the actual issues? We cannot here answer the question as to how this peculiar 'unity' of two such opposed attitudes is to be explained. In brief one might say perhaps that this 'unity' is symptomatic of the transition from an individualistic to a 'collectivist' age. People (still) wish to think individualistically and yet belong to a community of a similar mind. We cannot deny that such an intention has its justification and is – correctly understood – a task for a meaningful future. The question is only how both can be joined in one in a genuine manner.

II

In a situation like this, which will surely last for a long time, the former ways and means of doctrinal leadership are evidently insufficient. Today all authoritative representatives of doctrinal world-views (not only the Catholic Church) are faced with the question of how the unity of the obligatory doctrine can coexist side by side with the much quicker development of knowledge in freedom, and how those who make authoritative decisions in these matters are to respond in this situation.

There has been as yet far too little reflection on this matter. The letter also seems to be a symptom of this now inevitable embarrassment, which is, however, without doubt a healthy sign: one is rightly aware that one cannot do simply everything and commit everything to the 'free discussion' of 'autonomous scholarship', and at the same time one cannot see precisely how and what one is to decide clearly, in order that the decision is both correct as far as the particular issue is concerned and also effective.

It is here that the bishops themselves have a task, so that they need no longer simply wait for authoritative decisions or 'doctrinal political' measures from Rome, as was mostly the case before, content to be relieved of this difficult office of teacher in the modern Church by the Congregation for the Propagation of the Faith. Here we see a strange convergence between the theoretical teaching of Vatican II concerning the bishops' teaching authority, which they possess *iure divino* and on which they must themselves lay hold, and the concrete situation which calls for such a teaching authority. The bishops cannot pass on this task of theirs either to the authorities in Rome or to the theologians.[8] What the dogmatic constitution on the Church of Vatican II said about the office of a bishop is not to remain mere pious print. Furthermore it would be highly dangerous if Rome's effectual authority – the effectiveness of which is not unlimited – were over-taxed. The bishops can address themselves to a particular, regionally diverse situation with better prospects of actual effectiveness than Rome. For while Pius XII was in office Rome did not always proceed sufficiently carefully and sympathetically, with the result that (if we are seeing things as they unfortunately are) it doubtless lost a certain amount of effective authority even among those who were not in principle opposed to this doctrinal authority. Therefore that authority of the bishops which is humanly speaking more effective in particular concrete circumstances, should not be by-passed. It can be more effective – in the human sphere above all – because it can react more appropriately to a concrete situation, confronting and appreciating not only opinions

[8] It is interesting to observe the parallel situation that Bishop Lilje too has to defend himself against the accusation that he is not exercising his episcopal teaching authority (cf. supra, p. 85 note 3).

but also those who hold them. It is, or could be, therefore practically speaking more capable of dialogue. Ultimately too it is more effective since, being the penultimate authority, it can 'risk' more (and should have the courage to do so).

In not a few cases the clergy must understand more clearly than before that by no means everything which is discussed in theological science is also suitable for the pulpit. The pulpit is not the proper place for dubious 'demythologisings'. This distinction does not imply in any way that the preacher may say things in the pulpit which he could not defend before the honest and truth-seeking conscience of the scholarly Church theologian. The distinction is based on insight into the sermon's purpose: the salvation of man in the concrete, of the man who is listening and who can be hurt even by what is, in the abstract, a correct statement, if it is said wrongly. Indeed, the letter itself says that the bishops themselves are to do something about this and not merely make reports, and to this extent the letter is 'post-conciliar' in the best sense.

One ought to try as far as possible to foresee doctrinal and practical developments, to lay hold on them in good time and direct them into right paths, separating what is inevitable and correct from what is extreme, eccentric and mistaken. Many of these tendencies which are just becoming apparent to us will very soon become more pronounced and more threatening. We must take that into account quite soberly. The questions which are also raised in the letter will be asked more loudly and more publicly; e.g. the question of 'error' in scripture; the relationship, in theory and practice, of the man who is both Catholic and theologian to non-definitive decisions of the Church; the manner of knowing God; the nature of original sin; the virginity of the Mother of God; the meaning of God becoming man etc.; also the more practical questions of life and piety will become more urgent, e.g. the concrete forms of the Eucharist (Benediction, 'visits', processions, Exposition); of the confession of devotion; of sexual morality; of mixed marriages; the ethics of education (confessional questions concerned with schools); the celibacy of the secular clergy etc. We can imagine that these and many other similar questions will be asked more insistently and clearly everywhere in the foreseeable future. Something ought to be done in this respect in good time. If false views have already become entrenched and are proclaimed loud and clear in the Church's public consciousness, it is already almost too late. But much is still possible now, at the beginning of the development. It should therefore be actually taken in hand. Nothing is gained by a fearful, deadly silence.

In this matter it is inadmissible to think that everything is clear and that only muddle-heads have new problems with the old questions, which have been answered clearly long ago. For instance, there still seem to be canonists (and bishops too?) who proceed as though a Catholic is morally not permitted – by virtue of divine law – to contract a particular marriage if the children cannot be guaranteed a Catholic upbringing. That is incorrect.[9] Or it is thought to be completely left to the Church's discretion – not only according to canon law, but also morally – under what conditions a mixed marriage may be permitted. That is not right. The question of the 'infallibility' of scripture has not been answered and solved by the Council alone in such a way as to do real justice, in a positive manner, to the legitimate difficulties and problematical situations of the exegetes (and nowadays of the laity too). The question of Christ's knowledge concerning himself is one for which the exegete demands a better answer of the dogmatician than before, in order to deal with his problems. Nowadays, in spite of 'Humani generis', one may surely be permitted to assume that a theory of polygenism does not contradict the doctrine of original sin as defined at the Council of Trent. But this ought to be substantiated in greater detail and it ought to be shown that a polygenism of this kind does not require such a reinterpretation of the doctrine of original sin which would dissolve the dogma effectively into a weak rationalism. The doctrine of original sin must be re-thought no less in other points too, even if one is obliged to respect completely the teaching of Trent on this issue. The open questions in practical sexual morality are well known. Text-book theology has often arrived at an answer too easily. What degree of moral maturity is needed to constitute an indissoluble marriage is a dark question, and its answer has very practical consequences which the canonists have by no means been considering clearly enough or long enough. There are plenty more examples like this.

In many cases Rome itself will only be able to give a 'skeleton answer' (like the Council). Such an answer is important. But it is often not sufficient to protect the orthodox doctrine in a way which does not demand an unjustified *sacrificium intellectus* or permit the propounding of actual heresy or theological error under cover of an apparent verbal respect for authoritative doctrine. A certain formal and juridical mental attitude which one finds in Rome (and which is understandable and even unavoidable) cannot deal on its own with this situation, in the first place

[9] Details in the *Handbuch der Pastoraltheologie* II/2 (Freiburg, 1966), pp. 99–103; also the thorough study by J. G. Gerhartz, 'Die Mischehe, das Konzil und die Mischehen-Instruktion', *Theologie und Philosophie* 41 (1966), pp. 276–400.

because, as the final authority of the whole Church, it cannot easily speak the theological and human language which is appropriate and understood in a particular cultural setting.

The bishops have a task here; but they must recognise that a solution has yet to be found and cannot be presumed at the outset. Furthermore the solution must not be present simply anywhere, but must be communicated to the general awareness of the clergy, in order to protect the latter from either reactionary or heterodox 'solutions'.

In the face of this situation of open questioning, the clergy in the first instance, but also the laity, must be made far more clearly aware than before that an attempt at a solution made by individual theologians in the Church is not automatically acceptable in respect of dogma – seen from a practical point of view – if it is presented by a personally respectable theologian and has received the episcopal *Imprimatur*.

Today it is absolutely impossible to discuss such problems *in camera caritatis*, excluding all public participation and exposing only the matured solutions to the public gaze. Here too it is no longer possible to conduct 'privy council politics', although that does not mean that any theological nonsense ought necessarily to be allowed to pass the episcopal censure. It is quite in order and necessary for the episcopal censuring authorities to be magnanimous and tolerant in the case of scholarly publications (and conversely stricter than usual with pseudo-pious products which are only apparently 'popular'). In the case of scholarly theological literature the episcopal censor should be limited to a 'coarse filter', simply because it is scarcely possible today to do otherwise without obstructing necessary theological discussion. The latter is indispensable today even in important theological questions, not only in questions which have been regarded as 'open' (and of no consequence) from time immemorial. If that is the case, however, it must be clear to the clergy (especially the young clergy) and laity that in actual fact an *Imprimatur* gives no definite guarantee of the objective reliability of the view expressed. Consequently it may be a theologian's right and duty to question the orthodoxy of another theologian's theory, even if the latter were published by episcopal permission. Of course, a challenge of this sort is stated at the particular theologian's own risk and carries only as much weight as the reasons he gives. But it can be permitted or even invited. In so far as this does not happen enough, the wrong opinion grows up that everything which appears beneath an *Imprimatur* is orthodox and may not be doubted. Because this false view prevails the episcopal censors are obliged to become more anxious and rigorous. As a result the theologian's function with respect to the ecclesiality of a new attempt at a solution of a theological question is excluded, to the disadvantage both of the issue itself and of episcopal authority, which consequently has to be over-strained. It is a false politeness and collegiality when theologians are too concerned to take pains to be 'indulgent' with one another. The indisputable decline in theological criticism is to be deplored in this respect, and it is an extremely dangerous situation.

One must not imagine that in relatively weighty theological questions there can or ought to be no continuing differences of opinion which even the Church's teaching office cannot resolve (at least after a lengthy period of time). The Council has declared the reverse to be fundamentally the case, and has given concrete examples of it. One could quote cases – even in post-conciliar Germany – where this freedom in disputed questions has not been sufficiently respected by Church authorities.

However, it must not be thought that today one can either leave each question alone or that it can be cleared up in a purely scholarly dialogue with the agreement of all theological parties, without the teaching office having to step in authoritatively. The bearers of doctrinal authority (each according to his fundamental and respectively different authority and according to the importance of the matter in hand) must have the courage to say No under certain circumstances, even if they have not been able to 'convince' each and every person beforehand by exhortation, theological discussion of the issue itself, etc. After all, the Church *has* a common confession of faith which must be protected; the Church is more than a theological debating society; furthermore it is not possible to distinguish what is purely 'fundamental' from what is 'secondary', guarding the former and unconditionally surrendering the latter. The sense of the Decree on Ecumenism No. 11 is that there *are* things which, although not fundamental or only peripherally so, all the same constitute indisputable dogma in the Catholic Church. On the other hand even what is fundamental is under certain circumstances threatened nowadays by erroneous interpretations, even if they are able to maintain a certain verbal reverence for Church definitions. What is 'indispensable' and what is not is decided in the final analysis by the theology of the *magisterium*, not by the theology of the theologians. The latter have, however, an irreplaceable function in the Church, such that today the bishops have less right than ever before to make decisions simply on the basis of what they learned at one time in some fashion or other, but must keep on continually informing themselves anew. We have already mentioned that in having the courage to take such a decision they must not only make the one which is correct according to the matter in hand, but must also proceed in a humanly understanding and 'winning' way. In this latter respect the bishops have moral duties as well; and it cannot be so readily assumed as people would sometimes have us think that these duties are objectively fulfilled.

Since the bishops are obliged, in the modern complexity of theological problems, to have recourse to advice from theologians, and since the Spirit's aid to the Church is not exclusively available to the bishops and to no others, the bishops will have the right, and under certain circumstances the obligation, to let a theological view go uncensured when it is supported by a considerable body (and this need not be a numerical majority) of theologians who have demonstrated their competence by their teaching and life in general. Certainly this rule presupposes that the bishops have the practical possibility of knowing when a view is present (and what it concerns) which is subscribed to by a considerable section of theologians who think it correct or open to discussion. On the other hand not every opinion of an individual is immune to episcopal objection simply because the particular individual is respectable from the human and scholarly points of view. Naturally every theologian maintains that his view (as being correct or open to discussion) is the result of theological 'science' or some other science, and everyone is only too tempted to regard himself as the mere spokesman of this particular objective 'science'. But that on its own need by no means keep back the bishop in his teaching office from saying an unequivocal 'No' in certain circumstances.

More of these rules could be set up and refined 'casuistically', but ultimately no rule can relieve the bishop of his 'decision' in the specific sense of the word. Ultimately he must decide according to his knowledge and conscience how much courage he needs to use his authority and what measure of caution must be prescribed for using it in the concrete instance. If, objectively speaking, he prescribes wrongly, he can act wrongly in either direction. But he must have the courage to take this risk all the same. He has no absolute security against such a contingency. It is not pleasant, where matters of truth and the intellectual integrity of individuals is concerned, to have to come to a decision under certain circumstances knowing that the decision cannot be regarded as 'irreformable'. But human life and the Church's life of faith are not thinkable without these vulnerable and yet valid decisions. Even theological scholars for the most part do not get beyond such provisional decisions – which are all the same valid here and now – even where they are pronounced under the strange conviction of being merely mouthpieces of 'objective science'. So the right to make decisions of this sort is all the more to be granted to the official authority. For the faith and the Church are not made in the theologian's retort, but are carried by apostolic proclamation in the message which is entrusted primarily to Church authority, to the bishops. The vulnerability of reformable decisions of this kind does not excuse the office-bearer from exercising the duty of his office. But the 'censured' theologian cannot at the outset fundamentally refuse to accept the decision of the bishop's teaching authority and guardianship simply because it is not *a priori* above the possibility of error, not 'irreformable'.

III

What measures can be taken practically to do justice to these – self-evident – observations and rules? To this question we shall give a merely partial answer in question form.

How can collaboration between bishops and theologians become concretely closer? Why does not the episcopate provide the highly somnolent 'dogmaticians' study group' with tasks, by giving particular advice and suggesting important themes for conferences, etc.? (The same applies to the similar 'society of exegetes'). In the late Middle Ages and in the sixteenth century there were more institutions than today through which theologians expressed themselves as unities and bore collective responsibility. Today it is surely even more necessary. Surely the practice of theologians acting as consultants for the commissions of the bishops' conference ought to be more clearly institutionalised, so that it actually functions correctly and one knows who is responsible for giving advice?

Ought not the episcopal book censorship to be reformed? And why in our case is the provision of canon law not observed whereby the censor has to be responsible by name for his decision? Ought he not to do this when a book is rejected too? Are the censors always competent? Are they both courageous and cautious? Is it certain that the preliminary censure has still more advantages than disadvantages today, or does it not lead to a false evaluation, i.e. an over-valuation of those books which have only just passed the censor? Would not other forms of episcopal reaction to theological work and views be more effective and appropriate today?

It is not necessary today for the episcopal teaching office (in addition to agreeing to the appointment of professors and the filling of similar posts, sermons, the pastoral letters which for the most part seem rather antiquated, and the episcopal book censorship) to be exercised in other ways, best of all perhaps as the official statement of a bishops' conference?

E.g. by the bishops' conference issuing teaching letters and publishing its recommendations etc.? Theoretically the bishops' conference has for a long time had an institution for implementing the work of critical and productive contact with theology today and current cultural life as it is theologically relevant. One sees little sign of it and is tempted to doubt whether this institution, as it appears to exist, is even capable of informing the episcopate adequately on all these questions. Is it sufficiently provided with the necessary personnel and technical equipment for such a task?

Could not the 'priests' council' which is to be formed in the individual dioceses be in addition an instrument for keeping the bishop informed about doctrinal tendencies and unrest among the clergy, and for instructing the clergy correctly on such questions? Are the possibilities provided by deanery conferences, theological conferences for priests, conferences for Catholic academies (why not also for members of the clergy themselves?) sufficiently exploited for the purposes we have mentioned? Could not the bishops, without interfering with the free play of theological scholarship by excessive direction, influence the specialist theological journals to apply themselves more to modern questions of theology than to merely learned historical research (the importance of which we do not contest)?

Are the bishops really sufficiently aware of theology's urgent need of their encouragement at an academic level? Are all the bishops definitely willing enough to choose carefully and make available people who will eventually take up theological lectureships? Can this still be left to the individual bishop? May it still happen that a bishop refuses to free theologians for further study on account of a shortage of priests, in the hope that another bishop will do so in any case? Is it not possible to believe that the future of Christianity and the Church will be better served by a highly educated and lively clergy, able to deal with the mentality of our time, than by a quickly trained clergy prematurely expended in the routine work of the care of souls?

Is it not the case that educated people in the Church are very defectively taught by the mass media as regards theological questions? We do not mean to recommend that a more anxious watch be kept over religious broadcasting etc.; that would be quite out of place; but it is possible to have the impression that the bishops do not make available people of high enough qualifications for such a task. Is one not struck by the fact that in a broadcast religious discussion the lay contribution is often better and more relevant than what is presented by the Church in a narrower sense?

The solution of the problems referred to by Ottaviani will depend in the future largely on the training of young theologians. Is the new programme of studies which was committed to the bishops' conferences by the Council being pursued energetically enough? In practice is it not in danger of withering away or being wrecked by the specialist egoism of the individual professors? Are people aware that under certain circumstances professors, who are only exalting their own subject, do not make good advisers in the reform of studies, especially if, as is sometimes the case, they do not understand very much about modern pastoral care, the mental outlook of young people and the level of intelligence of the people who are nowadays coming to theology? So far what has been made known as a result of deliberations about the reform of theological studies in Germany seems merely like a tedious bargaining over lecture timetables. Do people seriously think that that is enough? If the subjects studied are left as they are, unless the ultimate aim, i.e. the training of future pastors, emerges more clearly than heretofore as the principle of form and organization of the studies, unless the actual level of intelligence of the young theologians is more realistically taken into account, unless the theologian's academic instruction is brought into a closer relationship with the existentially religious forming of his personality, the reform of studies will collapse.

Is it not possible to come to a clearer understanding as regards those questions touched on in Ottaviani's letter? How does one transform a mere defence against erroneous or dangerous views and tendencies into a theology of 'offensive'? Could not the bishops encourage such a theology (and not just tolerate it benevolently) where traces of it are to be found?

Without diminishing the Church's basic duty to conserve and defend the whole inheritance of faith, has not the Church's teaching authority the right (and perhaps the duty), trusting in the inner power of Christian truth, to organise centres of concentration instead of fighting battles on all points and frittering away its not inexhaustible resources of strength, gaining a victory nowhere? It ought not to be thought that man has always to be doing 'here and now' all the things which he *could* do. For instance one *can* fight false views regarding the theory and practice of Indulgences; but the fight against atheism, conducted properly, is certainly a more pressing problem.

Would it not be possible to pursue quite generally a more offensive theological 'cultural politics' (in the best possible sense), with bishops and theologians more clearly forming a community than is the case at present, where theologians constitute merely the critical element and the bishops represent merely the conservative element in the Church? – a strategy in which the theologians themselves take a clearer part in the offensive of defending the Church's doctrine, and the bishops' role is more clearly that of critically examining this same doctrine? Collaboration between bishops and theologians proved its worth at the Council. Will it be continued, or will everything back in the home situation, after the passing of the Council, remain as it was before the Council?

Everything that has been said is to be understood as a few observations upon Cardinal Ottaviani's letter. It would be truer to say that the letter has provided the stimulus rather than the subject-matter of these remarks. For it is plain that our observations have not entered deeply into the individual theological problems enumerated in the letter. They are thus concerned with a preliminary area of discussion. It may be that some readers have the impression that these notes hover between 'reaction' and 'progress' in theology.[10] But perhaps the author may hope that such an impression is fundamentally a false one after all. Not every compromise is dishonourable. Insight and action are always aiming for a centre which cannot be reached directly. For many, the extremist cuts a better figure than the one who continues patiently to seek this centre anew. But there is need today of that patience which seeks the centre.

[10] On the serious and difficult nature of the questions posed by the Council cf. the author's essay 'The Second Vatican Council's Challenge to Theology', in this volume, pp. 3 ff.

6

PRACTICAL THEOLOGY WITHIN THE TOTALITY OF THEOLOGICAL DISCIPLINES

THE question raised in this paper[1] is 'What does practical theology expect of the other fields of theological study?' First of all we must define the limits of our discussion of the matter in question. The approach and the situation of modern practical theology among the Protestant churches cannot be described. And as far as practical theology within the Catholic Church is concerned, the author is really more of a dilettante who has strayed into this field by a number of chance occurrences. There may be advantages in this if one regards it as a sign that a dogmatician *can* be interested in practical theology and that, therefore, such an interest can justifiably be expected from him. Seen thus it is perhaps not so untoward that practical theology's demands upon other theological studies should be put forward not by a representative of practical theology but by an 'ousider'.

Since there is no really clear and generally accepted agreement on the Catholic side as to what practical theology is and should be, and consequently there is amongst us no general consensus as to its relationship with the other departments of theological study and as to what demands it can and must make on the latter, the author has no choice but to say – on his own account and at his own risk – what he himself imagines practical theology to be. Anything which follows as a result of this is subject to the proviso that one *cannot* speak in the name of a *single* Catholic theology. At the same time of course this does not mean that the author's view is simply unique within Catholic theology or claims any patent for its personal originality. In any case we possess a sketch of a practical theology of this kind in the *Handbook of Pastoral Theology*, even if such a composite work naturally reveals many deficiencies, since not all its contributions adequately realise the fundamental conception

[1] cf. the details in the list of sources at the end of this volume for the occasion of this lecture.

equally well if at all.[2] H. Schuster gives an account of the history of practical theology's understanding of itself from the Catholic point of view in the first volume of the *Handbook*.[3] The author regards the name 'practical theology' as better than our more usual 'pastoral theology' because the latter indicates a false constriction of the discipline's field of activity, as we shall mention directly.

I

Practical theology is that theological discipline which is concerned with the Church's self-actualisation here and now – both that which *is* and that which *ought to be*. This it does by means of *theological* illumination of the particular situation in which the Church must realise itself in all its dimensions. We shall now amplify this essential description. For a detailed justification of this we refer to other studies.[4]

The Church is a historical quantity. Without endangering its abiding essence it is true to say that the Church not simply *is*, but must be continually 'happening' anew. This 'occurrence' of the Church, however, is not simply its being in essence perpetually present in a space-time always external to it, but the historical form of this essence – unique in each instance – to which the Spirit of the Church calls it through its particular and unique historical situation. Because of its Spirit's eschatologically

[2] cf. F. X. Arnold (from Vol. III onwards F. Klostermann), K. Rahner, V. Schurr, L. M. Weber (ed.), *Handbuch der Pastoraltheologie. Praktische Theologie der Kirche in ihrer Gegenwart* I (Freiburg, 1964), II/1–2 (Freiburg, 1966); III. Several translations are in preparation.

[3] cf. the second chapter, 'Die Geschichte der Pastoraltheologie', I, pp. 40–92; cf. also F. X. Arnold, 'Pastoraltheologische Ansätze in der Pastoral bis zum 18. Jahrhundert', I, pp. 15–39.

[4] cf. apart from the contributions of H. Schuster and K. Rahner in the *Handbuch der Pastoraltheologie* (esp. I, pp. 93–114, 117–215, 323–332, 333–343; II/1, pp. 181 ff., 233 ff., 256 ff.; II/2, pp. 19 ff., 46 ff.) esp. H. Schuster, 'Wesen und Aufgabe der Pastoraltheologie', *Concilium* 1 (1965), pp. 165 ff.; K. Rahner, 'A Theological Interpretation of the Position of Christians in the Modern World', *Mission and Grace*, Vol. I (London, 1963), pp. 3–55; K. Rahner, 'The Second Vatican Council's Challenge to Theology', in this volume, pp. 3–27; also 'On the theological problems entailed in a Pastoral Constitution' and 'Practical theology and social work in the Church', *Theological Investigations* X; cf. also F. Klostermann, 'Pastoraltheologie heute', *Dienst an der Lehre*, ed. Catholic Theology Faculty of the University of Vienna = *Wiener Beiträge zur Theologie* X (Vienna, 1965), pp. 51–108; F. X. Arnold, 'Was ist Pastoraltheologie?', *Wort des Heils as Wort in die Zeit* (Trier, 1961), pp. 296–300; K. Delahaye, 'Überlegungen zur Neuorientierung der Pastoraltheologie heute', *Gott in Welt. Festgabe für K. Rahner*, ed. J. B. Metz, W. Kern, A. Darlap, H. Vorgrimler, Vol. II (Freiburg, 1964), pp. 206–218.

triumphant grace the Church cannot be untrue to the particular 'occurrent' form of its self-realisation to such an extent that it simply ceases being the Church of Christ; but that does not alter the fact that the Church has the task of making a commitment to realise this particular historical form in responsibility and freedom, and can therefore also fall far short of it. Consequently the Church must reflect consciously upon the question how the Church's self-actualisation is to take place arising out of and in response to its particular given situation in each instance. Practical theology is the scientific organisation of this reflection.

This practical theology is a unique, independent science, a fundamental one in essence in spite of its reciprocal relationship with other theological disciplines, since its business of scientifically critical and systematic reflection is a unique quantity and its nature is not deducible. For it is reflection orientated towards committal. It follows from a correct evaluation of the relationship between theory and practice; from an appropriate understanding (from the point of view of existential ontology) of the nature of freedom; from a right theology of the intractability of the Holy Spirit as the principle of the Church's history; from a correct understanding of the nature of hope; from all this it follows that the Church's committal to the particular self-realisation to which it is called at any one time cannot adequately be deduced from its *essence*. And so the aim of practical theology – precisely this continually new self-actualisation in committal on the part of the Church – is not the mere consequence of an 'essential' theology of the nature of the Church, the Word of God and the kerygma, the nature of the Sacraments, the service of love etc., however possible and necessary this may be. If, in spite of this, this non-deducible factor which inheres in each committal is to be the object of a reflection *sui generis* which sees into the future, seeking what is to be done here and now, extending the horizons of the possible future, trying the spirits which are proclaiming the future, then the process of reflection upon it, scientifically organised, is an independent and primary science and not only an 'application' of the results of the essential sciences within theology, whether the latter be systematic or historical. It is true that the decisions of the Church are not really made in practical theology, for that is a matter for the whole Church (and within this totality it is a matter for official authority), even if the theory of practical theology, as actually carried on, is itself one factor in the Church's practice. But in being this kind of theory practical theology is not simply an 'essential' science but a quite unique one, a testing of the spirits with a view to the act of committal; it implies a prophetic element – which one may be permitted to call 'political' – since it must be aware of the impulse of the Church's Spirit, which is not simply identical with the perpetually valid truth in the Church, but translates the latter into the concrete challenge valid at the particular hour. Practical theology can and must be this, because the *theoria* realised in actuality is also an internal factor of the Church's practice and only remains genuine *theoria* under this presupposition. In a word, it is 'theory' and thus science. But it is the *theoria* which indwells the practice itself as an internal factor and which is thus not simply identical with the objectifying 'essential' sciences, which simply ascertain from a 'neutral' position what is the case, or what must always be, or what will surely occur independently of decisions. Consequently it is 'critical' towards the Church although it cannot annexe the latter's decisions. It attempts to be of service in continually overcoming the Church's given deficient self-realisation and transcending it in the next new form to which the Church is being called. It exercises a critical function in respect of the other theological disciplines since it is always questioning whether they are adequately making the particular local contribution required of them (and of which they are capable) towards the Church's self-realisation in committal. In spite of this critical aspect practical theology is an essentially ecclesial discipline, since it is not only concerned with the Church in its relation to its activity, but comprehends itself as the factor of reflection which inheres in this activity and is not merely applied to it from outside. As a result it is dependent on everything which constitutes this Church's continuing essence.

Practical theology's subject-matter is everyone and everything in the Church, i.e. all those who participate in the Church's self-realisation, not only those holding office in the Church and in its official care of souls. Consequently its subject-matter is not only the 'care of souls' in the more narrow sense, but the totality of that particular action required of all members of the Church at any one time, in so far as this action is a factor in the life of the Church as such.

Everything is its subject-matter; i.e. the Church's self-realisation in *all* its dimensions. From this point of view homiletics, catechetics, the study of mission and welfare work are partial fields within practical theology as such, although this does not eliminate the question of these partial disciplines' technical and practical independence.

II

The task of practical theology as an original science demands a *theological* analysis of the particular present situation in which the Church is to carry out the especial self-realisation appropriate to it at any given moment. In order to be able to perform this analysis of the present by means of scientific reflection and to recognise the Church's situation, practical theology certainly needs sociology, political science, contemporary history etc. To this extent all these sciences are in the nature of ancillary studies for practical theology. However, although the contemporary analysis provided by these profane sciences is necessary and sufficient for its use, it cannot simply draw on it uncritically as though it were already complete and given. Practical theology must itself critically distil this analysis within a theological and ecclesial perspective, a task which cannot be taken over by any other theological discipline. This contemporary analysis does not remain its only task, but it is indispensable. For the committal to the Church's particular relevant self-realisation cannot be unequivocally deduced solely even from a *dogmatic* knowledge of the essence of the Church and the reflex insight into its contemporary situation. Practical theology, on the other hand, can supply – asymptotically at least – the element of reflection and the offer of possible solutions. Beyond the confrontation of the Church's essence with the contemporary situation, practical theology should contain an element of creativity and prophecy and be engaged in critical reflection.

At this point we take the liberty of adding a small observation, even if it is perhaps not absolutely necessary for our subject. Today it is possible to observe that the concrete achievements of science as such are by no means exclusively due to university scientists. Besides universities there is an increasing number of other places of research, institutes, learned societies, etc.; even in public and economic administration itself there are scientific organisations which do not merely apply science but carry out actual research. We cannot here enter into the reasons for this – no doubt inevitable – partial migration of science away from the universities. But it can be questioned whether, as regards practical theology, an analogous process is not to be expected and even thought necessary and desirable. In concrete terms: can today's and tomorrow's practical theology be *merely* a university study sustained by the confidence that its work and its results will to some extent be taken note of benevolently by the 'practitioners' in office in the Church, while in general these practitioners still continue in actual fact to live, make decisions and take action in the future on the basis of their own individual experience of life, which has not been subjected to critical reflection? Or would it be desirable, for instance, for the Church's authorities to have something in the nature of a practical theology being studied scientifically alongside them, since they stand in need of it and since much of what is needed from it can only be seen in enough detail as a result of the closest contact with the practice of the Church? University theology, almost as a result of its very nature, lacks this rapport to a large extent. The politician is someone quite different from the student of political thought. But if it is the case today that life is becoming irresistibly subject to science, the student of political thought and the politician must carry on their work in such close collaboration – organisationally too – that the study of politics can no longer be pursued exclusively in the university. Is not the same sort of thing valid for practical theology too? Would it not be fruitful if the university were to train representatives of practical theology who would then continue to work scientifically within the Church's official organs and in direct contact with it and its tasks, exercising an advisory, critical and prompting function on the basis of this work?

III

What does practical theology, understood in this way, expect of the other theological subjects, and what must it demand from them?

Firstly it demands the *recognition of its originality and significance as a theological discipline in its own right.* As far as the other disciplines are concerned that is by no means a readily acceptable view. For the most part the representatives of the other disciplines look on practical theology as a mere hotch-potch of practical consequences which follow automatically from these disciplines. In the Romance countries, for instance, we do not yet have any really serious and distinct discipline of 'practical theology' and in this respect the demands of the Second Vatican Council have not yet begun to be met. Or else the representatives of the other disciplines regard practical theology merely as a collection of psychological, didactic, sociological rules of prudence, gained directly from the ordinary practice of the care of souls. No wonder that one's instinctive attitude – not explicitly stated of course – is to make for the most part less imposing demands on the practical theologian's intellectual and scientific competence than in the case of the other theological disciplines. So the first thing required of the other theological studies is a right epistemological understanding of practical theology – with all its consequences. Although we are not able to pursue this matter further here, it implies certain effects as regards the number of and the manner of appointment to professorial chairs, the arrangement of courses, and the provision of the necessary finance, etc

The *second* demand – still of a general character – is the demand that *the other theological disciplines should recognise the element of practical theology which must be contained within themselves, and that they should cherish it.* The whole of theology is an ecclesial field of study in all its disciplines, precisely because (and in so far as) it exercises its critical function with respect to the Church as well, since this criticism is always immanent in the Church's faith as such. But this also means that all theological disciplines must serve in the Church's self-realisation, and therefore contain within themselves an element of practical theology. As a discipline in its own right it cannot deny the relatedness of the other disciplines to the Church's self-realisation and thus to her faith, her message, her sacramental practice, to the life of the Church, her love issuing in works and her critical service to the world in all its dimensions, although in this respect practical theology always has to act in stimulation and criticism of the other disciplines.

For instance it cannot itself actualise the Gospel message in an existential hermeneutics intended for its proclamation today; exegetics and systematic theology must do this together; the *material* content of homiletics is, at least fundamentally, the province of dogmatics itself. Practical theology will leave the more precise formulation even of the *ius condendum* to canon law, even if by its very nature it must press for a continually new *ius condendum* appropriate to the Church's situation at any particular time. If it carries out itself an analysis of the Church's present situation by means of theological reflection, practical theology does not thereby become engaged in contemporary Church history, simply because this analysis is impossible *without* Church history and particularly contemporary history. However, by criticism and new ways of questioning it will make Church history (as a *theological* and ecclesial science) aware that a Church history studied theologically is not the satisfaction of historical inquisitiveness but the critical implementation of that anamnesis of the Church's past without which she cannot sufficiently take possession of her present, adopting it as the germ of her future. Practical theology will not itself carry on the dialogue with man's profane understanding of existence, as that is a matter for fundamental theology and dogmatics; but it will continually make these disciplines aware that their tasks are not to be fulfilled in the unhistorical and sterile realm of eternally valid truths, but in the historical situation which is ours at any one particular time.

When we said previously that practical theology is concerned with the Church's self-realisation in the continually new given contemporary situation, which it illuminates theologically, that does not mean that it either must or can itself determine the *content* of the Church's self-realisation in all its dimensions by means of theoretical reflection, but that it is to submit to reflection the tasks of the other disciplines as they touch the Church and arise from the contemporary situation. By means of its own analysis of the present, which is not the business of other theological disciplines, it will carry out a process of reflection which can now no longer be provided in a scientifically responsible and satisfactory manner by these other disciplines. Today they must allow the compass of their tasks, *in so far as* they are set by the Church and her future, to be prescribed by another discipline; by practical theology. To this extent practical theology takes precedence over the other disciplines, although the reverse is the case in other respects, i.e. to the extent that these other theological disciplines, as the essential fundamental alignment, constitute the precondition, perspective and standard for practical theology.

Practical theology challenges the other theological studies to recognise the task which inheres immanently in them, orientated to the practice of the Church; the second demand it makes is that they should apply themselves to this task. Of course that does not mean that practical theology is *only* a sort of formal conscience for the other theological disciplines. For on the one hand it implies, as its subordinate departments, the study of mission, catechetics, homiletics and the study of welfare work. However difficult it is to separate these individual disciplines from those which they presuppose as their foundation, it is in any case immediately apparent that practical theology is not only the critical and formal conscience of the other disciplines. Then there are many concrete factors in the Church's self-realisation (i.e. the whole 'organisation' of the 'care of souls'), which are not considered by any other theological discipline, especially what is 'institutional' in the Church's self-realisation, which is not simply coextensive with its right to be so, but far exceeds it. Conversely, what has been said previously does not deny the fact that practical theology can take on in addition subsidiary tasks which in themselves belong to other disciplines but which, under certain circumstances, the latter are not actually dealing with. So far for example there are many questions which Catholic dogmatic ecclesiology has not considered sufficiently, although they are really its province and are of the greatest importance for practical theology. In such a case practical theology can pursue a piece of dogmatic ecclesiology in a subsidiary role. The same thing can happen as regards dogmatic sacramental theology, canon law, moral theology, ecumenical theology, etc.

IV

We shall now try to fill in the details of this fundamental demand as it is addressed to the individual theological disciplines, even if it is unfortunately only possible here to formulate these demands and expectations in a very general and vague way. In addition it must be observed that the epistemological kind of question as to how the theological disciplines are related to each other at a more intimate level, forming the totality of the theology of Christianity and the Church, must be set aside.

1. Firstly, as far as *exegetics* and *biblical theology* are concerned, the question as to how far this discipline itself has the task of actualising the Word of God in scripture and how far it shares it with 'systematic theology' is a problem which cannot be solved here. In any case, as Christian theology, which is something other than the mere study of religion, this discipline is in the service of the Church's kerygma and must make its contribution to the correct and effective proclamation of the 'Gospel' in the Church according to scripture. It is a basic conviction of the Christian Faith that this is possible, in spite of – or rather *because of* – the methods of modern scientific exegesis as genuinely practised. An exegesis which does not share this conviction ought to withdraw from theology and become attached to a profane field of religious studies, if it is still thought interesting. Christian exegesis must serve the Church's kerygma; it must not only supply the critical standard but also be of positive assistance. It is precisely practical theology which will have to put this fundamental demand to exegesis, clarifying it and showing its specific application. This does not mean that it interferes thereby in the autonomous field of exegesis, but speaks in the name of the whole of theology, of which exegesis forms one part, receiving its task, its justification and its autonomy from this whole. Here I must admit that I cannot say precisely what practical theology's demands upon exegesis would look like in more specific and concrete terms, nor how it could be executed technically. But to say this is only to touch upon the more general problem of how to overcome the mutual alienation of the sciences and also of the theological disciplines. In my estimation in any case, practical theology ought to ask exegesis and biblical theology to be providing continually (as well as the increasingly detailed studies which tend to become boundless, and which are no longer digestible from the preacher's point of view) the kind of theological literature which the theologian and preacher (who can no longer be an exegetical specialist in the strict sense) finds useful in his work and which keeps him close

enough to scholarly exegetical research. This may mean a new kind of 'middle' position between precise research and *haute vulgarisation*. The true exegetical specialist should not think it beneath his dignity to write such books, but regard it as a higher task. Of course these wishes on the part of practical theology will be largely identical with the wishes which systematic theology lays before exegetics. There is nothing strange in that; it is rooted in the very nature of the case.

2. As far as practical theology's demands upon *systematic theology* (i.e. chiefly fundamental theology, dogmatics and moral theology) are concerned, it must be said at once that a more intensive dialogue between both disciplines would be desirable, to discuss their different nature. We have already observed that systematic studies continually tend to be quick to misunderstand practical theology as the mere practical consequences of the theses of systematic theology or as a straightforward echo of actual practice.

Furthermore, practical theology must draw the attention of systematic theology to the fact that the latter does not carry on its business in a vacuum, not subject to history and for its own sake, but in the concrete situation of the times and of the Church. It cannot set its own tasks and priorities just as it likes. It seems to me then, that this implies the following consequences for Catholic theology: Catholic systematic theology in universities – together with the historical work which accompanies it – seems to me today still to have too strong a flavour of historicism, too calmly pursuing historical theology detached from the question of proclamation today. It still tends to deal too intensively with peripheral dogmatic questions, to concern itself too little with the central issues involved in a new reflection upon the fundamental assertions of the faith, and (since Vatican II) it is in danger of focusing its whole attention on the Council's explicit theses, which neither were nor could have been the themes laid upon us today. It might very well be one of practical theology's tasks to investigate the strategy and 'politics' which lie unexamined and inexplicit behind the study of systematic theology; it would have to initiate an examination of the hidden tendencies and governing images of systematic theology as it is actually practised, from the point of view of a sociology of the Church, including statistical investigations; for the actual practice of theology is one factor in the Church's self-realisation and thus also subject-matter for practical theology. This kind of analysis of what is actually done and not done in the rest of theology could then lead to the question as to what *should* be done and what ought *not* to be done, or at least, not done with such over-emphasis. To my knowledge for instance there is today nowhere a text-book of fundamental or dogmatic theology for the young theological student which presents the subjects wholly in a way which is both good from a didactic point of view and appropriate to the demands of the present situation. And we simply accept this fact without a qualm. Ought not practical theology to protest loudly about this matter? Surely it is part of its real task, if it is to reflect critically and creatively upon the Church's particular self-realisation presented at any one time in all its dimensions (i.e. also in the field of theology)? While maintaining all due respect for the freedom and autonomy of the individual theological disciplines, it is surely part of the dignity of these disciplines that they can accept criticism where they are proceeding against their own aims, at least by default. Surely this kind of admonition cannot today be based merely on an unregulated private experience, but rather it must be established in a very precise and exact manner? But by whom, if not by practical theology?

3. As far as *Church history* is concerned, practical theology will first of all be surprised to find that we – as Catholics – have a greatly underdeveloped theological reflection concerning the real nature of Church history. Consequently the compass of Church history and its relation to the other theological disciplines and to the Church itself in its concrete form remain highly obscure. Of course, as such Church history has to do with the past and not directly with the future, it is not a prophetic oracle, nor is it a drawing-office of creative programmes as to what is to take place in the Church today or tomorrow. But if it is really interested in genuine theological issues and looks into the past from this standpoint, it could recognise – in accordance with its own true nature – much of the past as initiating future possibilities and tasks for the Church. For instance, is our Catholic Church history aware of a *theological* structure principle of its object of study in its temporally occurrent form? If it had this knowledge, the real significance of 'what happens' could be made clearer, and this would be of the greatest importance for the Church's practice tomorrow, even if it were not just an easy recipe for it. From the point of view of the open questions of the future which practical theology endeavours to uncover, the past could be asked to reveal its own theological mystery, thereby shedding more light on these questions and bringing into view a horizon in which an answer could be sought. If a Christian can only grasp the Old Testament in its deepest essence from the standpoint of the New, why should he not understand the Church's past better from the standpoint of *that* theology which anticipates the Church's future in its *formal* nature and tries, in

practical theology, to plan out its more immediate possibilities in concrete terms?

In truth, an answer is not an answer unless it is surprising and unexpected. But it is also true that no-one receives an answer if he has no question. The horizon opened up by a correctly formulated question in no way violates the answer – if one is forthcoming – so that one only hears what one wants to hear. If history (*Geschichte*) is to be the teacher of the present and the future – and to say this is not an unscientific self-alienation of history (*Historie*) – one must know to some extent (including all possible surprises in one's calculations) *what kind* of instruction for the future one expects from history. And on *this* matter surely practical theology could have something to say to Church history, and might expect the study of Church history to take advice from history on these matters? It is unfortunately impossible here to clarify by means of concrete cases what we have said in this very abstract manner. Ultimately the Church's past achievements are only interesting in connection with what lies ahead of her. If the Church historian is imbued with this awareness, he will write Church history which is also of service to practical theology. But not otherwise.

4. The relationship between *canon law* and practical theology is or ought to be very close. First of all practical theology must cherish its independence *vis-à-vis* canon law. Practical theology is not identical with the sum total of observations concerning the more concrete implementation of canon law. Only a small portion of the life of the Church is accessible to legal ordering. Practical theology ought to defend the remaining sphere of the Church's life which is not subject to legalistic manipulation. That is not as obvious as it sounds, since our Catholic canon law tends to formulate *moral* norms in its own sphere, which on the one hand are not really *legal* norms at all, and on the other hand it tends to manipulate them as if they *were* legal norms. In so far as canon law is not only concerned *de lege condita* (historical, interpreting and casuistic) but is also seeking the correct law which ought to exist and yet does not at present, the *lex condenda*, and in so far as this law of the future is not *only* that law which develops out of the immanent dynamic of the currently valid law, it is the task of practical theology to discover aims and horizons for canon law in respect of this *lex condenda*. Today this can only take place as a result of a scientifically critical and simultaneously theological analysis of the contemporary situation. This, however, cannot be the task of canon law. For it is not a legal matter and at the same time constitutes such a difficult and extensive reality, demanding its own metho-

dology for study, that it cannot be investigated as an appendage by canon law merely because the latter as the science *de lege condenda* happens to need some knowledge of it. Criticism of current law and fundamental exposition of the recommended law are therefore tasks of practical theology and imply as many demands of practical theology upon canon law. The relationship here is similar to that between the study of politics, sociology, etc. on the one hand and jurisprudence on the other. Just as profane jurisprudence must accept observations from these other profane disciplines although they are historically junior to it, the same applies also to canon law in relation to practical theology.

5. Finally something must be said concerning practical theology's demands upon the *study of liturgy*. This question depends to some extent on whether liturgiology is to be understood as a subordinate discipline of practical theology or not. However that may be, modern liturgiology has taken as its object the scientifico-theological reflection of a liturgy yet to be created, and deals no longer primarily with the history and appraisal of existing liturgy. Thereby it has developed a broader and more comprehensive concept of liturgy than was the case previously within a markedly ritualistic and rubricistic understanding of liturgy. As a result, in any case, liturgiology has come into the immediate neighbourhood of practical theology. The question of the *liturgia condenda* is above all a question of practical theology seen from the standpoint of its whole task, or at least one requiring an answer for which practical theology must create the presuppositions. For one can only answer the question as to *how* liturgy ought to be done *today* if one knows what Christians are like as contemporary men, if practical theology approaches its problems with the help of sociology of religion etc. Precisely because liturgiology has now become in actuality quite independent, practical theology as a whole will continually have the task of delivering liturgiology from the dangers of a romantic glorification of the old forms of the liturgy, the danger of an aesthetic view, of a rubricistic legalism and also of the private whim of the connoisseur. It will lead to a liturgy which can really be a liturgy of the People of God here and now.

We cannot discuss here the question of the relationship between practical theology and the profane disciplines which constitute its necessary ancillary studies (like psychology, sociology, etc.). It will be clear too that we have only touched upon the relation of practical theology to those theological disciplines which to a certain extent have a fundamental and normative significance for practical theology. The prime intention of this contribution has been to demonstrate the urgency of the basic task. If we find ourselves only at the beginning of our endeavours and deliberations it may be all the more a health-giving challenge to pursue the matter with more energy and with greater sensitivity. If that were done, even to a small extent, it would be a good beginning.

PART TWO

The Doctrine of God and Christology

7

THE NEED FOR A 'SHORT FORMULA' OF CHRISTIAN FAITH

In order to be effective *vis-à-vis* modern unbelief the mission of the Church calls for a kind of witness to the Christian faith which can be really intelligible to modern man. This truism implies a demand, however, which is by no means easily fulfilled and is often neglected. For this message must be so expressed that what is essential is clearly distinguished from everything of secondary importance and can be actually 'realised'. Otherwise a modern 'pagan' is not able to distinguish this essence of Christianity from the Church's often uninviting and repellent appearance (in sermons, religious practice, social conditions, etc.), and consequently applies his – partially justified – opposition towards Christians to Christianity itself. Thus the Christian message must be such that it clearly criticises Christians and concrete Christianity. This message must be able to express what is essential *in brief* to today's highly preoccupied men, and it must go on saying it. Such repetition is not wearisome so long as it is really concerned with what is decisive and essential, not as an 'ideology' which impinges on man from outside (and which changes nothing as far as the 'facts' are concerned), but as the experienced and lived reality of man's life itself.[1] Such a 'short formula' is especially urgently required in our *pluralist* society. In earlier times a homogeneous society itself 'lived' Christianity, at least as a 'religion', even if perhaps not always as a personal 'faith'. In a situation where one was already impregnated with Christianity as social custom and 'ideology' *before* being capable of and compelled to a personal decision of faith, it was possible to be unconcerned as to the doctrinal mode of communication of Christianity. This kind of 'postponement' was true of Baptism and also to a certain extent of life in general. It was not necessary to be very concerned about the correct proportions of what was said; secondary things could be communicated more urgently as if they were primary; one could

[1] This statement cannot be suspected of Modernism if one bears in mind that the grace of Christ always precedes the external preaching of the Gospel.

permit oneself rather to neglect that *single whole* of Christianity as such, whereas nowadays it is precisely this 'whole' which is the precondition for a correct understanding and realisation of the 'particular' within it. Nowadays the baptised person too, even if he is born into a Christian family, lives in a situation of existence which largely does not communicate Christianity. Simply from the fact of the situation in which he finds himself, even a baptised person is in many respects more 'pagan' than ever anyone has been since Constantine. He must understand sufficiently clearly what is particular and really distinctive in Christianity, those things by which he is to be distinguishable from his environment.

I

If one considers this and other requirements, one must needs be surprised that there are so few 'short formulas' expressing the essential nature of the Christian message briefly and in terms which are intelligible today. 'Briefly' is here of course a very relative concept. Such a 'formula' does not need to be as short as the Apostles' Creed or any other authoritative confession of faith. But on the other hand the modern 'Shorter Catechism' is definitely much too long, and furthermore, it does not really correspond, for other reasons too, to what is meant here. Nor is it a question of finding an identical formula for all countries and all of today's culturally and socially differentiated groups. In our continually and rapidly changing world a short formula of this sort would be doubtless short-lived by comparison with something like the Apostles' Creed. It is therefore all the more necessary that there should be such formulas to be appropriated by man's spirit, heart and mind. They must be capable of being directly and 'existentially' assimilated, self-explanatory and not requiring a long prior elucidation, in order to commend themselves to men. They must be illuminating within the particular man's perspective of understanding and experience of life, as far as possible using his modern vocabulary and employing those presuppositions which are self-evident to modern man (whether they are actually so *per se* more than others or not). They must not presuppose as already given anything which is not immediately intelligible as 'given' and cannot be fundamentally experienced. These requirements of a short formula of this kind are not indeed as clear and evident as one might be inclined to think.

We may illustrate this with a small example: probably *all* these short formulas of faith[2] – beginning with the New Testament – presuppose that

[2] It is possible to understand the Old Testament Decalogue as a short formula of

the hearer understands the word 'God' correctly and can easily realise this correct meaning existentially. But is that the case today? Is it still possible today to say with Thomas that *Quid est Deus* is 'clear' and 'familiar' *to everyone* and that accordingly the question only remains as to whether this 'God' also exists? Things are simply not like this today.[3] Nor is a quickly proffered 'definition' of 'what' is *meant* by the word sufficient, however logically lucid it is. Ought not a short formula of this kind to begin much 'earlier', where what is really meant by 'God' is experienced in one's own actualisation of existence? But where could a point of departure be found for such a modern understanding of the meaning of the word 'God' and for its existential realisation? What kind of starting-point is it which would have to be actually expressed *explicitly*, even if only briefly?

From this simple discussion it is immediately apparent to how large an extent the scope and proportions of a modern 'short formula' of this kind would differ from those of other times. The chief question would be therefore, what such a short formula would look like if it were to be suitable for a situation of which real atheism is a decisive co-determinant for the first time in the history of the world. The same would be said as regards the *Christological* assertions of such a short formula. This Christological content must be formulated from the very beginning in such a way that it does not sound like a myth of a distant age and so that modern man does not have the impression that it is at the outset impossible to ascertain *what* really happened in times past, and that therefore what is past certainly *cannot* be important for today.

Before directly presenting such an attempt – intended only as an experiment[4] – we shall say something further to a deeper knowledge of 'short formulas'. We are only drawing attention to a *demand* which must be made upon the concrete proclamation of the Gospel, on dogmatic theology and also on pastoral theology in this age, which is characterised by an ideologically pluralistic society and by atheism.

Here we mention one or two things in support of this demand. The history of these 'short formulas' is as old as Christianity itself. In the

---

this sort, for it should be thought of as the charter of the covenant rather than as a codification of mere moral norms (or even norms of natural law) for the individual.

[3] cf. Karl Rahner, 'Bemerkungen zur Gotteslehre in der katholischen Dogmatik', *Catholica* 20 (1966), pp. 1–18; in this volume pp. 127 ff.

[4] In the following section (II) the author presents an extended version of an earlier attempt. Cf. K. Rahner, 'Kurzer Inbegriff des christlichen Glaubens für "Ungläubige" ', *Geist und Leben* 38 (1965), pp. 374–379.

New Testament the formula 'Jesus is the Messiah' (cf. e.g. Acts 9:22; John 20:31) was a formula which more or less told a Jew of the Old Testament religion everything he needed to know and confess in order to be a Christian. It was a formula which was basically directly intelligible to him.[5] Romans 10:9 (Jesus as the Risen Lord) is also a short formula of this kind, expressing clearly and distinctly in its concentrated form the minimum of the Christian faith necessary for a 'theist' at that time. If one had grasped what was said in this way and adopted it in reality, one was at that time without doubt a Christian. 1 Thessalonians 1:9 is likewise a short formula directed particularly at the situation produced by the meeting of paganism and Christianity. If one wanted to write a patristic history of these short formulas, part of it (but not the whole) would be the history of the creeds, bearing in mind that in addition to official Church confessions of faith in the stricter sense there were always the more 'private' formulations of faith (as, for example, bishops' declarations on the occasion of their taking office). Similarly under this heading come small writings like Augustine's *Enchiridion* (in spite of its more detailed character: *PL* 40, 181–196). For instance, Luther's powerful paraphrase of the Apostles' Creed in his Short Catechism is also such a short formula. The most recent attempt at – or rather the most recent demand for – this kind of short formula (in a single sentence) can be found in Vatican II's Decree on the Church's Missionary Activity: in his fundamental position as a baptised person the believer must grasp the fact that in Christianity he 'has been snatched away from sin and led into the mystery of the love of God, communicated to him in Christ' (No. 13). Naturally even a short statement like this is on its own by no means equivalent to a short formula, but it implies the demand for such a short formula and to a certain extent it shows the way towards it. For it is plain that the statement is not afraid of an 'anthropological' perspective on the part of the affirmation of faith; it presents the substance of faith in the form of a statement about man; man is the one to whom the divine self-communication is addressed and who, in receiving this divine self-communication, comprehends both what he is himself and what God is.

In everyday life today there are advertising slogans, party programmes and manifestoes by means of which social groups aim to tell other people what they are and what they intend to do. These communications are produced as a result of the greatest care and trouble, and they cannot be replaced by weighty volumes or a long series of lectures, whilst at the

[5] For a thorough treatment of the approach to these early confessions of faith in the New Testament cf. K. Lehmann, *Auferstanden am dritten Tag* (Freiburg, 1968).

same time they must fulfil all the necessary conditions so that what is said can really strike home and take effect in our situation of a pluralistic mass society. Something like this is also needed for the Church's proclamation in the Age of Atheism.[6] Such a short formula of the Christian message – and today we probably need several – cannot be found in the ancient creeds even if the latter remain the *regula fidei*. Perhaps dogmatics and catechetics will soon take up this challenge, if it is recognised as valid. It signifies a task not only for the teaching of religion, but also for dogmatics, philosophy and the history of ideas. The proper starting-point for a correct expression of faith in God is a question which reaches far beyond the problems of the teaching of religion.[7]

II

In what follows we shall present an attempt at this kind of 'modern' confession of faith. It is indeed no more than an attempt. The emphases could be placed differently and it could be longer or shorter. Naturally it can only be intelligible to educated western man, if at all. But I do not find this in itself a drawback: ought we to try to make a thing suitable for everyone by rendering it not really acceptable to anyone? Was not the ancient Creed 'generally intelligible' as a traditional sacral formula by being suitable for only a very small cultural field? If anyone says that he finds this attempt useless we shall certainly not take offence at his opinion, provided that he himself knows better how to communicate just *what* we Christians actually believe to an 'unbeliever' of our own time, in his own environment, and can state it briefly. How would it be if the new Secretariat for Unbelievers in Rome were to produce examples of a short catechism for unbelievers? These examples would follow the teaching of the Decree on Ecumenism that there is a very important distinction between the 'fundamentals' of the faith and other truths, and they would underline the abiding value of the ancient formulas not by repeating the latter but by explaining them. And must this decidedly necessary process of explanation (which even the most stubborn defender of the abiding validity of the ancient formulas recognises as justified and necessary)

[6] There is no need to explain in detail that 'religious propaganda' of this kind is inseparably connected with the specific intimacy of personal faith. Cf. K. Rahner, in F. X. Arnold, K. Rahner, V. Schurr, L. M. Weber (ed.), *Handbuch der Pastoraltheologie* II/1 (Freiburg, 1966), pp. 146–151.

[7] For the historically different ways of access to faith cf. K. Rahner, *Handbuch der Pastoraltheologie* II/1, pp. 142 ff.

always be very much longer than the formulas it is supposed to be explaining? Why? If this is not the case, even our stubborn defender must be able to produce a short 'creed' containing the ancient abiding truth and yet expressing it in a different way as compared with traditional formulas. As we have said, the present attempt is to be understood in this sense. Its only purpose is to enable many other people to do the same thing more quickly and better.

Whether he is consciously aware of it or not, whether he is open to this truth or suppresses it, man's whole spiritual and intellectual existence is orientated towards a holy mystery which is the basis of his being. This mystery is the inexplicit and unexpressed horizon which always encircles and upholds the small area of our everyday experience of knowing and acting, our knowledge of reality and our free action. It is our most fundamental, most natural condition, but for that very reason it is also the most hidden and least regarded reality, speaking to us by its silence, and even whilst appearing to be absent, revealing its presence by making us take cognisance of our own limitations. We call this God. We can ignore him, but even in an act which professes to be unconcerned about him, God is once more affirmed as the sustaining fundamental of such an act, just as logic is still operative even in an act which denies the validity of logic, or just as an action which affirms absolute meaninglessness considers itself more meaningful than the acceptance of a meaning for existence, thus explicitly affirming once again that meaning is fundamental to reality. In its capacity as the very ground of the individual absorbed in knowing and acting, the holy mystery we call God is at once what is most internal to ourselves and also what is furthest from our manipulation and has no need of us. Our proper response to it is reverence and worship; Where these are present, where man accepts his being in an attitude of absolute responsibility, seeking and awaiting this ultimate meaning in trust, he has already found God, whatever name he may give him. For his ultimate name can only be uttered, finally, in loving silence before his incomprehensibility.

However hard and unsatisfactory it may be to interpret the deepest and most fundamental experience at the very bottom of our being, man does experience in his innermost history that this silent, infinitely distant holy mystery, which continually recalls him to the limits of his finitude and lays bare his guilt, yet *bids him approach*; the mystery enfolds him in an ultimate and radical love which commends itself to him as his salvation and as the real meaning of his existence (provided only that he allows its possibilities to be greater than his own finitude and guilt). This love –

experienced at the ground of being, which is nothing other than God's absolute self-communication, in which God gives himself and not only what is finite, in which he becomes the infinitely wide horizon of our being – we call divinising grace. It is offered to everyone as light and as the promise of eternal life, working freely and graciously in every man, welling up from the origin of his existence and – even though perhaps not named as such – appearing everywhere where in the history of man courage, love, faithfulness to the light of conscience, endurance of darkness by faith in the light, or any other witness to the ground of his being is at work and is made plain as the holy mystery of the loving nearness of God. That history which reveals more and more clearly God's pledge of himself in radical self-communication to man, accepted in faith, hope and love, we call salvation and revelation-history. It is the 'categorial' historical form in which God's self-communication, 'transcendentally' given from the very beginning in the ground of man's being (by virtue of the deification of man through grace, effected by this self-communication), becomes more and more apparent. It is true that this history is often marred and darkened by the history of the guilt by which humanity shuts itself off from the grace of God in the mystery of self-refusal and wishes to understand itself from within itself alone. But in spite of this it is always and everywhere present, since the mystery of the God who reveals and communicates himself in love is more powerful than the mystery of human guilt.

This history of man's self-discovery as one who is (at least as far as God's offer is concerned) divinised in the ground of his existence, the history of the concrete expression in space-time of this self-discovery in God (both always by virtue of the divine self-pledge, called grace) reaches its historical apogee and unsurpassable goal – which secretly sustained this whole historical movement from the very beginning – in the one in the midst of divinised humanity whom we call simply the God-man. It is he whom everyone seeks, not expressly but in reality all the same, in wishing the ultimate question (of one's own being and of one's destiny in death) and the ultimate acceptance (of this question by God) to appear together, experienced in the concrete terms of one's own history, and thus be completely existent and finally affirmed. To this extent every man who is true to his conscience is for us an Advent Christian, looking forward to the *one* Man in whom his own question (we do not merely *put* questions; we *are* questions) and God's acceptance have become one and have finally appeared in one person. As Christians we have the courage to believe that this looked-for one is found. He is Jesus of Nazareth.

The man who has experienced God in Christ in this way wants to and must confess him. Not as though he thought that the others, who are not able to call the consummation of their secret experience by name, are not embraced by God's mercy (by which he gives himself to us, provided only that we do not refuse him). But the man who has found Christ must bear witness to him before his brethren. In the first place that simply means that he obediently accepts life and death as they are. In this way he meets Him. Further, it means looking towards God and the continually renewed acceptance of His forgiveness, and finally the explicit confession of His Name, of the hope we find in Him.

Christ is the one in whom God's self-communication to man and man's acceptance of him have become materially and existentially 'One' by the action of God. In him, God is unsurpassably and irrevocably *present* where we are, and in him man exists not only as the question in respect of God, but, as God's pledged acceptance, has become God himself in appearance: *the* Son of Man, the Son of God in the true and unconditional sense of the word. The Christian recognises in faith that the historically concrete realisation of this goal of salvation-history, which sustains and perfects the latter and causes it to triumph irrevocably over the history of evil, is given in Jesus of Nazareth. Throughout its whole history humanity looks for the God-man as the fulfilment of its own salvation-history; it has found no-one but Jesus of Nazareth in whom it is able to recognise the God-man; by his wonderful life, his death and resurrection he shows himself to be this God-man, the presence of God himself in the history of mankind. In him, God is irrevocably the one who has accepted us in love and has made us possessors of his infinite wealth of truth, life and eternity. The Christian believes in the death of Jesus, in which mankind has delivered itself with its own ground and goal to the grace of God, and in the complete perfection of the man Jesus (called his Resurrection), in which mankind has already begun to possess the life of God himself directly, breaking the bounds of its space-time history.

In so far as God, in his self-communication, still remains the holy and inconceivable mystery who, in giving himself away, does not lose his divinity, we call him Father. In so far as God communicates himself to us as our most real and eternally valid life by the means of divinising grace at the ground of our being, we call him Holy Spirit. In so far as the genuine truth of our being appears in history in the God-man, we call him the Word and the Son of God. In so far as these two mutually sustaining and determining ways of God's self-communication actually communicate God himself and not a creaturely, finite representation of God, we acknowledge that in his own life God himself, while remaining one, is distinguished as Father, Word and Spirit, so that we call him the threefold God, or the Three Persons: Father, Son and Spirit, one God.

The community of those who come together in faith around Jesus, in hope waiting to participate in his perfection and in him bound together in love with the Father and with each other by his Spirit – this community we call the Church. He himself founded this Church in the persons of his first disciples and provided it with his Spirit in the 'twelve' messengers to whom he entrusted his commission. He united this apostolic community in Peter as its head and gave it a constitution which these authorised messengers had authority to hand on. Thus he gave the Church the task and the powers of representing him and witnessing to him throughout history until its end, so that he should remain God's self-committal to the world in the dimension of historical concreteness, and as such should be continually at work. In this way, in its origin in and in its witness to Christ, the Church is the historical sign of God's victorious will for Salvation, conquering all man's guilt. To this extent the Church is the 'sacrament' (i.e. the holy, effectual sign) in which the world's divinisation appears and, in appearing, establishes itself. As the historical presence of God's unrevoked pledge of himself in Christ, the Church's testimony, wherever it is expressed in a definitive witness on the part of its authoritative teaching office, is protected from slipping from God's truth; and in so far as the word spoken by the Church by means of holy symbols communicates grace (which lives in the Church) in its full measure to the individual in the decisive situations of his life, it is an effectual word, carrying with it what it signifies: this word is itself a sacrament.

Just as man in his personal life is familiar with words which involve him totally and which reveal precisely what is happening *while* they are being said – for instance, words of ultimate love or of forgiveness – so in a similar way the Church is acquainted in its own field with words by which it pledges itself to man as what it actually is: the sign of mercy and of the love of God to all.

Seven of these effectual words of grace are known to the Church: the sign of grace (called Baptism), in which the sinful human being is dedicated to the triune God by the rite of washing and is also accepted into the Church as a member – in the concrete historical dimension – by the forgiveness of his sinfulness and by sanctifying by God's Spirit; the express promise of the Spirit in conjunction with the imposition of hands (Confirmation), enabling and empowering the baptised person to be a witness by life and testimony to the fact that God loves the world, even in the presence of those who think they are unable to believe in his love; the word of judgment and forgiveness (Penance), in which the Church reconciles the culpable person to herself and to God; the word by which the Church commends the baptised person in imminent danger of death to the God of eternal life (Holy Unction); the word (Ordination) by which the Church imparts to one of her members by the imposition of hands a share (in three stages) in her authority and the power of that authority; the word (in the Sacrament of Matrimony) which lays the foundation for the marriage bond and at the same time reveals it as the reflection of the unity and fertility of the love of God towards human kind gathered into the Church in Christ. In addition to these six signs of sanctifying grace there is the seventh and greatest in the holy meal of the community of Christ, in which the latter is mindful of the death and resurrection of its Lord as its salvation and is united anew with Him in the rite of the meal under the signs of bread and wine: the Sacrament of the Altar. Thus the Church is at the same time the visible community of the redeemed and also the sign by which God's Spirit effects the world's salvation and renders it visible in concrete history.

To the extent that the Christian is united with his Lord by his Spirit in faith, hope and love, he knows that he has already been set free from all intramundane forces and powers (sin, law, death) into the infinity and finality of the life of the true and living God. But he also knows that he must share with his Lord his destiny of death, until he too, at the point where his life and death seem to enter the most extreme degree of forsakenness by God, the ultimate darkness of guilt, lays his existence into the hands of the living God. He knows that his life must be an act of unconditional love to God and his fellow men, which far exceeds the fulfilment of all law. He confidently looks forward to the end of his life and the end of the history of mankind, when what is already present now in faith and lowliness will appear unveiled and perfected to all who have loved: the life of God, who is all in all.

8

OBSERVATIONS ON THE DOCTRINE OF GOD IN CATHOLIC DOGMATICS

THERE is always something dubious about methodological investigations: it is only too easy for the thing under discussion itself to slip out of sight. But we may observe further limitations in such a procedure. For several reasons we cannot undertake here a *new* and *basic* foundation for the methodology of the Catholic Doctrine of God. We are really presenting only 'observations'.[1] Nor is it our aim to do any more than this, in a way, for it is not our intention to propound any particular, strikingly new thesis in order to contradict what is usual in Catholic theology, or which would develop a new programme, proclaim a radically new orientation and seek once more to revolutionise theology. Nothing is further from our intention. Not only because it is contrary to the nature of Catholic theology but because it seems contrary to the reality with which we are concerned here, namely God. For if one can think of anything at all under this heading which repays constant pondering, it is clear at the outset that it would be to go sadly astray and to miss the point completely if one were to say of a particular radicalism of a system, a thesis or an opinion – as opposed to any other system, thesis or opinion – that 'this is God, and not that'; that 'this is the true experience of the true God and that is not'. The true radicalism in the doctrine of God can only be the continual destruction of an idol, an idol in the place of God, the idol of a theory about him. What it cannot be is a statement about him which distinguishes him from another object on the same plane, or which distinguishes this particular way ofhaving-to-do-with-him from any other mode of approach to him. If it tries to do this

[1] The author may be permitted to refer in addition to other studies which will perhaps supplement the thoughts expressed here (apart from the references given below in the subsequent footnotes): *Theological Investigations* III (London and Baltimore, 1967), pp. 385–400; *Theological Investigations* IV (London and Baltimore, 1966), pp. 36–73; *Theological Investigations* VI (London and Baltimore, 1969), pp. 3–20; *Theological Investigations* VII (London and New York, 1971), pp. 25–46.

it must come under the hammer of its own principle of 'destruction', for one cannot gain control of God by a wild radicalism in negative theology either, since negative theology cannot give Him to us if He had not always given Himself to us already.

This principle is found in the sober humility of the true relationship with God. The unique character of our relationship with God and his existence for us is shown by the fact that when we have renounced a knowledge of God which *conquers* him by means of affirmation or negation, God does not disappear, but precisely at that point commits himself to us; furthermore it is shown by the fact that this renunciation (ultimately the renunciation of being God) is not *one* pole in the human dialectic between Yes and No, but is rooted at the very basis of this dialectic, and that God only appears when he is accepted simply, humbly and unselfconsciously in worship and obedience and when he is not torn to pieces in all the talk of reflection. Finally it is also characteristic of our relationship with God that all these considerations must be thought out in very strict terms all the same, notwithstanding the foregoing. Anselm says: *consideratio rationabiliter comprehendit incomprehensibile esse.* If this truth were given pride of place as the very first condition of our existence, as that which upholds everything else, itself unsupported by anything (such that every attempt to reach down to the basis of this primary condition finds itself still 'upheld' by the latter, thus placing *us* before the question whether we are to accept it or not), all reflex dialectic – which is necessary and must opt for saying Yes or No – is only preliminary; but it *is* a necessary preliminary. Consequently a certain calmness of approach is justified with respect to theological reflection about God. But for this very reason we may not proclaim any theological affirmation in opposition to others in too absolute a manner, as theology itself does not do, so long as it is genuine and erects no idols to be worshipped. However – and this is what I really wanted to say – this seems to me to be the ultimate legitimation for my making a few observations on the theme committed to me. What is said in systematic terms is only true here provided that it is understood as something occasional and fragmentary, and provided that it is prepared to disintegrate into 'observations'.

I intend to arrange these observations, loosely related as they are, by first presenting some remarks concerning the Doctrine of God within Catholic dogmatics, chiefly as regards its scholastic form.[2] (This is to a certain extent an issue internal to Catholic theology; however, in an age

[2] This is a kind of revision of the remarks given by the author in the *LThK* IV (Freiburg,[2] 1959), cols. 1119–1124.

of ecumenism it may also claim to be of interest to Protestant theologians.) Then in the second part I shall append some further observations in an attempt to reach beyond the confines of this Catholic academic question.

In this *first* part I make some observations which arise from a simple glance at the *history* of this treatise in Catholic dogmatics. In line with the beginning of each of the Creeds, it is an uncontested practice in Catholic theology (although it is not really as evident as it seems) that dogmatics must begin with the doctrine of God if it is to be anything like systematic in its procedure. Of course, this way of beginning in Catholic theology has been called in question to a certain extent because, since the advent of modern times and the Enlightenment, the 'beginning' of so-called 'fundamental theology' has been prefixed to this original 'beginning'. Naturally, a problem has arisen in this way which, if the unity of theology is an ultimate necessity, cannot be solved by saying that this 'fundamental theology' is a discipline on its own with its own method and its own subject-matter, distinct from dogmatics as the study of the *content* of dogmatics. The issue becomes even more difficult because today, on account of theology's object being seen in salvation-history – which bars the way to a systematic treatment – the question of a fundamental and formal theology[3] as the starting-point for dogmatic theology has been recently raised. (Not to be confused with 'fundamental theology' in the usual sense.) Furthermore there is the fact that today the problems involved in an existentially effective fundamental theology apart from and prior to dogmatics have again been seen more clearly in Catholic theology, and so the tendency is to merge the two together.[4]

However that may be, it was certainly the case in the earliest epistemological discussions of the theology of the Fathers that the θεολογία came before the οἰκονομία, the doctrine of salvation. For instance, the doctrine of God stands at the beginning of Origen's περὶ ἀρχῶν, the first systematic treatment of the faith of the Church. Behind this tendency there are naturally the presuppositions of Greek metaphysics, the theoretical interpretation of man as a contemplative being orientated towards eternity; these presuppositions cannot be justified without further ado by appealing to scripture. But in any case it remains an open question whether man – *ultimately* at least, both within and in spite of such historically determined

[3] cf. K. Rahner, *LThK* IV (Freiburg,[2] 1959), cols. 205–206; *Theological Investigations* I (London and Baltimore, 1961), pp. 1–37.

[4] For a preliminary treatment see K. Rahner, 'Reflections on the contemporary intellectual formation of future priests', *Theological Investigations* VI (London and Baltimore, 1969), pp. 113–138, esp. 123 ff.

and unsupported presuppositions and perspectives – does not always remain a being who is freely open even with regard to his own systematic endeavours, and who thus always knows more than the formal method of his systematics should actually permit him to know. Consequently even such a problematical beginning need not constitute a mortal blow for a genuine faith. In mediaeval theology, where theology's formal object is 'God as such' (e.g. Thomas I, 1, 7), this way of commencing dogmatics with the doctrine of God must have seemed even more obvious. But even in circles where this definition of theology's formal object was not held in such esteem, Catholic theology has almost always assumed that dogmatics should start with the doctrine of God and not, for instance, with the reality of Christ, 'Sophia', the Kingdom of God, faith, justification, man's religious subjectivity, or the like. And this is perfectly understandable. For according to a Catholic understanding of grace God does not apply a saving 'something' to man, but gives his very *self* as our salvation in a most radical manner, so that God-in-himself and the God-of-our-salvation are strictly identical. If as a result of this the idea of the priority of the Doctrine of God is not utterly compelling, for this very reason *every* dogmatic treatise must speak of this God who communicates himself in grace, and of this God *alone*; thus we can say that a correctly understood Doctrine of God, placed at the very beginning, expresses precisely that. In doing so it avoids making such a doctrine of God a purely regional and isolated study, but on the contrary takes the shape of a formal anticipation of what all theological studies are concerned with. Understood in this way the almost universal practice of the priority of the Doctrine of God in Catholic Dogmatics is – if not utterly compelling – sufficiently justified, especially since man, not being God, never has such an ἀρχή at his disposal. In expressing it he can never really have said everything, he can never completely comprehend the flow from its source; for in reality he only has the source by entering the flow many times at many points.

Even historically speaking, the relationship between the general doctrine of God (De Deo uno) and the doctrine of the Trinity is more problematical. One cannot elicit a unified conception of this relationship from a study of the history of Catholic theology. The order of the treatises which is almost universally accepted today – first De Deo uno, then De Deo trino – has probably become general custom only since Peter Lombard's Sentences were ousted by Thomas' *Summa Theologica*. The Apostles' Creed with its trinitarian structure would only provide a clue to solving the problem of the unity and diversity of these two treatises if one were to understand – in common with the ancient θεός terminology[5] – the word 'God' as the Father of the trinitarian confession, and, taking a Greek kind of trinitarian theology (linear with respect to the world), to discuss in addition the whole 'being' of God in the first chapter concerning the Father. It is noteworthy that Peter Lombard subsumes the general doctrine of God under his doctrine of the Trinity, which M. Grabmann,[6] for instance, regards as one of Lombard's 'chief errors'. Noteworthy is also the fact that we do not yet find a clear division in the *Summa Alexandri* either, whereas Thomas, for reasons which have not yet really been explained – whether in opposition to the Arabic systems or from apologetic or pedagogic motives – clearly follows the Augustinian and Latin method: he does not treat the general doctrine of God as the doctrine of God the Father, the sourceless origin in the Godhead, but, by way of anticipation, as the Doctrine of the nature of God which is common to all the Persons. Only after that does he commence his doctrine of the Trinity. And so it has remained in general right up to today. For example the new Spanish Jesuits' Dogmatics gives an uncompromising and explicit defence of this method.[7] In still more recent times, for instance in the case of Anselm Stolz and M. Schmaus, one can sense this problem again. M. Schmaus subsumes the treatise De Deo uno as the doctrine of 'the fulness of life of the three-personal God' under the first section of his dogmatics which deals with 'God the Three in One'.

Furthermore, the doctrine of God of all the more recent Catholic dogmatics always contains a section on man's *knowledge* of God. That may seem strange, for at a first glance the theme seems to belong rather to dogmatic anthropology. For this accepted procedure to be really substantiated, as is quite possible, it would be necessary to deepen this section of a doctrine of God so that the following were made clear: Firstly it is concerned with that *particular* knowledge about God which arises, in an ultimate and indissoluble unity, from that experience which grasps in an original unity human existence, creatureliness transcendentally situated in the sphere of grace and of revelation-history, the consequently implied

[5] cf. K. Rahner, *Theological Investigations* I (London and Baltimore, 1961), pp. 79–148.

[6] *Die Geschichte der kath. Theologie seit dem Ausgang der Väterzeit* (Darmstadt,[2] 1961), p. 42. On the relationship between the two treatises 'De Deo uno' and 'De Deo trino' cf. K. Rahner, *Mysterium Salutis* II, ed. J. Feiner and M. Löhrer (Einsiedeln, 1967), pp. 317–397, esp. 323 ff., 340 f., 395 f., and in the same volume M. Löhrer, pp. 291–315.

[7] Patres S.J., in 'Hispania Professores', *Sacra Theologiae Summa* II (Madrid,[4] 1964), pp. 12 f.

possibility of a 'natural' knowledge of God, and the continual temptation to atheism in man's tenacious sinfulness. In this case the question of 'natural' knowledge of God alone, in the terms of Vatican I, cannot occupy the centre of attention, but must take its place as the reductive element within a total experience of God. And secondly it must be made clear that in this case knowledge and what is known, belief and what is believed stand in a particular, unique relationship with one another, such that the knowledge of God cannot (or can only retrospectively) be regarded as constituting a regional sphere of knowledge side by side with other regional spheres of knowledge, but is the fundamental source and ultimate horizon of all knowledge whatsoever in the unity of human existence. This knowledge of God is always there and can always be 'held fast'; its conceptual interpretation is always one factor of it itself to some degree and in some form, but it is not simply identical with it. As a result of this, knowledge and what is known can only be grasped by reflection *in one*, the doctrine of God *is* dogmatic anthropology *and* the doctrine of God itself, just as, by analogy, ontology is precisely onto-logy, i.e. the doctrine of being *and* also the doctrine of the knowledge of being, in an indivisible unity.

As far as the inner structure of the treatise is concerned, where the doctrine of God is distinguished from the doctrine of the Trinity, it has been customary for a long time, following the presentation of the theme of the being of God, to supply a discussion of the *attributes* of God. In such a discussion it is usual for issues to be dealt with which find a place equally well in the doctrine of Creation or in the doctrine of Grace, like the questions of God's foreknowledge (sovereignty) and of predestination. The discussion of God's attributes pursues an almost exclusively metaphysical, i.e. not originally theological path: we usually divide them into active and passive attributes, and the latter are again distinguished as transcendental and categorial. We shall say more about this shortly.

However, these clear and tangible features in the history of the treatise's inner structure do not supply any considerable impetus towards solving the theological issues themselves; the Catholic treatise De Deo uno is to some extent aware, at second hand, of the questioning or contesting of a rational knowledge of God, and against such a denial it repeats the Anathema pronounced by Vatican I. But so far the reformation, the change from the technical Greek way of thought to the correct anthropocentricity of modern times, the historical shift from the question of a gracious God to the question of where and how one can find God and man at all (and both at the same time), the question of reconciling transcendence and historicity, transcendence from above and from past origins and transcendence from ahead in the future, the question of the interweaving of faith, hope and love in the knowledge of God itself, the question of the constant possibility of atheistic unbelief[8] as an internal factor of faith in God – all these have not really become a part of the history of the treatise. And to allow these issues to affect its future history would not be to deliver a mortal blow.

In the second part of this section we shall make a few more *systematic* observations (if that is not a contradiction in terms).

We have already said that in its own particular dogmatics – notwithstanding 'fundamental theology' and the possibility of a formal and fundamental theology – Catholic theology places the doctrine of God at the beginning. Let us leave it so. Revelation-history and salvation-history (and consequently the nature of theology) as God's self-revelation, together with transcendental and 'eccentric' man, whose fundamental vocation is to obey this self-revealing God in faith (and who can only be himself by receiving his being from the mystery which envelops him, and would not find the true God if he only considered him from the standpoint of *ad nos*, i.e. by measuring the *ad nos* from our point of view instead of accepting it from God) – these two factors demand that man should not speak first of his own salvation, but of God. In other words he must *begin again*, and correctly this time, *after* he has finished talking about himself and his sorry state. This time he must say that his true salvation is precisely the God who does *not* exist solely to be our salvation, and that our true salvation – which is wrought by him and not by us – disappears into his incomprehensibility. This does not exclude, but includes the fact that all remaining dogmatics is already contained in this doctrine of God. But besides being said *in toto* in each treatise (and hence necessarily more than once, since we cannot say everything *in toto* at the same time), the whole of dogmatics must first of all be uttered as the doctrine of God so that it remains clear that we must speak of God and not, after all, of ourselves, even if this speech is only meaningful as the final sound indicating the adoring silence before God. Instead of excluding it, this way of beginning includes the fact that this very treatise, because it is theology, reflection, and not the original source of the history of faith, must not forget the origin of our real knowledge of God in Christ and must make all affirmations whatever about God in such a way as to include the experience of salvation-history. Thus it will (as far as possible) strive against the danger of tacitly making an abstract metaphysical

[8] cf. J. B. Metz, *LThK* X (Freiburg,[2] 1965), cols. 496 ff.; J. B. Metz, 'Unbelief as a theological problem', *Concilium* 1 (June 1965).

schema into the *norma non normata* of what, how and who God 'can be'.[9]

The mere *sequence* of the treatises De Deo uno and De Deo trino, as if the second treatise were only supplementary to the first, and as if only the second contained affirmations going beyond metaphysics (even though of a metaphysics requiring to be confirmed and secured), is apt to obscure the concrete history of theology, i.e. the two possibilities which present themselves in the orthodox conception of the doctrine of the Trinity itself, and it presupposes wrongly that the history of revelation itself followed such a sequence, i.e. from the revelation of God's being to the revelation of the Trinity. One could just as well say – indeed it would be more correct to say – that the history of revelation first of all shows God as a Person without origin, the Father, who has then revealed himself (as we say in technical terms) within this relationship with the world as a self-communication, as the source of divine life-processes, capable of creating persons. These life-processes reveal their divine immanence characteristically in the economic trinitarian relationship of God in Christ and in his Spirit which is given to us. So the sequence whereby the treatise De Deo uno precedes the doctrine of the Trinity is not *necessarily* to be seen as the result of the infiltration of philosophy. Thus the question seems to be more didactic than fundamental whether and in which order the two treatises should follow one another, or whether they should be assimilated to each other. But on the other hand it is most important, if the general doctrine of God is placed first, not to present it as though there were no doctrine of the Trinity at all (as occurs in standard Catholic dogmatics). If the creation of what is not divine is understood dogmatically at the outset as a factor and a condition for the possibility of God's absolute self-communication, in which absolute Love gives its very self and not something other than itself, creation as the freely uttered Word of the unfathomably Inconceivable is then seen as the beginning and the 'grammar' of the divine self-expression communicated into the void. Thus it is the beginning of the trinitarian self-revelation.

It may be counted as a positive achievement of the more recent academic tradition (although the latter does not have a real understanding of itself everywhere as yet) that the study of the knowledge of God is taken as a part of the doctrine of God. For as we have already said, there is a unique relationship between this knowledge as a subjective act and what is known thereby, a relationship which essentially cannot be found elsewhere. Thus

[9] A typical example of this is the *undialectical* idea of God's 'immutability' which pays little or no heed to the dogma of the Incarnation. Cf. K. Rahner, *Theological Investigations* IV (London and Baltimore, 1966), pp. 112 ff.

we can see a transcendental factor at work in man's necessary recourse to God in knowledge and freedom in respect of any object whatsoever, and this inevitably involves an implicit, non-objective experience of God which is always unthematic and capable of being overlooked. Hence too the unique character of the religious act in general[10] (above all with its original and integrated structure), the necessity of a total involvement flowing from the very essence of this knowledge, since the *concept* of God in this knowledge only avoids being an idol by referring to the God who, without an image of himself, standing fundamentally over against man, gives himself.[11] In the same way we can understand man's basic constitution in the experience of God, according to which man does not experience himself as an autonomous subject who creates a subject/object relation or anticipates it in his transcendental autonomy, but is aware of himself as the one who is destined, consigned and 'uttered' by the inexpressible Mystery.

All this means that one is justified, even obliged, to maintain the unity of the treatise on God and on the knowledge of God. Furthermore it must be made more radical so that the treatise on the knowledge of God is not only one *piece* of the whole doctrine of God but the doctrine itself, and so that it actually speaks only of God and not about ourselves, since talk about ourselves is ultimately nothing but the challenge to be silent, to adore, to hide oneself in the inexpressible Mystery, which commits us to ourselves in order to commend itself to us and sustain us. Where this unity of θεολογία and θεὸς λέγων is reflected upon – a unity which is not produced by us, but which itself sets us in existence – we must naturally speak of the possibility of such a reflection, which is always already present. In other words we must be aware of the possibility that we must not only be silent about God, but may also speak of him (and therefore *must* speak of him). Expressed in Catholic terms this doctrine of the transcendental necessity of the priority of the experience of God and its necessary expression in explicit speaking about God (with all the dangers of conceptual idolatry) refers to a knowledge which is both transcendental *and* unavoidable and is always sustained by the offer of God's self-communication in *grace*. Consequently the doctrine of the *natural* knowability and knowledge of God is not a knowledge which appears in isolation, but one element, only subsequently isolated, in a single knowledge of God, authorised by him in its direct relation to him, which, when

[10] cf. J. B. Metz, *LThK* I (Freiburg,[2] 1957), cols. 256–259.

[11] Not, of course, in the sense of ontologism, but as a result of man's transcendental being-in-reference-to God.

it is accepted, is already faith. Needless to say, this supernatural transcendentality (if we may term it thus) of the knowledge of God must be understood from the very beginning such that it only exists in the encounter with history, and consequently not only is it always open towards salvation-history and the revelation of the Word but it experiences the latter as its own history.

From this it is clear that the doctrine of God cannot (and not even primarily) be concerned with making statements about God's metaphysically necessary attributes, but above all concerning the workings – maintained throughout salvation-history – of God's freely adopted disposition towards man and the world. These two things are for the most part not clearly enough distinguished and related to one another in the official Catholic doctrine of God. His faithfulness, mercy, love, in short the concrete relationship of God to us which we experience in the unity of the transcendental experience of grace and salvation-history, and which we have to express in the doctrine of God, are not merely the theologically attested necessary 'attributes' of God's metaphysical being, but considerably more. For God could deny us the very faithfulness, love etc. which he actually shows towards us, without ceasing to be faithful and loving in a metaphysical sense. And to recognise this possibility, to confide in the marvel of the *free* love of God, is to open up the horizon within which his attributes can really be grasped as being *divine*, i.e. such that a knowledge of them does not give us any power over him. From this point it might be possible for the Catholic doctrine of God to find a way of approach towards understanding and using the Lutheran *theologia crucis*. Even less than his attributes, God's dispositions cannot be united in a single, positive concept by us; we can only say formally, aiming at the unity of God asymptotically, *that* in God they must be one, transposed into each other in perfect harmony. For us they remain materially and positively unamenable to synthesis, and thus the way they affect us has a history (which as a result of the divine act of *self*-communication to us is the genuine history of God), and the consequent history of our response therefore neither can nor needs to consist in a metaphysical equilibrium in our attitude in respect of God's free disposition towards us. For instance we have more reason to praise his mercy than to fear his justice, because he has allowed his grace to overflow and not his anger, and we must not let this fact be obscured by a dialectic balancing between divine attributes of God in themselves, in an attempt to manipulate him by means of the understanding. In a similar way other themes usually treated in a doctrine of God, like God's foreknowledge, predestination, God's freedom in grace, could be liberated from an abstract formalism; it could lead to the theological counterpart of Heidegger's secularised concept of the history of Being (*Seinsgeschichte*).

II

Following these semi-systematic observations on the doctrine of God in Catholic dogmatics I take the liberty of adding some further unsystematic remarks more or less at random, concerning particular points arising in connection with the doctrine of God. At the very outset it is strange to be talking 'about' the doctrine of God, as opposed to stating it, for in the nature of the case the affirmations of this doctrine can only refer to what is meant in a very indirect way. However, that may perhaps excuse the unsystematic nature of these remarks.

1. First of all, the following plain threefold presupposition characterises the Catholic doctrine of God.

(a) The calm and unembarrassed acceptance of the pluralistic structure of human knowledge and thus of theology too. Our knowledge has an ultimate subjective and objective unity. But so far as we think in terms of propositions, we are not standing at the focus of this unity, but are situated in a plurality of modes of knowledge. Consequently there is no formula which can say everything at the same time, no single idea from which everything else could be deduced. We are rightly always engaged in *systematising* (however we are to understand this word more precisely), but we never *have* a system; we always know more than what we have already systematised, and this unsystematised extra in our fundamentally plural experience is not merely supplementary to what we have mastered by system, but constitutes an incommensurate challenge and threat to it and is its future corrective. God is the presupposed objective and subjective unity, but he is also the God whom we can only *approach* by thought; we cannot ourselves join with him in realising this pluralism which he established and sustains in his creativity. It is thus clear that, as the first treatise, the doctrine of God is not complete until the end of the last dogmatic treatise. It is only possible at all in so far as we have continually exposed ourselves patiently to the claims of the many theological treatises. Hence it is also clear that we must always be aware – without letting ourselves become irritable or annoyed – that in a doctine of God we have forgotten and omitted much that we could and should actually have known.

(b) The patient desire for historical continuity in theology also applies in the case of the doctrine of God. If we wish to say something new and find what has been said of old to be inadequate, we may calmly count on finding implications of it in earlier theology. In spite of *Seinsgeschichte* and the recognition that the history of theology reaches right down to a real history of revelation and a real salvation-history and is not merely the playing of surface waves above the unmoved depths, the religious man, the man of faith, standing in the midst of his history where the issue is the issue of God, already possesses the totality of what can and must be pondered upon by theology. For genuine and fundamental knowledge consists in the unreserved surrender in faith to the absolute Mystery, the surrender to the self-communication of this Mystery, which, though holy, yet gives itself and forgives in direct intimacy, the surrender to its inscrutable ordering of history. This being so, we cannot really proceed in a revolutionary manner, as if the men of old did not know the God of whom we wish to speak. We can only claim to use the speech of reflection about him in such a way that it introduces *us* better to the faith which was always there. And this we must do with the painful and sobering thought that when we have poured out our pail of knowledge into the ocean of the incomprehensible God, we have really poured it back into the ocean whence we drew it in the first place.

(c) The courage to engage in metaphysics. There is no theology which does not carry on metaphysics, simply because in theology too there must be the process of thinking. I am sometimes amazed that theologians are quick to declare that a metaphysics must be false or unsuitable for theology simply because it is a matter of dispute. How can they not see that their own theology too is itself a matter of dispute, and yet they do not straightway regard this as a criterion for saying that their own theology is false? The man who has not the courage to pursue a metaphysics (which is not the same as a closed system), a metaphysics which can be contradicted, cannot be a good theologian. Even when one is conscious of possessing a constantly inadequate metaphysics, it is still possible to rely on it, to use it in addressing the true God and in directing man towards the experience which he always has already from God. For it is man's inalienable blessing that his words say more and purer things than he himself knows and can enclose in his impure words, provided, that is, that his pride does not make him keep silent just because, as soon as he begins to speak about God, his words immediately sound foolish. In using them one always becomes ridiculous, even if neither the others nor oneself notice it straight away; the same is true if one uses the ancient words, the tired and rickety words of tradition.

2. It seems to me that Thomas separated the question *an Deus sit* rather too much from the question *quid sit Deus.*[12] Of course one can ask whether there is such a thing as that which everyone calls God, without first of all explaining in greater detail what is meant thereby. Naturally, as individuals always determined by history, we would not think about God unless we had already heard of him indirectly. But if it is not to be merely a question of the existence of a mere empty cipher, the question of the existence of God must be launched as a question concerning the *real* God. And as opposed to more arbitrarily chosen objects of knowledge, which can be known as *possible* prior to a knowledge of their existence, in the case of God possibility and actuality can only be grasped in a *single* act of knowledge. Thus from the point of view of ontology, the theology of creation, the theology of grace and of existence (and all four in one) the question of God can apparently only be stated as one which has necessarily already been asked and which has the answer *in itself* and has not received it from elsewhere. Hence at the *same time* the question itself says both that God is, and also who he is. If we are not to miss God right from the very outset, the question of God must on no account be put as a question about an individual existent *within* the perspective of our transcendence and historical experience, but only as a question concerning the very ground sustaining the 'question' which we ourselves 'are', concerning the origin and future of this question. Consequently it already of necessity contains within itself simultaneously the answer to the questions 'whether?' and 'what?'

3. Naturally I cannot at this point give a sufficient answer to the question of the so-called proofs of the existence of God in themselves and as an element in a doctrine of God. However, I may be permitted to make a few observations. Usually, the Catholic dogmatic doctrine of God does not discuss these proofs as such but assumes them as a task of metaphysics which has been successfully completed. Even in the section of the doctrine of God concerned with the 'natural knowability of God' it is usually said that according to dogmatic sources such proofs are possible and actually exist. But on a closer investigation one would have to say that this dogmatic doctrine of God ought itself to present these proofs, at least *in nuce*. For can it say that there are such things without giving an idea of what is actually meant by them and what may not be meant? But can one give an idea of the essence of the proofs without actually performing them if (as is surely the case) their 'essence' and their transcendental necessity – their 'existence' – can only be grasped together at

[12] cf. e.g. *S.T.* I q.2, a.2, ad 2 et 3.

the same time? Furthermore, can the proofs be understood in any other way but as one element in the single, ultimately indissoluble experience of God in faith, as that element which is present (though rejected and repressed) even to the real unbeliever in so far as his unbelief is capable of leading to his judgment and loss of blessedness? That is the real theological reason why Catholic dogmatics holds fast the possibility of the so-called proofs, the possibility of a natural knowledge of God, just as it maintains the distinction between nature and supernatural grace. But that is not to deny that this 'proof of the existence of God' is absolutely *sui generis* and cannot be calculated as an individual item of knowledge by the formal and univocal procedure used in the case of any other piece of knowledge, nor is it the application of general axioms (in themselves quite independent of any application) to a particular case. Rather it is the result of the manifestation of the very ground of all such axioms, which is and remains the ultimate Mystery. In Thomas' theology and ever since, in spite of his *quinque viae*, there is and can be only *one* proof: in the whole questionable nature of man seen as a totality, which man is aware of in the concreteness of his existence striking him in a perpetually novel and existential way, provided that he does not run away from it.

4. In a Catholic doctrine of God the question of atheism ought to be considered much more seriously than is actually the case as a rule. And the first question must be the 'atheism' of the believer himself. If there can and ought to be a Catholic doctrine *simul justus et peccator*,[13] its modern historical form should be concerned with the man who, by virtue of the grace which he simply assumes without proof, is always breaking out of his atheism into faith in God.[14] There would have to be an exposition of the fact that theism can be the mask of a concealed atheism and vice versa, and that in this sense ultimately no-one can say of himself whether he believes in God or not, in the same way that the Council of Trent taught justification's existential hiddenness from the reflection of the individual conscience. We shall only be able to speak in justice, love and humility of

[13] R. Köster's 'Luthers These "Gerecht und Sünder zugleich"', *Catholica* 18 (1964), pp. 136–160, 210–224.

[14] Because the concrete and actual free realisation even of a 'natural' knowledge of God is a moral act which, 'elevated' in the existing order of salvation by supernatural grace, is also materially *faith*. For supernatural saving grace constitutes a transcendental horizon for freedom and knowledge, and the deliberate acceptance of these automatically implies an element of non-propositional, transcendental 'revelation'. Cf. K. Rahner/J. Ratzinger, *Revelation and Tradition* (Freiburg and London, 1966).

the atheists outside when atheism is admitted as the constant inner temptation of the theist, as a condition of faith.

I regard it as an oxymoron, which does not really lead us any further, when Tillich[15] says that it is just as much atheism to affirm the existence of God as to deny it. If that were true, one would be obliged to abandon the question of God as something about which essentially nothing can be said. But the only possible absolute atheism would be if one said one could manage to leave the question of God alone to such an extent that it *did not arise* at all, and thus did not even need to be dismissed. This cannot really be disproved by *a priori* metaphysics but by the *a posteriori* historical and yet unavoidable fact that man's existence actually *does* ask the question. This question can become stifled and suppressed; it may be necessary to dig for it; if it were not present already, it would be senseless to wish to inculcate it. That it can only be disproved in this way is what is really meant by scholastic theology where it says that God can only be known *a posteriori*. For this *a posteriori* point of departure is not intended to make the knowledge of God into a particular individual pursuit within the homogeneous field containing all other items of knowledge; it only says that, like his existence itself, the individual has laid upon him the transcendental necessity of being aware of himself and of the question (in whatever form), and that this necessity is his destiny, communicated to him as the question of the freedom committed to him and of the necessary nature of this freedom. The only thing which seems to me to be correct in Tillich's statement is that, if God is included as one object in an arbitrary series of other objects (similarly demonstrable) and knowledge of him is treated like any other knowledge, *this* kind of theism is in reality atheism, because it has no understanding whatsoever of the God referred to by genuine theism. A theism of this kind would be erecting an idolatrous image upon a foundation laid and ordered by ourselves, instead of reaching God on the intractable foundation which sustains us and which is God himself.

5. Is God in the doctrine of God, or does it only consist of talk about God which actually conceals and drives him away? Certainly he is not identical with this way of talking; for it is *our* way of talking, and we are finite and sinful. Similarly it is *our* speech when we talk of God according to God's revelation. For we only possess this revelation as one which has reached us, which we ourselves have heard, and so too as a revelation spoken by us. And it is certainly true that there is a radical distinction

[15] Paul Tillich, *Systematic Theology* (Nisbet, 1953 [University of Chicago, 1951]), Vol. I, p. 227.

in the relation of the form of what we say to the content of what is said, depending on whether we are speaking of some temporal thing within our speech horizon or of God, who is not of this nature. Our speech is indeed strange and uncanny when we are obliged to speak of God with temporal words – since we have no others. And least of all can we *compare* what we say with the One of whom we speak, since for the purposes of such comparison, he would be present only in the terms of our speech. Strictly speaking, in theological talk as such it is not God who is present, but ourselves.[16] But we are the ones who are spoken of, related to and destined from the Incomprehensible. And so it happens that talk about God comes from him, without itself possessing him. If we *speak* of our origin and destiny in this way, and thus speak of God, it is still speech. But it speaks of what we are *as* what we are. And there we have God, as the unutterable Mystery, banishing us from him and yet in his grace promising and giving us himself. That which we ourselves are, which gives us God himself, and whence we speak, does not make God subject to us, does not make theology into anthropology. On the contrary it actually makes us subject to God and yet at the same time – how can we say it in any other way? – his children.

This nameless something which we can neither grasp nor circumscribe, which lies behind us as our perpetual creation in grace, is both revelation and mysticism; as creation it always lies behind us and as the absolute future it lies ahead of us, confronting us with the concreteness of our individual and collective history and bidding us enter in (ultimately into the love of one's neighbour); this is how it actually presents itself to us; this is how we possess God himself. Provided that our explicit talk of God in the dogmatic doctrine of God really comes from this source, it possesses God although it is ours, although in itself it only *refers* to its origin. Whether, when a particular person is talking, it really comes from this source or is ultimately only the moribund babblings of what was once genuine in other people, no individual can know for certain. He can only tremble and hope. But since a man can believe that Jesus of Nazareth spoke in such a way because through death and resurrection he was 'uttered' absolutely by God as his Word; since a man, in loving his *neighbour* – and not, in the first instance, himself – must believe in hope

[16] It cannot be objected that this is always the case whenever one talks 'about' something. For when, in talking about other things, we are presented with ourselves, we have already anticipated the world (that which is referred to in speech), at least as far as its formal structures are concerned. But where God is concerned this relationship never exists.

that other men can speak in this way; since a man in the fellowship of Jesus believes in hope that this very speech, springing from its original source in God, is really present, he can as an individual confidently join in this speech about God, boldly entrusting his theological issue to God. He too will assuredly possess something of this genuine speech; he must not think of himself and of his sinfulness but calmly pursue his theology and commit it to God, from whom it *can* originate. And when he has spoken he should once more be silent in adoration, drinking draught by draught the everyday cup of God-less-ness, waiting for death, giving thanks for the joy of life – i.e. accepting it as sent to him in love – holding on to the *theologia viatoris et crucis* until at last the eternal light dawns. For the present we are held suspended in the very midst of it; even in the realm of thought we have no abiding city, even in theology we are pilgrims. But that is how it must be.

6. In the doctrine of God there is no real difference between the *Deus in se* and the *Deus extra se*. At least since Christ and in him we are both obliged and empowered to be continually overstepping this distinction. For to communicate himself to us 'in se' is exactly what he desires. And it is the paradoxical miracle of his love (i.e. of himself 'in himself') that he is able to do this without becoming finite and without violating our creatureliness. This process of *becoming* identical (and not just *being* identical) is the real content of salvation-history, which is the history of the unchangeable God. He really can *become* something in this history, precisely because ('and in the final analysis not 'although') he is infinite and unchanging, the absolute power, capable of doing this.

7. Can it be said that in this age there can no longer be an alliance between theology and philosophy in a Catholic dogmatic doctrine of God? If anyone thought that there were no metaphysics in theology, the answer to this question would have to be Yes. For in theology at least very accurate thought is needed; but any thought which questions and ponders itself as a whole (and how could one avoid doing this in the case of the doctrine of God, which is concerned with God and the knowledge of God, i.e. the onto-logical origin of everything?) is metaphysics. For that reason it is nonsense to talk about the end of *metaphysics*, however much one may wish to say that a particular form of metaphysics has been eclipsed. So the Catholic doctrine of God will always imply and maintain a fundamental unity of theology and metaphysics, even if one would not wish to speak of an 'alliance' between them. Of course, this does not answer the question as to the precise relationship between metaphysics and theology, nor the question as to how these two disciplines

have come, in a historically justified manner, to separate out from one another into two independent units, although from their very nature neither of them can be or wish to be 'regional' disciplines, but rather are concerned fundamentally with everything (including themselves).

The questions we have just raised will be answered sufficiently when reason and metaphysics understand that it is they which pose the open question and refer man back to the experience of his interior and external history, and when theology grasps the fact that it can only give God's answer – God as the answer for all time – provided that it keeps the question open. (For the question into which the answer is projected has always been answered already by God – not by us.) And both philosophy and theology – in their different ways – must understand that in answering the sinner too and man in general, God has granted the question. If this question were not granted, both the answer given would lack a question and the question would lack an answer, or both would dissolve together into a flat commonplace. Of course all this does not mean that the old alliance between theology and metaphysics is to remain exactly as it was before. For above all in theology the doctrine of God must not talk in terms of its *own* metaphysics, but the metaphysics which is committed to us today as our lot in history, whether through our own fault or not. The actual form of this metaphysics certainly no longer has the homogeneity, the balance of language, and of presuppositions and perspectives calmly assumed which was once the case. Consequently Catholic theology no longer has simply *one* language; it must learn many languages, and thus it probably speaks them all thoroughly badly. But it will be of the opinion, furthermore, that in being obliged to speak today in many metaphysics, it is not simply uttering propositions which oppose each other with an absolute lack of mutual understanding – like a simple Yes and No – but rather that there is a philosophia perennis *in* them, not besides them, for which one must listen sympathetically, as it cannot be distilled out. Thus a dialogue is possible with these diverse metaphysics; and theology can be expressed in their language, for theology is a human language too, and every human language which is not itself dead points, questioning, towards the unutterable Mystery with which alone theology is ultimately concerned.

9

ATHEISM AND IMPLICIT CHRISTIANITY

I

IMPLICIT Christianity – it could also be termed 'anonymous Christianity' – is what we call the condition of a man who lives on the one hand in a state of grace and justification, and yet on the other hand has not come into contact with the explicit preaching of the Gospel and is consequently not in a position to call himself a 'Christian'.[1] Theologically there can be no doubt that there are such people, as we shall show later in more detail. It is in itself a question of secondary importance whether this particular state should be called 'implicit Christianity' or not. Yet if one attends to the implications of this phenomenon the question can be answered unreservedly in the affirmative.

In addition there is technical justification for the use of the concept. For everything which is explicit in the proclamation, the sacraments and institutions of Christianity is instrumental in securing the possession of the grace of justification (and maintaining it until the end as the foretaste, the initial instalment of eternal life), to such an extent that, as the 'pars potior' and goal of everything else which is 'Christian', it may itself be called 'Christianity', especially since this grace is the grace of *Christ*. Furthermore the concept of being 'implicit' is thoroughly common in theology: it even occurs in a related context in *fides implicita*, *votum* (*baptismi*, *Ecclesiae*) *implicitum* etc. However, we have no objection to anyone wishing to avoid the term 'implicit Christianity' for various reasons (e.g. the danger of misunderstanding). But he would be obliged to provide another term saying what is meant in just as clear and brief a manner. The same applies to the synonymous term 'anonymous Christianity', which is distinguished from the other only by underlining the implications of this state as such *for other people*.

[1] cf. K. Rahner, 'Anonymous Christians', *Theological Investigations* VI (London and Baltimore, 1969), pp. 390–398; further reference in Kl. Riesenhuber, 'Der anonyme Christ nach Karl Rahner', *Zeitschrift für katholische Theologie* 86 (1964), pp. 286–303.

For the sake of full conceptual clarity we must emphasise this: By virtue of God's desire for universal salvation, the 'objective redemption' constituting a fundamental factor in every man's 'subjective' state of salvation, the 'supernatural *existentiale*' and the continual offer of the grace of God's supernatural saving activity, even the unbaptised person (in the state of original sin as well) is in a unique situation. Prior to any existential attitude which he takes up, whether in faith and love or unbelief and sin, he is in a different position (and he himself is different too) from what would be the case if he were only the result of his 'nature' and his original sin. He can never be simply a 'natural' man and a sinner. By virtue of the grace of Christ (as possibility and obligation), which is at least a constant offer, he is always in a Christ-determined situation, whether he has accepted this grace or not.

Terminologically, however, it is better not to call this existentially (but not *existentiell*) 'Christian' position on the part of every man 'implicit' or 'anonymous' Christianity straight away. Otherwise we obscure the radical distinction between grace merely offered and grace existentially accepted in faith and love.

The basic thesis of this study is that even an atheist may possess this kind of 'implicit' Christianity.

This basic thesis is by no means self-evident. For it must be said that right up to most recent times official text-book theology has fairly unanimously supported the view (in spite of various theological qualifications) that it is impossible for a normal responsible human being to entertain a 'positive atheism' for any considerable time without becoming personally culpable.[2] Since in this context there is no sense in weakening this culpability as though it were only 'venial', the official view involves a denial of the possibility of 'implicit Christianity' for any length of time in an adult atheist.

On the one hand one is obliged to appreciate the weight of the official view: in scripture God's knowability seems so clearly *given* and atheism seems to give evidence so definitely of being man's most terrible aberration, that it was only thought possible to understand it as a *sin* in which a man *freely* turns away in the *mysterium iniquitatis*, evilly suppressing the truth which everywhere impinges on him (Rom 1:18).

On the other hand it must be said that until now neither text-book theology nor scripture has been confronted with the experience of a

[2] A more detailed treatment is given in K. Lehmann, 'Die Auseinandersetzung mit dem westlichen Atheismus und der pluralistischen Gesellschaft', *Die Zukunft der Kirche*, ed. O. Mauer (Herder-Vienna, 1968).

world-wide and militant atheism, confident of its own self-evident nature and because of this it was possible to regard the earlier, ubiquitous, theistic 'common opinion' as something necessarily so, as an eternally valid quality of human nature. This was a mistake: it led to the official text-book view we mentioned being taken as self-evident.

Next, for the sake of brevity, it will be simplest if we have recourse to the doctrine of the Second Vatican Council in order to illustrate our basic thesis theologically. The texts concerned are Nos. 19–21 of the first chapter of the first part of *Gaudium et spes*, the fifth paragraph of No. 22 of the same chapter, No. 16 in Chapter 2 of *Lumen gentium* and finally – since what has been said about the polytheistic religions of mission lands also holds good in the case of atheism as the product of a different historical and sociological situation – No. 7 of the Decree on the Church's Missionary Activity.

It emerges from our definition of 'implicit' Christianity that the basic thesis can be suitably demonstrated in two stages:

1. According to Vatican II not every instance of positive atheism in a concrete human individual is to be regarded as the result and the expression of personal sin.

2. Such an atheist can be justified and receive salvation if he acts in accordance with his conscience.

II

1. In the first place, therefore, although it is relatively exhaustive in its treatment of atheism, the Council makes no reference to the traditional text-book view that positive atheism cannot be entertained for any considerable period of time by a fully developed person of normal intelligence without involving blame on his part.[3] Furthermore it is safe to say that the Council not only left this thesis[4] alone, but actually *assumed a contrary thesis*, i.e. that it is possible for a *normal adult to hold an explicit atheism for a long period of time* – even to his life's end – *without this implying moral blame* on the part of such an unbeliever. It is true, however, that this view is not taught explicitly: for example it is not pointed out that on the one hand we are faced with an explicit atheism, very widely

[3] In what follows the author is taking up some observations which have already appeared in *Concilium*: 'The Teaching of the Second Vatican Council on Atheism', *Concilium* 3 (March 1967), pp. 5–13.

[4] For its foundation and a more detailed interpretation cf. e.g. 'Patres Societatis Jesu facultatum theol. in Hispania professores', *Sacrae Theologiae Summa* II (Madrid,[4] 1964), pp. 23–24 and notes 21–22.

extensive in society, characterised by a straightforward self-confidence, and on the other hand that in accordance with general Christian principles we do not have the right to declare these atheists to be living in a state of unequivocal and severe moral blame before God. The *absence* of the traditional view seems to be at the same time highly suggestive and most remarkable if one considers that, provided that it were assumed to be correct, the text-book answer would be *the* decisive statement concerning atheism. But in the description of atheism in Nos. 19–21 the traditionally held view appears to such a small extent; in No. 19 (third section) where the question of blame is touched on in half a sentence, there is reference to the evident truth that the holding of atheism is culpable *provided* that the person intentionally banishes God from him or intentionally and wilfully excludes religious questions from his consciousness. But by no means is it said that *every* concrete case of atheism in a man can only continue for a considerable period of time if he is wilfully trying to exclude God or the religious question in this way. When we come to demonstrate the second part of our basic thesis as the teaching of the Council it will be even clearer – it will be conclusive – that we are right to interpret the Council's silence thus. For if it is possible for an 'atheist' to be justified by grace, not every instance of atheism can be the result of the personal culpability of the atheist in question. It is an artificial and ultimately nonsensical excuse to say that atheism of this kind is always culpably induced, but can persist afterwards even if the guilt itself – which need not necessarily have consisted *formalissime* in the culpable reception of atheism as such – is cancelled by a moral change of heart: it does not dispose of the decisive issue, which is the possible coexistence of atheism and justification.

Later on we shall come to speak about the possibility of coexistence of a conceptually objectified atheism and a non-propositional and existentially realised theism. From this it will also be apparent that the Council's pronouncements in Nos. 19–21 concerning the unavoidability of the religious issue do not contradict what we have just said. Of course the Council's reticence with regard to the question of blame in atheism does not imply a trifling with the problem, for: 'the Church has already repudiated and cannot cease repudiating, sorrowfully but as firmly as possible, those poisonous doctrines and actions which contradict reason and the common experience of humanity, and dethrone man from his native excellence' (No. 21).[5] But after the Council, Catholic pastoral

[5] For an authoritative condemnation of atheism previously cf. *Sacrae Theologiae Summa* II, p. 20, and K. Rahner, 'Atheismus (systematisch)', *LThK*[2] I, col. 985.

theology today will no longer be immediately under the impression, even when confronted with a committed atheist, that it is dealing with a fool or a knave; hence in a totally new way it will have to consider – with the Council (cf. No. 21) – what the *real* causes of modern atheism are, if it cannot be attributed simply to dullness of the mind or perversity of the heart. Without intending to give an exhaustive list or a deep analysis of such causes of atheism, the Council itself has indicated some of them. But in doing so it has not released Catholic theology, and Christian philosophy, pastoral theology and the teaching of religion from their task, a task which has not, as yet, been adequately tackled.

2. The second element in our basic thesis on atheism which is confirmed by the Council and which – judged by the accepted traditions of scholastic thought and religious practice – may cause offence is the conviction *that even an atheist* (holding the concepts and theory of atheism, as we shall explain in detail later) *is not excluded from attaining salvation, provided that he has not acted against his moral conscience as a result of his atheism.* We have already said that this proviso cannot be taken for granted, i.e. the atheist's blamelessness is thus not simply an immaterial hypothesis. This is observed by the Constitution on the Church *Lumen gentium* (No. 16): 'Nor does divine Providence deny the help necessary for salvation to those who, without blame on their part, have not yet arrived at an explicit knowledge of God, but who strive to live a good life, thanks to His grace.'[6] But for salvation both supernatural faith and the grace of justification are necessary. Technically speaking it cannot be here a question of those (entitatively natural or actually supernatural) graces which constitute an as yet remote preparation for justification and the consequent attainment of salvation which are mediated by (among other things) an explicit theism. For otherwise we would be merely stating the obvious, saying in effect that by the grace of God an atheist can become a theist and *thus* can be finally justified. Nor would this fit the context of the constitution, which is concerned with the different kinds of non-Catholics *in so far as* they are and actually *remain* non-Catholics. Thus No. 22 of the Pastoral Constitution says: 'All this' – the blessed Resurrection – 'holds true not only for Christians, but for all men of good will in whose hearts grace works in an unseen way. For, since Christ died for all men, and since the ultimate vocation of man is in fact one, and divine, we ought to believe that the Holy Spirit in a manner known only to God offers to every man the possibility of being associated

[6] cf. the commentary on this text by A. Grillmeier, *Commentary on the documents of Vatican II*, ed. H. Vorgrimler (New York and London, 1967).

with this paschal mystery.' There is no reason to exclude atheists from this declaration. For it refers explicitly to No. 16 of the Constitution on the Church which concerns those who have not yet come to a conscious recognition of God. Moreover, mention of 'ways known only to God' is also made in the Decree on the Church's Missionary Activity (No. 7), where the 'heathen' who have not yet been reached by the Gospel are recognised as having a real possibility of supernatural faith and salvation even in their condition. But it would be arbitrary to wish to attribute a fundamentally much greater chance of salvation to a polytheistic heathen, who according to Paul is still 'without God' (Eph 2:12),[7] than to a modern atheist, whose 'personal' atheism is in the first place no less a product of his cultural situation.

With regard to all the texts quoted, as we have already said, it obviously cannot be a question of assuming at the outset that these atheists will become conceptually and theoretically *explicit* theists before death and *thus* saved. For in that case the texts would be merely repeating the platitude that an atheist can attain salvation when and in so far as he ceases to be one. Such an interpretation would deny any serious meaning to the texts; in producing them the Council would have been wasting its time.

III

Something really new has been said in these two elements of the Council's authoritative doctrine. If we consider the explicit statements of Scripture[8] and the traditional verdict on atheism, as well as the cautious reticence of Protestant theology with respect to the unbaptised person's possibility of salvation, we cannot say that this 'salvation optimism' as regards non-Christians (including atheists) is simply a theological truism for here we can see the development of something which really only began with Pius IX (*DS* 2865–2867) and led to the Holy Office's declaration of 8th August, 1949 (*DS* 3866–3873). Moreover this line of thought has really been developed *further* to the extent that, in a much clearer way than before, *atheists too* have been *explicitly included* in this 'salvation optimism'.

[7] cf. H. Schlier's exegesis of this passage: *Der brief an die Epheser* (Düsseldorf,[4] 1963), p. 121.

[8] cf. the concise synopsis in *LThK*[2] I, cols. 985–986. Many scriptural statements about the fate of unbelievers need to be understood more clearly than has been the case until now in Catholic exegetics, as eschatological, prophetic 'admonitions' in a very particular literary form.

These declarations have rendered obsolete even the earlier, *moderately* optimistic interpretations of the situation of non-Christians and heathen and atheists too which were to be found in text-book theology. According to the latter, such people outside the jurisdiction of Christianity were recognised as capable of attaining a 'natural' salvation (similar to that which the text-books acknowledged in the case of children dying without being baptised) but excluded from a really *supernatural* salvation. The Decree on the Church's Missionary Activity (No. 7) expressly states that these people too, by the grace of God and in ways not known to us, can reach a real *saving* faith even without having accepted the explicit preaching of the Christian Gospel. And wherever the word 'salvation' occurs in the other texts we have quoted, what is meant is genuine supernatural salvation, more particularly since it is expressly declared that all men have only *one* vocation to salvation, and since the attainment of this salvation is understood as participation in Christ's Easter mystery.

Thus according to the teaching of Vatican II it is possible for an atheist to be living in the grace of justification, i.e. possessing what we have called 'implicit Christianity'. In this short investigation it cannot be our business to show how this conciliar doctrine is deduced from the genuinely original sources of revelation, nor how it is defended against the seemingly weighty objections which could be brought against it by Scripture and Tradition. The Council itself only gives a very brief and general justification for its approach. To a certain degree the Council makes its own case – the possibility of the unbaptised non Christian's salvation without contact with the Gospel (thus including the atheist) – more difficult to defend by requiring a real supernatural faith even in such a case, i.e. not escaping the issue by saying that such a person attains supernatural salvation at the end of his life on the basis of a mere 'natural' morality.

In connection with the Council's teaching our basic thesis implies:

1. the thesis of God's will for the salvation of all men in Christ (he will is understood as 'infralapsarian'), and the availability of his grace, and the doctrine that there is only *one* supernatural goal for all men; and

2. the conviction that not every individual atheist can be regarded as a gravely culpable sinner.

The Council neither poses nor answers the question of how one arrives at the second part of this argument from a theological point of view. In this matter one can only say that on the one hand it rests on the theological conviction that one cannot and must not judge any man, but that each particular empirical state of affairs, ambivalent in itself, appeals to the judgment of God alone; and on the other hand that the modern historical situation of the previously nonexistent experience of a world-wide and growing atheism, whose culture and social forms are not directly conditioned by morality, makes it improbable that in each case atheism is the result of the incurring of personal guilt.

All the same, our basic thesis, confirmed as it is by the Council, has provided us with difficult theological problems. This is clear in the Council's statement that the 'ways' in which such non-Christians reach salvation and justification are 'known only to God'. Naturally a statement like this does not forbid further theological study of these 'ways', but it shows that the Council was aware of a certain tension in what it said, even if this tension did not weaken its courage, in faith, to speak of this universal salvation optimism.

So far our observations on the possibility of implicit Christianity in an atheist have only served to set the task, not to give the answer we are looking for. We must now attempt to do this.

IV

In saying that according to the teaching of the Council an atheist does not automatically forfeit salvation, even if under certain circumstances he remains an atheist to his death, the question arises from the theological point of view as to whether in that case simply a 'good will' suffices to replace the knowledge about God and belief in God.

We have already seen that the Decree on the Church's Missionary Activity (No. 7) teaches the possibility of salvation for all men, and we have included atheists too in this category in so far as they are without blame. But the Decree expressly says that the people referred to attain salvation in so far as they come – by paths known only to God – to a saving *faith*.[9]

The question, therefore, is whether and how an atheist can demonstrate the preconditions under which this faith is at least conceivable. Here one cannot immediately refer to the minimum content of faith[10] which traditional theology, basing itself on the Epistle to the Hebrews (Heb 11:6),[11] declares to be sufficient under certain circumstances for a super-

[9] See the study already quoted in note 6 and the further literature mentioned in it.

[10] For the dogmatic side of this doctrine cf. *Sacrae Theologiae Summa* II, p. 804 (see note 5 above), with the differentiated views of Mitzka, Beraza, Pesch.

[11] cf. especially the commentary by O. Michel, *Der Brief an die Hebräer* (Göt-

natural, saving faith. For this minimum content is precisely belief in the existence of God and in him as guarantor of the moral order. Put differently, the problem is that if belief is required as assent to the divine revelation, '*something*' must be believed. Even if we were to avoid the question as to how the atheist is to recognise this content as a revelation from God and not as the result of natural insight, the question remains just *what* this particular individual can embrace as an object of faith, in order for us to be able to talk about it being 'faith' at all.

In this connection the Council's texts which we have quoted always assume that the atheist in question is one who *acts in accordance with his conscience*, *seeks truth and fulfils the demands of his moral consciousness*; for to be considered free from blame and within the sphere of God's will for salvation, although he has not (yet) found God, he must act in line with the demands of his conscience. But is this 'content' of the atheist's awareness sufficient to provide an adequate object for *saving* faith? We must answer this question in several stages.

By reference to the doctrine of the Epistle to the Hebrews one is justified in answering *provisionally*: Yes, *provided that* this conscious content includes *at least implicitly* a knowledge about God, and moreover that this 'content' is affirmed by a free act elevated by grace in the manner of faith. Now this is in fact the case. It can be maintained as such, at least under certain epistemological conditions. The person who accepts a moral demand from his conscience as *absolutely* valid for him and embraces it as such in a free act of affirmation – no matter how unreflected – asserts the absolute being of God, whether he knows or conceptualises it or not, as the very reason why there can be such a thing as an *absolute moral demand at all*.

This preliminary answer needs a deeper grounding, and we shall attempt to do this in a more thorough treatment. Once we have assumed this kind of affirmation by the conscience of an absolute demand, it is not so important how far, in such an act, a man *is or is not consciously aware* of these presuppositions (both objective *and* subjective) which inform his concrete knowledge and action. It may even be that he is *not able* to reflect conceptually upon the subjective factors involved in his concrete spiritual action. Whenever a simple man in his everyday life acts sensibly and with insight, i.e. also logically, the ultimate principles of logic are not only found as the objective basis of his intelligent insight and

ingen,[12] 1966), pp. 386–387; E. Grässer, *Der Glaube im Hebräerbrief* (Marburg, 1965), pp. 132 ff. *et passim.*

action; he has also embraced them, they are his spiritual 'possession', although as a simple man he would be probably quite incapable, even after instruction, of understanding the abstract principles of Aristotelian logic as such in its abstract formality.

This modest observation from everyday life can be heightened theoretically and applied to our question. In every one of its acts, human knowledge is to a certain extent *dipolar*: it implies a subjective knowledge of the knower himself and his act on the part of the subject as such, while at the same time this same knowledge has a known and conceptualised object which is its goal and with which it is concerned. In knowing about oneself and one's act one always knows *something*. The objective content of such an act can also be something which is known without reflection on the subjective side of the same act, i.e. when the subject, knowing itself subjectively, makes itself in addition the *object* of its judgment. But even in such a case the dipolarity, the difference between the subject present to itself and the known object, between knowing-ness and what is known, is not detroyed. Furthermore it is quite possible for such an act, the content of which the self-knowing subject of this act wishes to present to itself, to be inadequately or falsely interpreted by this selfsame subject, although on the subjective side what has been interpreted is present in its known reality. For instance, a man who performs an intellectual act knows 'subjectively' what an intellectual act is, because the subject with its intellectual act is present to itself in a real identity. In spite of this, however, a theoretical psychologist who is a sensist, denying in a materialist manner the subject's intellectuality, is *bona fide* capable of giving quite false theoretical explanations of his own intellectual act; i.e. what he experiences subjectively he may translate objectively falsely into objective concepts and statements.

Now in so far as every instance of intellectual knowledge and freedom on the part of the subject and his act is a 'transcendental experience', i.e. an experience of the intellect's unlimited rootedness in absolute Being, on the subjective side every instance of knowledge is a real, even if implici (i.e. not necessarily objectified) knowledge of God, although we canno show this in greater detail here. What we commonly call 'knowledge o God' is therefore not simply *the* knowledge of God, but already th objectified conceptual and propositional interpretation of what w constantly know of God subjectively and apart from reflection. Knowledg of God is certainly *a posteriori* to the extent, on the one hand, that eve the subjective act – which by virtue of its transcendental nature alway knows about God – is historically contingent; in order to be itself th subjective act always requires an 'objective' object, without which it cannot exist at all, but which it experiences *a posteriori.* Besides this, knowledge of God is also *a posteriori* in so far as the conceptual and propositional objectification of the transcendental experience first needs a vehicle to pass among the *a posteriori* given objects of knowledge of the world, in the way expounded in detail in the classical 'proofs of the existence of God'. On the other hand the knowledge of God is not *a posteriori* simply in the sense in which the knowledge of any external object is, e.g. the knowledge of the existence of Australia. It is true that there is no innate idea of God in the sense of an inborn conceptualised content, but nevertheless the conceptual and propositional knowledge of God is the objectification of that rootedness of the intellect in absolute Being which is always present to man's transcendental intellectuality; that rootedness which is a concomitant experience in every intellectual act, whether of knowledge or of freedom, irrespective of the particular object with which this act is concerned.

V

If we adopt these assumptions (which we have really only touched upon here) we can draw up a sort of table of the fundamental types of man's relationship with God. In doing so it must always be borne in mind that a conscious or known reality present to man's mind may exist in the mode of free acceptance or free rejection, since man is not merely a being who is intellectually knowing, but is also always a free being.

First possibility: God is present in man's transcendental nature and this fact is objectified in a suitably and correctly explicit and conceptual theism, and moreover is also freely accepted in the moral affirmation of faith (in the practice of living). In this case we have what constitutes simply correct theism, what we might call transcendental *and* categorial theism, accepted and affirmed by man's freedom in both these dimensions. In this way it represents in every respect a proper relationship between man and God such as we may assume in the case of a justified Christian.

Second possibility; Both transcendental and categorial theism are present, man knows of God in his transcendental experience and also his reflection upon the latter is correct, but in his moral freedom he rejects this knowledge, whether as a sinner, denying God, or going on to reject the God whom he has correctly 'objectified' conceptually in real free unbelief. This is the category in which the 'atheist' was thought of previously in religious and in specifically Christian matters. It was assumed that he had an objectified and more or less correct idea of God but rejected him in sin or freely turned away from him either in a merely practical 'godlessness' or in theoretical atheism as well.

Third possibility: The transcendental experience of God is present of necessity and is also freely accepted in a positive decision to be faithful to conscience,[12] but it is incorrectly objectified and interpreted. This inadequate, false (and under certain circumstances totally lacking) *idea of God* as such can be again the object of free acceptance or rejection in various ways, but we need not concern ourselves with that in any greater detail here. For instance, consider the case of a polytheist who, in the dimension of free reflection, freely 'believes' this polytheism or freely and 'atheistically' rejects it, without replacing it by a correctly conceived theism. In either case this third instance is the sort of atheism which is innocent in the sense of Vatican II. It is atheism on the plane of categorical reflection, coexisting in the subject with a freely affirmed transcendental theism. There can be such a thing as innocent atheism because of the difference between subjective transcendentality and categorial objectification in concepts and sentences, producing this coexistence of transcendental theism and categorial atheism. For the said 'difference' is necessarily present in every act of the mind. The components of this innocent atheism are: *on the one hand* the subject's continual transcendental dependence on God and the free acceptance of this dependence, especially in the moral act which respects absolutely the demands of conscience – i.e. a transcendental theism 'in the heart's depths' – and *on the other hand* the free rejection of the objectified concept of God, i.e. a categorial atheism in the forefront of conscious reflection, a rejection which cannot in itself be regarded as culpable.

Fourth possibility: The transcendental dependence on God is present; objectively it is interpreted falsely or insufficiently correctly in a categorial atheism, and this transcendental dependence on God is itself simultaneously denied in a free action by gravely sinful unfaithfulness to conscience or by an otherwise sinful, false interpretation of existence (as being 'totally absurd' or of no absolute significance, etc.). In this case the free denial does not refer merely to the categorial interpretation of man's transcendental nature, but to existence and thus to God himself. Here we have culpable transcendental atheism, which excludes the possibility of salvation as long as it persists.

[12] Whereby the consciously reflected object of this act of obedience to conscience is not explicitly God, but another moral object as envisaged by the conciliar texts quoted above, where the atheist is conceived as acting morally.

By presenting these four basic types of man's relationship with God we do not wish to suggest that the table could not have been drawn up differently, especially as we ourselves have indicated further subordinate possibilities within this 'system'. Furthermore, by naïvely distinguishing the correct from the false conceptual objectification of man's necessary transcendental dependence on God we have made an over-simplification which does not correspond to concrete reality. For here there are naturally correct and less correct conceptualisations (e.g. an idea of God revealing partially false, pantheistic or polytheistic tendencies and blemishes). Indefinite transitions and fluid boundaries are also compatible with the exercise of freedom. So the system we have outlined is no more than a rough preliminary sketch. But it may be sufficient for our purposes all the same.

VI

Our whole concern here is to reach an insight into why there is in fact in man the possibility of innocent and of culpable atheism, and the knowledge of how on the one hand a man's innocent atheism by no means destroys every really fundamental relationship with God, created by man's constant transcendental rootedness in God; and how on the other hand, in spite of this possibility, culpable atheism consists not necessarily merely in transgression in connection with any particular moral situation but in an *ultimate* 'No' to man's fundamental dependence *upon God himself*, i.e. in a free 'No' to God himself.

It must be further remembered that the categorial affirmation of God – as a theoretical and categorial action – is by no means a guarantee that the man concerned really seriously accepts his transcendental dependence on God at the very heart of his transcendental freedom of choice. Put simply, a man, even a 'Christian', can accept God as objectified in knowledge and freedom, and can even declare that he is a 'theist' and think that he is keeping to God's moral norms, *and yet deny him* through immorality or unbelief in the depths of his heart. This is just as possible as the coexistence of a categorial atheism with a (freely affirmed) transcendental theism. So, too, categorial theism can coexist with a transcendental theism which is itself freely rejected, thus becoming freely adopted transcendental atheism – in spite of the abiding experience of rootedness in God.

In the Pastoral Constitution the Council taught that there is also a culpable atheism. But it was not made clear enough how such an atheism is possible as an atheism really directed at God himself. The Council recognised the existence of innocent atheism, but without plainly showing how salvation and faith are reconcilable with it. The distinction we have indicated between transcendental and categorial atheism/theism provides a theoretical understanding of this teaching. Innocent atheism is always only categorial atheism, atheism on the plane of conceptual and propositional objectification, where it is ultimately immaterial whether this atheistic objectification as such is accepted or freely rejected by the person concerned, since this particular free act only involves the *categorial* object. On the other hand *transcendental* atheism (which is really possible) it always necessarily culpable, since God is always present to man in the dimension of man's transcendentality, and therefore can only be rejected by a free decision, not by knowledge as such. In this dimension the 'matter', namely God, is necessarily correctly present, so that his rejection cannot be justified or thought to be justified on the grounds of an inadequate or falsely objectified concept of God in the dimension of categorial reflection.

VII

If what has been indicated here in very few and inadequate words is understood, pastoral insights emerge concerning the correct approach on the part of the person proclaiming theism or the Gospel. These insights might suitably serve to deepen and systematise the Council's necessarily very brief remarks on this approach. The preacher of the Gospel is never confronted with an atheist who has so far had simply nothing to do with God; the preacher's relationship to this particular listener is never like that of a geography teacher teaching a small boy for the first time that there is such a place as Australia and demonstrating the fact. Where free, responsible human beings are concerned, the preacher of the Gospel is confronted fundamentally with a man who already has a real experience of what is meant by God, but who for various reasons (either free from blame or – under certain circumstances – culpable) is not able correctly to interpret his own experience of God in conscious reflection and consequently rejects the concept of God presented to him from elsewhere, as being either false or meaningless for him. To combat a categorial and conceptual atheism of this kind one must not remain solely on this particular plane as such; one must not only present proofs of the existence of God as if the latter were of the same structure and amenable to the same methods as the existence of an object which is merely accessible in purely *a posteriori* experience. If *this* were the case, under certain circumstances a man might be justified in rejecting the existence of such a God as being a matter of no interest and not worth bothering his head about.

Even if it is possible at all to speak to an atheist on the level of the 'proofs' so well known to us, to be successful today such a dialogue unavoidably presupposes that the atheist has been made aware of his own transcendental knowledge of God through a kind of 'mystagogy'. If he is really acquainted with unconditional faithfulness, absolute honesty, selfless surrender to the good of others and other fundamental human dispositions, then he knows something of God, even if this knowledge is not present to his conscious reflection. Of course, in a particular concrete instance, it can be very difficult to bring to the surface the theological implications of these fundamental dispositions and objectify them in conceptual form. In any particular case the attempt may simply fail. In itself that is no more strange than the fact that it is sometimes impossible to make formal logic clear to a person *in the mode of theoretical reflection* although he employs this very thing in his everyday affairs and has insight *into* the 'logic' of these affairs. In any case, however, the traditional 'proofs' can only be presented successfully to a person who is not already an explicit 'theist' provided that rational reflection is joined by this kind of 'mystagogy'. Depending on the case in question, this mystagogy must naturally also deal with the difficulties from which arise, according to the Council's Pastoral Constitution, the various forms of modern atheism; the protest against evil in the world, the supposed lack of any religious experience, the supposed threat to mankind in the idea of God, the strange ideas which people connect with the concept of God, etc.

Provided one understands what is meant by the transcendental theism we have described it is clear, furthermore, that according to genuine theism God is not present in our everyday experience like the other objects of our *a posteriori* experience. He is not an existent within the sphere of our experience but the precondition of our transcendental horizon. A theist or an apologete of theism must not proceed, therefore, as though God were – not of course an object directly present to our sense-experience, but – to all intents and purposes capable of being known rather like an electric current, which, not itself directly visible can be deduced from its effects.

Here we have a way in to an understanding of the phenomenon in atheism referred to by the Council itself when it says that certain atheists are held fast in a 'scientistic phenomenalism' and are unable to understand, so they say, what might be meant at all by the word 'God'. According to a proper understanding of the nature of the knowledge of God there can be no question of expanding and deepening the area of empirical experience by the *same* methods. What is required is rather to help man to appreciate that there is another mode of experience, a transcendental experience in intellectual knowledge and freedom, according to which what we mean by 'God' can be understood and known as real; and furthermore that what is meant by this transcendental experience, referential to God, is the precondition for every *a posteriori* experience whatsoever, whether in everyday matters or in science, even if it is not and cannot be the task of these *a posteriori* disciplines to reflect upon their own presuppositions.

The first Vatican Council expressly defined that God is incomprehensible (cf. *DS* 3001). No Christian doctrine of God and his knowability denies this. But the dogma is often forgotten in the practice of our apologetics of theism. For one cannot first of all know God – as one knows anything else according to its existence and nature – and then subsequently 'add on' the attribute of incomprehensibility. Both the proof of God's existence and the 'mystagogy' which is absolutely necessary if the former is to be successful must relate, from the very beginning, to the absolute mystery[13] which pervades and penetrates our whole existence; this mystery must be brought together with theoretical knowledge and the existential actualisation of life, and then one can say: This is what we mean when we speak of 'God'.

VIII

So far we have only taken the first of the steps (cf. V above) leading to a theological understanding of how an atheism which is not blameworthy can constitute 'implicit' Christianity. For what we have said up to now only serves to make it clear that a blameless categorical atheism can be a freely accepted, transcendental theism. But on its own this does not constitute the 'implicit' *Christianity* in which a man by grace accepts the self-imparting God in faith, hope and love.

In order to proceed further we must bear in mind that in the actual order of things the 'atheist's' transcendental, freely accepted theism, which here concerns us, is elevated by supernatural grace because of God's will for universal salvation, and man's essential transcendentality – at least in so far as it is freely accepted – finds its ultimate goal, by grace, in the God of Eternal Life. Although one must admit that the Council has expressed itself cautiously and somewhat indefinitely, it may certainly be said that as far as the texts we have quoted are concerned the Council professes no acquaintance with a merely 'natural' morality. Of course the latter does

[13] cf. K. Rahner, 'The concept of mystery in Catholic theology', *Theological Investigations* IV (London and Baltimore, 1966), pp. 36–73.

exist, but it is integrated into the concrete order of God's desire for mankind's supernatural salvation as a distinguishable, but not isolated, factor in a larger whole, of which God's offer of saving grace to all is also a part.[14]

In Catholic theology no-one can deny the possibility of justification and supernatural sanctification prior to Baptism (given the presence of supernatural faith, of which we shall say something in particular later, and an implicit *votum baptismi*). Thus there is in any case a divine offer of supernatural grace and the possibility of freely accepting it prior to Baptism, apart from the sacrament.[15] We have only to assume that this offer and the free acceptance of it (thus made possible) is *always* and *everywhere* present (on account of God's desire for universal salvation, not because of the natural goodness of a moral act) where a man freely accepts his own transcendentality – which includes an implicit, transcendental theism – by means of a moral decision in absolute faithfulness to his conscience, by means of 'righteousness of life' etc. We assume, therefore, that under these conditions there is *always* an occurrence of what Thomas calls *infusio et acceptatio gratiae*. In that case the concrete order of salvation together with the freely accepted transcendental theism which can even be found in an atheist, produces *implicit* Christianity.

The reason why traditional theology up to now for the most part has always counted on there being a phase of merely 'natural' morality in the course of a 'heathen's' life (and so too has been inclined to acknowledge only a 'natural' moral goodness – if any – even in the case of a bona fide atheist) is because on the one hand it is correctly assumed that justification is impossible without revealed faith, nor can a *fides virtualis* be a substitute for it, as for instance Straub suggested; and on the other hand it was thought impossible to imagine such a revealed faith in the case of a 'heathen', let alone an atheist. The reference in the conciliar texts to the 'ways known only to God' witnesses above all to this difficulty, but also shows that the Council, particularly in the Decree concerning the Church's Missionary Activity, nevertheless has no doubt that this faith is possible even in the instances which are of interest here; moreover it does not restrict this possibility to cases of extraordinary, miraculous

[14] It would be arbitrary to wish to understand the 'grace' which is continually referred to in these texts with regard to the non-Christian or atheist merely as God's entitatively natural assistance towards the fulfilment of the natural moral law as such. For this theological issue cf. K. Rahner, *Theologie des Todes* (Freiburg,[5] 1965), pp. 79 ff.

[15] For extra-sacramental justification cf. K. Rahner, 'The Word and the Eucharist', *Theological Investigations* IV (London and Baltimore, 1966), pp. 253–286.

intervention on the part of God such as have been appealed to by previous text-book theology (private revelation, special illumination, etc.).

This obscure issue can be pursued further if one bears in mind, in *this* context as well, the well-known Thomist doctrine that every supernaturally elevated moral act on a man's part has, in connection with its essential elevation, a supernatural formal object which cannot be reached by any merely natural intellectual or moral act on his part, even if in both cases the material object, the objective, *a posteriori* content of the act, is the same.

If we assume this thesis, which Thomism has rightly regarded as fundamental to its 'system' and which can be held to be *at the very least* above reproach in theology, and apply it to our context, it gives us the possibility of revealed faith which we require for our cases: The communication of a supernatural formal object (in other words, the supernatural perspective within which, in a non-reflex but real manner, morality's material objectivity is grasped; the revealing of man's intellectual and spiritual trancendentality in its direct relation to God) is in a true sense 'revelation' already. It is constituted as such by the offer of saving grace itself (logically or temporally) prior to the *a posteriori* and historical communication of an objective content by means of historical revelation. The supernatural elevation in grace automatically involves revelation and the possibility of faith.[16]

Naturally *this* revelation is not simply identical with revelation as it is usually (and correctly) understood. It is obvious that much ought to be said about the relation of this 'transcendental' revelation (or rather, the transcendental *element* of revelation) to the categorial, historical, verbal revelation (or the categorial *element* of the *single* revelation). Certainly this relationship must not be thought of as if the transcendental element of revelation (constituted by grace) rendered the categorial element superfluous or threatened its meaningfulness.

But in the *first* place, if one considers that in any case this transcendental element is present in revelation and faith because the verbally objectified, categorial revelation can only be spoken in 'Pneuma' and heard in faith; and *secondly*, if one does not wish to have recourse to improbabilities (i.e. original or private revelation); and *thirdly*, if one still wishes to maintain the possibility of saving, supernatural faith and, in line with the Council, the existence of revelation for *all* men; then the only possibility

[16] For this concept of revelation cf. K. Rahner/J. Ratzinger, *Revelation and Tradition* (Freiburg and London, 1966); K. Rahner, *Hörer des Wortes* (Munich,[2] 1963).

left is to say that the elevation through grace of man's freely accepted transcendentality is in itself revelation, because it involves an *a priori* formal object of man's mind, not necessarily reflected in consciousness, which, *qua* formal object, cannot be reached by any natural intellectual ability but arises from God's self-communication in grace. It is a revelation without which a categorial, historical, verbal revelation – although it could constitute an utterance to do with God and 'about' him – could not be the 'Word of God' in its most proper sense.

These brief notes must suffice here to demonstrate how transcendental theism freely accepted on the part of a categorial atheist can be – or rather, actually *is* – revelation and the possibility of saving faith.[17] This is the case if it is assumed that this transcendentality of the mind, implying a theism, with its free acceptance, is elevated by grace. And we *may* assume this because of God's desire for universal salvation. Under these presuppositions the Council's optimism concerning salvation is theologically justified. Now a theism which is elevated through grace and which is freely accepted (by the grace supplied by the possibility of faith) is a justifying theism and hence an implicit Christianity. And this kind of existential transcendental theism (although not necessarily the object of reflection) is also possible in the case of a (categorial) blameless atheist, whose actions are good and arise from an absolute commitment; therefore *this* kind of atheist can be an implicit Christian.

In its Pastoral Constitution Vatican II most strongly emphasises that modern atheism requires new and most serious thought on the part of the Church and the preachers of the Gospel. This declaration must not remain a mere pious tag, a part of the inventory of courtesy used in dealing with an opponent. There really are questions which must be asked and answered *anew* if it is really intended to engage modern atheism in a real dialogue. These questions do not merely concern the 'didactic' and 'pedagogical' methods best employed in speaking with today's atheists. They are questions to do with the *thing itself*. Thus the question in pastoral theology as to how to come to grips with modern atheism changes very quickly into the question as to what is actually meant by

[17] For a treatment in greater depth cf. the author's studies: 'Concerning the relationship between nature and grace', *Theological Investigations* I (London and Baltimore, 1961), pp. 297–317; 'The Christian among unbelieving relations', *Theological Investigations* III (London and Baltimore, 1967), pp. 355–372; 'Nature and Grace', *Theological Investigations* IV (London and Baltimore, 1966), pp. 165–188; 'History of the world and salvation-history', *Theological Investigations* V (London and Baltimore, 1966), pp. 97–114; 'Konziliare Lehre der Kirche und künftige Wirklichkeit christlichen Lebens', *Schriften zur Theologie* VI (Einsiedeln, 1965), pp. 479–498.

'God',[18] and how we theists and Christians come to have a direct approach to this incomprehensible mystery of our existence, which sustains us and at the same time constantly calls our whole being in question, a direct contact which cannot be reduced to the sociological phenomenon of Christians sharing common assumptions and talking among themselves about God, merely *thinking* they know *who* he is and *why* our life itself is meaningless without God.[19] In maintaining this one has uttered an ultimate truth about our life; but to really grasp it, life must first be *experienced* as meaningful, one must face the question whether one accepts this experienced meaning or not and know, in this experience and its acceptance, what is really meant by 'God'.[20]

[11] For details in this issue cf, K. Rahner, 'Christian living formerly and today', *Theological Investigations* VII (London and New York, 1971), pp. 3–24.

[19] Cf. K. Lehmann's 'Some Ideas from Pastoral Theology on the Proclamation of the Christian Message to Non-believers Today', *Concilium* 3 (March 1967), pp. 43–52.

[20] cf. K. Rahner, 'The concept of mystery in Catholic theology', *Theological Investigations* IV (London and Baltimore, 1966), pp. 36–73.

10

'I BELIEVE IN JESUS CHRIST'

Interpreting an article of faith

TODAY one cannot say anything of religious and theological significance about Jesus Christ himself without also describing the essence of *faith* itself as an act whereby Jesus is seen as the Christ. In referring to this faith first of all as an occurrence – and as having a 'content' only within the particular context of that occurrence – it must be clear at the outset that this faith is to be understood as more than the merely private subjectivity of which we today are justly suspicious, by being faith within the *Church* and under obedience to what the Church's authoritative faith says. Hence we can immediately see the point of a mandatory Confession of Faith today too. The man Jesus commits himself to men in the faith of the Church and with the Church. To wish to find this faith by relying solely on oneself would be a fatal individualism.

This faith occurs as a result of an absolute trust, by which one commits *oneself* to the other person and thereby embraces the rights and privileges of such a total self-abandonment with a hope without reservations. This extends to all areas of existence which, on account of the absolute quality of this self-abandonment, do not need to be seen *in toto* nor to be specified in advance. The person to whom one thus commits oneself can be addressed in the most varied ways depending on the dimensions of one's own self and the nature of one's absolute committal: simply 'Lord', 'Son of God'; 'Pardoner', 'Saviour' and a thousand other names which have become his since the New Testament. Hence it is an important but secondary question, which of the many aspects of this total claim is most suitable for any particular man's encounter with him; whether the apparently completely private aspect, for instance, whereby one confidently lays hold on his forgiveness of one's own guilt, or within the cosmic perspective of universal history, whereby one accepts him in trust as the Omega of the development of the universe, the meaningful conclusion of history. The most diverse approaches to him are all intended to be gateways to the one radical self-committal of the whole man to Jesus Christ and it is only in this sense that they have any meaning at all. Similarly we are not concerned here with the question of what is required for a person so to find the concrete man Jesus that this act of total self-surrender to him successfully takes place. Although it is no less decisive for the understanding of Christology and the subject under discussion, we cannot here enter into detail as to why what we mean when we say 'God' is the same as what is known and accepted as the ultimate ground of this free act of confident, hopeful and loving self-surrender to the other person. Once we have assumed this, we can say the following: where someone is *justified* in trusting himself to another person *absolutely*, and where this other person *on his own account* is able to accept this absolute trust and give it a basis, authorised by God and by no-one else, then this other person is in such a unique and radical union with God that the relationship can be rightly and radically interpreted for all time in the way orthodox Christian faith affirms – irrespective of how such a committed person himself understands and interprets the experience.

If we are honest, we modern men will admit that the doctrine of God's Incarnation seems at first sight like pure mythology which can no longer be 'realised'. But if we listen closely to what *real* Christian doctrine says about the God-man, we notice that there is nothing to be 'demythologised' in this fundamental dogma, but that it only needs to be understood correctly to be *completely orthodox and at the same time worthy of belief*. If we say 'God is made man' in the ready-made patterns of our everyday speech, we either think automatically of God being changed into a man or else we understand the content of the word 'man' in this context as an outer garment, a body in its constituent parts or something similar, by means of which God himself renders himself visible on the stage of his world's history. But both interpretations of this statement are nonsensical and contrary to what Christian dogma really intends to say. For God remains God and does not change, and Jesus is a real, genuine, and finite man with his own experiences, in adoration before the incomprehensibility of God, a free and obedient man, like us in all things.

Then what does this fundamental affirmation of the Christian Faith mean? It is unexceptionable and legitimate from the point of view of Dogma if we consider on the one hand that, in the sense we have outlined, a man who is able to receive an act of unconditional trust in God authoritatively and on his own account, must be in a quite unique union with God; and it is conversely also legitimate to try to formulate the fact of this union, the abiding mystery of the Divine Sonship of Jesus and of the Incarnation, in primarily existential categories, i.e. in terms which express man's total spiritual and cognitive nature. Man exists all the time as one who comes from somewhere and as one who is spoken to; as one who answers Yes and No and who comes from and returns to the mystery we call God. This fact of issuing from an origin and proceeding to an end is the essence of the spiritual creature. The more radically this fact is realised in actuality, the more independent, i.e. the freer man is. Therefore the realisation of thus originating in a source and being bound for an end is to an increasing extent the gift of God *and* man's act. If a man receives this human essence from God in such absolute purity and integrity and so actualises this relationship with God that he becomes God's self-expression and his once-for-all pledge of himself to the world he calls into existence, we have what we call 'Incarnation' in a dogmatically orthodox sense. Similarly in the doctrine of the Unity of the one Divine Person and the two – Divine and Human – Natures, the mystery described in ontic and substantial categories is the same as that which can also be expressed in existential terms. The only necessary condition for interchanging the types of statement is the awareness that every existential statement automatically includes an ontological one and vice versa.

It is essential, however, that we understand that this act on the part of such a man is already the act of God in creating and sustaining him as he is. It is also absolutely necessary not to misunderstand the relation between God and the human person as a merely peripheral and supplementary 'state of mind', leaving man's actual existence basically untouched, and unable to influence it radically. To understand this correctly one only needs to grasp the fact that God has not merely 'uttered' man as the open question which we are in respect of him, but that he has uttered this question in such a way as to provide it with the possibility and potential of accepting itself as such unconditionally and totally – thereby accepting God himself.

The message of the faith concerning Jesus Christ is neither myth nor fairy-tale, but it tells of the unique occasion which saw the radical achievement of the *ultimate* possibility of man's existence. Faith has the courage to accept Jesus of Nazareth as the one who, from the depths of his being, grounded in God, has surrendered himself in obedience to this God and has been accepted as such by him – this is made plain by the Resurrection. He was *able* to do this because he was and is the one who *had always* been accepted by God. What he is in reality occurred and appeared in history in his life, namely in God's pledging of himself to the world, made irreversible in and through the radical, divinely-initiated acceptance of this pledge in the true man Jesus.

Looking now from the other angle, whoever experiences in faith that he trusts Jesus of Nazareth absolutely, that in him God gives his pledge unconditionally and irreversibly, that in respect of Jesus his own concrete encounter with another person in trust and love becomes absolute and he *thus* experiences what is meant by 'God' – such a man may interpret this experience how he will, well or ill, adequately or unsatisfactorily; in reality he believes what we orthodox Christians call 'Incarnation': the uncompounded and inseparable unity of God and man, in which God remains totally God, man is radically man, and both are One, uncompounded and inseparable, in this Jesus who is the Christ of faith. If we entrust ourselves to him in a radical way, and exist in attendance on him alone, we experience directly *who* he is, and this trust of ours is *founded* on who he is. This circle cannot be broken. Whether one knows it explicitly or not, one is always seeing God and man in one. The Christian believes that in Jesus of Nazareth he finds both as One. Love for all other people finds its justification here and discovers its ultimate ground, and all such love leads to the one man in whom this union of God and man, intended for everyone, appears in its historical uniqueness and utter finality – Jesus Christ.

The Church is right to value highly its ancient Christological formulas, the product of a long and troubled history of the faith. Every other formula – and there may be others – must be tested to see whether it clearly maintains that faith in Jesus does not acknowledge merely a religious genius or the prophet of a passing phase in the history of religions, but the absolute Mediator of Salvation now and always. But wherever and in whatever way a person accepts this in faith and trust, he enacts in such faith what Christianity confesses concerning Jesus of Nazareth, Crucified and Risen.

11

ONE MEDIATOR AND MANY MEDIATIONS

I

In itself this title could be said to mean several different things. However, if we look at it in the context of theological controversy, the theme will be obvious to everyone: 'orthodox' Protestant Christendom – above all in its theological dispute with the Roman Catholic Church – witnesses to its belief in the *one* and *only* Mediator of salvation (forgiveness, justification and sanctification): Jesus Christ. It is believed that although the Catholic Church subscribes verbally to this same belief (which no-one can seriously deny), it is not in actual fact genuinely and unequivocally faithful to it,[1] since Catholic doctrine and especially its actual religious practice are very familiar with many other mediations of salvation 'besides' Jesus Christ.[2] These could be divided into personal and institutional mediations: on the one hand Mary and the other Saints, and on the other hand the whole wealth of institutions, like the institutionally protected authority for doctrinal truth[3] and the *opus operatum* of the sacraments.[4] Here we must restrict ourselves to the question of personal

[1] There is a summary of the contemporary discussion in C. A. de Ridder, 'Maria als Miterlöserin?' = *Kirche und Konfession* 5 (Göttingen, 1965).

[2] cf. the tendency towards this criticism in G. Miegge, 'Die Jungfrau Maria' = *Kirche und Konfession* 2 (Göttingen, 1962), pp. 150–172 (Miterlöserin), pp. 200–212. The same accusation is implied if one tries to look at Mary from the point of view of the phenomenology of religion, and fit her into a general, undifferentiated trend of religion as a whole as 'mediatrix omnium gratiarum'; cf. *RGG*³ IV, 769 and 1064. Cf. also W. Delius, *Geschichte der Marienverehrung* (Basle, 1963), esp. pp. 154, 160, 165, 259, 266 f. (Mittlerin), 258–320. Cf. also A. Brandenburg, *Maria in der evangelischen Theologie der Gegenwart* (Paderborn, 1966), pp. 71 ff. (The encroachment of paganism into the Christian sphere through Catholic theology?)

[3] Of course this does not mean that these institutional mediations may be treated as though they were static, material objects, without reference to persons and their expression in and through persons.

[4] cf. also K. Rahner, 'Personal and Sacramental Piety', *Theological Investigations* I (London and Baltimore, 1963), pp. 109–133; also *Kirche und Sakramente* (Freiburg,² 1963), pp. 11–67.

mediations, setting aside the issue of mediating institutions.[5] Similarly we shall not raise the old controversial question as to whether the Catholic doctrine of justification concerning freedom and 'merit' in the process of salvation is or is not injurious to the 'merit' of the one Mediator.[6] Furthermore we shall not discuss the question of the relationship between the redeemed person's function as regards the Church within history and his function of heavenly intercession,[7] which must naturally not be thought of as a continuation of history, but as history's abiding validity before God.[8] Having thus narrowed our field, let us turn to our original theme. Catholic theology is reproached with having transgressed in a totally intolerable way against the dogma, verbally common to the whole of Christendom, of the sole and unique mediatorship of Jesus Christ:[9] we

[5] An initial approach to institutional forms is given in K. Rahner, 'The Church and the Parousia of Christ', *Theological Investigations* VI (London and Baltimore, 1969), pp. 295–312; *Handbuch der Pastoraltheologie* II/1 (Freiburg, 1966), pp. 61–79.

[6] cf. *DS* 1583. For recent discussion concerning 'meritum' cf. A. Forster, *LThK*² X, cols. 677–680; M. Flick and Z. Alszeghy, *Il Vangelo della Grazia* (Firenze, 1964), pp. 638–683 (literature); H. Küng, *Justification* (E.T. London 1964), pp. 257 ff.; P.-Y. Emery, *Le Christ notre récompense* (Neuchâtel, 1962). Most recently cf. O. H. Pesch O.P., 'Die Lehre vom "Verdienst" als Problem für Theologie und Verkündigung', *Wahrheit und Verkündigung. Festschrift für M. Schmaus*, ed. L. Scheffczyk/W. Dettloff/R. Heinzmann, Vol. II (Paderborn, 1967), pp. 1865–1907 (literature).

[7] For an introduction cf. K. Rahner, 'Some theses on prayer "in the name of the Church"', *Theological Investigations* V (London and Baltimore, 1966), pp. 419–438; P. Molinari, *Die Heiligen und ihre Verehrung* (Freiburg, 1964); B. Kötting, 'Heiligenverehrung', *Handbuch theologischer Grundbegriffe* I (Munich, 1962), pp. 633–641 (literature); K. Rahner, 'Why and how can we venerate the Saints?', *Theological Investigations* VIII (London and New York, 1971), pp. 3–23.

[8] cf. the author's studies referred to in the last note. In addition: 'The life of the dead', *Theological Investigations* IV (London and Baltimore, 1966), pp. 347–354.

[9] In the New Testament the concept of the mediator appears relatively seldom. (Cf. Gal 3:19 f.; 1 Tim 2:5; Heb 8:6; 9:15; 12:24.) Cf. esp. A. Oepke, *ThWNT* IV, pp. 602–629, esp. 624 ff.; F. J. Schierse, 'Mittler', *Handbuch theologischer Grundbegriffe* II (Munich, 1963), pp. 169–172; O. Cullmann, *Die Christologie des Neuen Testaments* (Tübingen, 1957), pp. 88, 99 f.; C. Spicq, 'Mittlerschaft', *Bibeltheologisches Wörterbuch*, ed. J. B. Bauer (Graz, 1959), pp. 563–573, also in II (Graz,² 1962), pp. 869–879; O. Michel, *Brief an die Hebräer* (Göttingen,¹² 1966), pp. 292 f., 468; O. Kuß, *Der Brief an die Hebräer* (Regensburg,² 1966), pp. 29, 32, 108, 112 119, 146, 155, 214; F. J. Schierse, *Verheißung und Heilsvollendung* (Munich, 1955) H. Hegermann, 'Die Vorstellung vom Schöpfungsmittler im hellenistischen Judentum und Urchristentum' = *TU* 82 (Berlin, 1961). For the use of the concept 'mediator in dogmatics cf. esp. J. Ratzinger, 'Mittler', *LThK*² VII, pp. 499–502 (with mor literature). Cf. also L. Thunberg, *Microcosm and mediator* (Maximus Confessor (Lund, 1965). Also: M.-F. Lacan, 'Le Dieu unique et son Médiateur, Gal 3:20

call on the Saints; we defend and justify this practice itself, not merely commending 'veneration' of the Saints;[10] above all not only do we teach theoretically the function of Mary as 'mediatrix of grace', but make her into an actual mediatrix 'between' ourselves and Christ in a popular devotion of vast proportions. In this way, it is held, Christ is for us not the one who stands between us and God as sole Reconciler and Mediator, but he stands over against us on the side of God as the one with whom we have to be reconciled, so that we need the many mediators, the Saints and chiefly Mary, in order to bridge this gulf.

It cannot be my task here – although in itself it is the more important issue – to present the statements of authoritative doctrine and Catholic theology in its received form concerning this problem. Instead I shall just refer to a few passages in Denzinger, chiefly from the Council of Trent and Vatican II. There it is stated that Christ is the principle of salvation itself,[11] that all our boasting is in Christ,[12] that he is the source of merit in justification, which occurs without our deserving it, the sole source and mediator of all grace.[13] It is maintained that the invocation of the Saints does not prejudice the honour of the one Mediator.[14] Furthermore the Second Vatican Council declares[15] that when we ask for the help of the Saints, the benefits which come from God are obtained through the supplication of Christ, who alone is our Redeemer and Saviour. Concerning Mary the Constitution on the Church says[16] that Christ is our sole Mediator and that whatever significance Mary has for salvation, it does not obscure the sole mediatorship of Christ but is a free gift to Mary from God, springing from the wealth of the merits of Christ, grounded and

L'homme devant Dieu. Mélanges offerts au Père Henri du Lubac (Lyon, 1963), Vol. I, pp. 113–125; N. Kehl, 'Der Christushymnus im Kolosserbrief. Eine motivgeschichtliche Untersuchung zu Kol. 1:12–20' = *Stuttgarter Biblische Monographien 1* (Stuttgart 1967), pp. 99-108.

[10] Studies of the veneration of the Saints by Protestant theologians: M. Lackmann, *Die Verehrung der Heiligen* (Stuttgart, 1958); H. Asmussen, *Maria, die Mutter Gottes* (Stuttgart, 1950); P.-Y. Emery, 'L'unité des croyants au ciel et sur la terre. La communion des Saints et son expression dans la prière de l'Eglise', *Verbum Caro* 16 (1962), No. 63, pp. 1–24. Cf. also L. Höfer, 'Ökumenische Besinnung über die Heiligen' = *Begegnung* 1 (Lucerne, 1962).

[11] cf. *DS* 3915.

[12] cf. *DS* 1691.

[13] cf. *DS* 1523, 1526, 1529, 1530, 1560, 3370, 3820.

[14] cf. *DS* 1821.

[15] cf. the Second Vatican Council's Constitution on the Church *Lumen gentium*, No. 50.

[16] cf. ibid., No. 60.

totally dependent upon his mediatorship, and drawing all its power from it.[17] Thus it by no means excludes a *direct* union of Christ with the believer.[18] Consequently the various possible forms of mediation must never be thought of like a succeeding series of 'instances'. According to the Council, if Mary's function in salvation-history as one who has abiding validity before God leads to her being addressed in terms such as 'Advocate', 'Co-helper' and 'Mediatrix',[19] it is to be understood as neither taking away from nor adding anything to the rank and efficacy of Christ the sole Mediator.[20]

So we see that Vatican II by no means ascribes to Mary the title and function of a mediatrix in the strict theological sense, but rather takes the freer language of pious affection under its protection[21] when the latter

[17] Ibid.

[18] Ibid.; cf. O. Semmelroth's commentary on the numbers quoted in *Commentary on the Documents of Vatican II* (New York and London, 1967), Vol. I. R. Laurentin, 'La Vierge Marie au Concile', *RSPhTh* 48 (1964), pp. 32–46. Further literature in Laurentin, 'Bulletin Marial', *RSPhTh* 50 (1966), pp. 496–545.

[19] We cannot go into the history of the various titles and their application to Mary. Cf. H. M. Köster, 'Miterlöserschaft', *LThK*² VII, cols. 486–487 (with comprehensive references). R. Laurentin gives references to the very important supplementary literature produced in recent years in the Bulletin just quoted. On this issue cf. esp. P. Sträter, *Katholische Marienkunde* (Paderborn, 1947 ff.) II, pp. 241–313; *Heilsgeschichtliche Stellvertretung der Menschheit durch Maria*, ed. C. Feckes (Paderborn, 1954); H. M. Köster, *Unus mediator* (Limburg, 1950), pp. 108–149, 171–183; H. Seiler, *Corredemptrix* (Rome, 1939), 'Die Lehre der Päpste Pius IX. bis Pius XI. über die Mitwirkung Mariens im Heilswerk und Auslegung dieser Lehre'; J. Bittremieux, *De mediatione universali B.M.V. quoad gratias* (Bruges, 1926); G. M. Roschini, *La mediatrice universale* (Rome, 1961); F. H. Schüth, *Mediatrix* (Innsbruck, 1925); R. Laurentin, *Kurzer Traktat der Marianischen Theologie* (Regensburg, 1959), pp. 76–116; W. Sebastian, *De BMV universali gratiarum mediatrice* (Rome, 1952): Franziskanertheologie 1600–1730; J. Ude, *Ist Maria die Mittlerin aller Gnaden?* (Bressanone, 1928), pp. 41–133. Also cf. the various studies in the collection *Maria. Etudes sur la sainte Vierge*, ed. Hubert du Manoir (Paris, 1949–1961). H. Lennerz, *De beata virgine. Tractatus dogmaticus* (Rome, 1957), pp. 197–230, 231–289. Cf. also the works quoted at the beginning of this essay by C. A. de Ridder, W. Delius, etc.

[20] The Constitution on the Church *Lumen gentium*, No. 62 (with the commentary by Semmelroth, loc. cit.).

[21] It must be borne in mind that the Church's commonly understood dogmatic terminology throughout history comprises very different literary genres. Besides the doxological, hymnic, catechetical, juridical and other styles, there is in dogmatic assertions the rather more speculative as well as the more devotional tone. One would have to show the respective justification of each of the various modes of expression. No doubt each one has its own particular danger. (A devotional mode of speech, for example, inevitably runs the risk of giving way to excessive emotion

has recourse to the title 'Mediatrix'. For in using this title it is expressing the fact *that in the economy of grace in Christ, as a result of and by virtue of his mediatorship, everyone depends on everyone else and is of significance for everyone else, that everyone has a task subordinate to Christ (munus subordinatum), and that the receipt of salvation also implies the receipt of the* TASK *of salvation, a 'participata ex unico fonte cooperatio'*.[22] For this reason it is applicable above all to Mary, whose function belongs to the plane of solidarity in salvation which is true of all the redeemed, not to the plane of Christ's sole mediatorship.[23] These 'mediations'[24] exist, therefore, because justification is God's unmotivated gift, the act of freedom set free in Christ, and because this act of salvation in Christ by grace always implies a significance *for everyone*; salvation is not solipsistic.

In saying this it is only our intention to reveal a starting-point for the authoritative teaching of the Church and the more general theological doctrine concerning the many 'mediations' and their relationship with the single, radically unique mediatorship of Christ. We cannot discuss and defend the further development and the details of the doctrine itself at this point. It is our intention rather to proceed in the opposite direction: we wish to conceive these 'mediations' not as dependent subordinate modes of participation in the unique mediatorship of Christ, but, reversing the process, we shall try to understand the mediatorship of Christ as the eschatologically perfect and consequently the highest, the unique 'case'[25]

---

and vague enthusiasm, undisciplined dogmatism and pious exaggeration.) But all this would have to be demonstrated in detail to clarify the above statement. Cf. *Lumen gentium*, No. 62.

[22] *Lumen gentium*, No. 62. Cf. also on this issue A. Brandenburg, *Maria in der evangelischen Theologie der Gegenwart* (Paderborn, 1966), pp. 118–145, 146–154; M. Thurian, *Maria* (Mainz, 1965), pp. 233–237; K. Rahner, 'Zur konziliaren Mariologie', *Stimmen der Zeit* 174 (1964), pp. 87–101.

[23] For a correct basic principle in Mariology cf. K. Rahner, *Maria, Mutter des Herrn* (Freiburg,[4] 1962), pp. 15–38; also 'Le principe fondamental de la théologie mariale', *RSR* 42 (1954), pp. 481–522.

[24] The existence of the thing itself cannot be assessed simply according to the verbal occurrence of terms like 'mediator', etc. In the New Testament even the mediating function of Christ himself is expressed in very diverse ways. Cf. *ThWNT* IV, pp. 624 ff. and *LThK*[2] VII, cols. 498–499. The same is the case in dogmatics with the titles accorded to Mary. A comprehensive example of what is intended in exegesis is provided in W. Thusing, 'Per Christum in Deum' = *Neutestamentliche Abhandlungen* NF 1 (Münster, 1965).

[25] Apart from the author's larger studies on the theology of the Incarnation cf. the small sketch 'I believe in Jesus Christ' in this volume, and the preliminary plan for a speculative doctrine of the Trinity in *Mysterium Salutis* II (Einsiedeln, 1967), pp. 317–401.

of human intercommunication before God and of the solidarity in salvation of all men.[26] This also makes it clear right from the very beginning that Christ's unique mediatorship does not suspend this saving intercommunication and solidarity, but perfects it, since the latter is both the necessary precondition for Christ's mediatorship, and also its effect.[27]

II

We shall therefore put forward the following thesis: *the condition required for the possibility of the saving mediatorship of Christ and its personal realisation in faith is the intercommunication of all men right down to the ultimate depths of their existence, to their very salvation, and the concrete and existential 'realisation' and experience of this radical intercommunication.* This intercommunication is part and parcel of man's concrete being[28] and is therefore a constant. The experience of it (whether accepted or rejected) is the precondition without which such a thing as the mediatorship of Christ could neither be understood at all nor held to be credible.

Here it is unnecessary to engage in a lengthy explanation of how, for a distinctly Catholic theological anthropology, this saving intercommunication and solidarity, as a factor in the constitution of man's concrete being, contains a 'natural' and a charismatic/pneumatic element. Both precede the individual's decision for or against salvation as its condition and perspective, contributing to making the decision possible and determining it in such a way that, in spite of its transcendental character as a condition of Christ's mediatorship, it can be understood as a condition which the Christ-event itself *actively* presupposes for its own actualisation. In this way it does not prejudice the majesty and independence of Christ's mediatorship.[29]

We shall now endeavour to elucidate and substantiate the proposed thesis piece by piece. Naturally we cannot do this here by referring in

[26] Not only providing a way to a deeper understanding, but also taking up a whole range of essential Old and New Testament motifs. Cf. J. Scharbert, 'Die Rettung der "Vielen" durch die "Wenigen" im AT', *Trierer Theologische Zeitschrift* 68 (1959), pp. 146–161; also *Heilsmittler im AT und im alten Orient* (Freiburg, 1964) (with literature).

[27] On the fundamental legitimacy of this view cf. the author's essay 'Theology and Anthropology' in this volume.

[28] For a few observations on this cf. K. Rahner, *Handbuch der Pastoraltheologie* II/1 (Freiburg, 1966), pp. 31 ff.

[29] cf. H. Küng, *Justification* (E.T. London 1964); and K. Rahner, *Theological Investigations* IV (London and Baltimore, 1966), pp. 189 ff.

detail to the sources of theology, Scripture, Tradition and their expression in authoritative Church pronouncements. We shall give a plain account in the hope that the listener will himself gather what is being referred to or will supply his own illustrations.

It must first be said by way of introduction that even in a context of theological controversy it is no longer permissible, in discussing a theme such as this, to treat the idea of Christ's mediatorship as if it were unquestioningly accepted. It is by no means self-evident just *what* this concept means or can mean, nor how it can be believed seriously today in this age of 'demythologising'. It is not as if we *only* had to ask whether this 'mediation' – as something self-evident both in its meaning and in actual existence – permits of another kind of mediation 'beside' or 'beneath' itself. For what does it mean to say that Jesus has redeemed us by his blood? How can we think of a *reconciliation* with God at all? How can the forgiveness of our radical sinfulness be conceived in any other way than as the pure act of God *alone*? Precisely *what* does one mean by saying that this very act of God alone, of which he is the *sole* subject and the unconditioned origin, has *happened* in Christ, has come to light in Christ and nowhere else, and is addressed to us in him? How can Jesus do more than give us courage to believe in the forgiving love of God, which *exists* but is not effected by him? What *is* a mediator, if he is constituted in the same way as those to whom he mediates? How can this mediatorship be conceived if it is to be valid also for mankind *before* and *outside* the compass of the preaching of the Gospel of the death of Jesus? When applied to our relationship with God, are not words like 'blood', 'sacrifice', 'propitiation', 'God's anger', 'Atonement' etc., verbal relics of a mythological age? Do we know what they really mean for us? Above all we are faced with this question: what is the transcendental horizon of understanding, and thus the hermeneutical principle, which will lead to an understanding of the mediatorship of Christ which can be protected from misconceptions? What and where is the unavoidable existential experience within the perspective of which we can really encounter the unique historical fact of the redeeming death of Jesus and find it credible?

There must be such a horizon of understanding, and nowadays it must no longer exercise its influence hidden from reflection; it must be especially and explicitly shown. This may be dangerous, because if it is interpreted falsely or incompletely, the wrong hermeneutical principle will also corrupt the reality and its expression which was to be rendered intelligible by reference to this horizon. It may be that the hermeneutical circle, embracing both the horizon of understanding and what is to be understood, in which each must clarify the other in a mutual exchange, and which itself has a history, cannot be broken. But all the same we must ask this question: Where can the experience of a horizon of understanding be found within which the message of Christ's mediatorship can 'strike home' at all? On its own, the experience of man's unavoidable guilt does not provide this horizon. Lostness does not itself automatically give rise to a rescue, let alone lead one to understand *how* such a rescue is conceivable.

III

This horizon of understanding is man's experienced, intercommunicative existence, which is always committed to us for us to accept or reject freely. It is ultimately a matter of no significance to what extent we succeed in reaching an adequate reflex interpretation of this intercommunicative existence. It is there and it is constantly experienced, whether it is interpreted well or ill, according to pre-philosophical or pre-theological categories or according to existential ontology or theology. Nor does it matter ultimately whether this experienced, intercommunicative existence is *explicitly* recognised in its express relation to the question of *salvation* or not. For this intercommunicative existence is experienced as being unlimited: the experience would automatically cease if it were thought of as limited to a particular area of human existence, e.g. to the biological or political area, or the private area of a love which excludes others. Intercommunication in all its tenaciousness, according to which the other person is necessarily always present, sustaining and making demands upon me, would be a mere surface appearance if I could withdraw to a region where I was simply alone, where no-one could follow me or was necessary for me any longer, and where there was no-one for whom I was partly responsible. If, therefore, the question of salvation is an unavoidable element of human existence, intercommunication is also a factor of existence, whether for or against salvation. Here too no-one is alone; each one supports every other person, in the matter of salvation everyone is responsible and significant for everyone else. The commandment to love one's neighbour[30] was not given to make our social or private lives bearable or agreeable, but to proclaim everyone's concern in everyone

[30] cf. K. Rahner, 'The "commandment" of love in relation to the other commandments', *Theological Investigations* V (London and Baltimore, 1966), pp. 439–459; 'Reflections on the unity of the love of neighbour and the love of God', *Theological Investigations* VI (London and Baltimore, 1969), pp. 231–249.

else's possibility of salvation.[31] It goes without saying that concepts like 'people (of God)' in salvation-history,[32] 'covenant',[33] 'Body of Christ',[34] 'Prayer for one another'[35] etc., presuppose this kind of intercommunicative existence. The reality and experience of this intercommunicative existence which is so important for salvation is made concrete in the absolute quality and unfathomable depths of the love of one's neighbour, in the puzzling experience that in the fate of any individual we are confronted and put face to face with the fate of all human kind, and that this experience cannot be explained away rationalistically as abstraction, induction or the seeing of all 'cases' in a single 'case'.[36] Everyone is aware of this in the experience of his being weighed down by a guilt which is not merely his own, in the experience of his own historicity. This historicity is on the one hand a co-determinant of the most ultimate aspects of one's own existence, and on the other hand it is itself partially the result of the historical decisions of other people. But one cannot draw a boundary between these two, between the passive and active effects of others.[37]

[31] cf. also the *Handbuch der Pastoraltheologie* II/1 (Freiburg, 1966), pp. 31 f., 271 ff. (with literature).

[32] cf. N. A. Dahl, *Das Volk Gottes* (Darmstadt,[2] 1963); H. J. Kraus, *Volk Gottes im AT* (Zürich, 1958); F. Mußner, 'Volk Gottes im NT', *Trierer Theologische Zeitschrift* 72 (1963), pp. 169–178.

[33] The fact that the covenant is made between unequals rather than equals does not contradict this principle. The structure of intercommunication must not be thought of as having a homogeneous and even surface. Cf. Kl. Baltzer, 'Das Bundesformular' = *WMANT* 4 (Neukirchen, 1960); D. J. McCarthy, 'Treaty and Covenant' = *An Bibl* 21 (Rome, 1963); also his 'Der Gottesbund im AT' = *SBB* 13 (Stuttgart, 1960); J. l'Hour, 'Die Ethik der Bundestradition im AT' = *SBB* 14 (Stuttgart, 1967).

[34] E. Käsemann drew attention very early to the collective structure of this concept, and maintains this biblical view of intercommunicative existence against all tendencies to individualism. Cf. E. Käsemann, 'Leib und Leib Christi' = *BHTh* 9 (Tübingen, 1933); and now E. Güttgemanns' study, 'Der leidende Apostel und sein Herr' = *FRLANT* 90 (Göttingen, 1966), pp. 199 ff., 206 ff.

[35] cf. note 7 above, including the author's studies.

[36] Thus it becomes once more apparent that the concept of neighbourly love to which we refer must not be understood in an introverted and 'private' sense, but, in an original sense, gains 'political' dimensions. Cf. on this aspect J. B. Metz, *Verantwortung der Hoffnung* (Mainz, 1968).

[37] cf. in the first place K. Rahner, 'Ursprünge der Freiheit', M. Horkheimer/K. Rahner/C. F. v. Weizsäcker, *Über die Freiheit* (Stuttgart,[2] 1965), pp. 29–49, esp. 34 ff.; also 'Der Friede Gottes und der Friede der Welt', *Der Streit um den Frieden*, ed. R. Schmid/W. Beck (Munich-Mainz, 1967), now also in this volume; also 'The theology of power', *Theological Investigations* IV (London and Baltimore, 1966), pp. 391–409.

It is impossible here to give a detailed account of how this intercommunicative existence always takes place *before God*, coming from him and proceeding towards him, however unconsciously and anonymously.[38] It would be of fundamental importance, however, for what follows. The experience of being-in-reference-to the absolute mystery we call God and the experience of intercommunication mutually determine each other, because the world, which, according to Catholic teaching, can lead to a recognition of God, is not only a world of things but the world to which self-experiencing man belongs: within himself and his intercommunication he recognises God. Consequently a closer knowledge of God's relationship to the world, together with the history of this relationship, are partial constituents of a closer understanding of man's intercommunicative existence. God himself initiates an absolute intercommunication between himself and man, i.e. in absolute *self*-communication – which we call 'grace' – giving himself in a direct partnership and intimacy, and not only showing himself to be the radically unapproachable Distant One, separating himself from the creature, the 'other'; to this extent (and only thus) we have the possibility of a radically serious, ultimate and secure interpersonal communication. (The mere formal concept of intercommunication cannot, of course, provide such a full content on its own.) But the reverse is also true: wherever this intercommunication is set free, accepted and experienced in its unlimited, unconditional and dynamic nature, there is – at least anonymously – the experience of the relationship of grace between God and man, springing from God's free self-communication. Man is loved in God, and God in man.[39] Where interpersonal communication reaches the ultimate possibility of its actual being (secretly supplied by and through God himself), it is already a meeting with God (whether this is acknowledged expressly or not),[40] since it is itself founded on God's self-communication.[41]

This union of men in an intercommunicative existence, which exhibits the most varied elements – although we cannot discuss them here (the

[38] A discussion of principles in K. Rahner, 'The concept of mystery in Catholic theology', *Theological Investigations* IV (London and Baltimore, 1966), pp. 36–73.

[39] Details in K. Rahner, 'Reflections on the unity of the love of neighbour and the love of God', *Theological Investigations* VI (London and Baltimore, 1969), pp. 231–249; also *Glaube, der die Erde liebt* (Freiburg, 1966), pp. 83–99; note 31 above.

[40] cf. K. Rahner, 'Anonymous Christians', *Theological Investigations* VI, pp. 390–398 (with further literature).

[41] In scholastic terms, because, as a theological virtue, the infused virtue of 'caritas' is a strict unity of the love of God and the love of one's neighbour. For further theological clarification cf. the essays referred to in note 30 above.

physical unity of the cosmos, the space-time unity; biological unity; intercommunication in the unity of a single history of truth and love, untruth and hate; the unity of rootedness in God, etc.) – itself has a history which is of relevance for salvation. It is a history in which the intercommunications sustaining it and taking place within it are never simply the same ones: each instance is unique, since this history of intercommunications is not built up out of equal atoms, but is shaped by persons who are unique at any one time. Furthermore, this history is a one-way history, and is proceeding towards a goal.

IV

When this *history* of human intercommunication and of the relationship between God and mankind together in one reach their eschatological meridian,[42] i.e. when the occurrence of the offer and the acceptance – both given quite freely – of the divine self-communication in God's Pneuma[43] becomes irreversible and *appears* historically as such for the believer, we have what Christian Dogmatics calls 'Incarnation', the death and resurrection of the divine Logos.[44] Naturally we have no time here to give a more thorough justification for this assertion,[45] We shall only draw out its implications for our particular theme.

If it is correct, it follows that the Father's Word made flesh is the Mediator of God's self-communication (which is also always a forgiving communication) in so far as he is the eschaton of the history of this self-communication. History hangs upon its own future and is mediated by it, i.e. it *is* as it happens throughout its *whole* course, and it takes place in reference to its fulness and its victorious end. Consequently it is in this sense that the Word made flesh is the Mediator of God's self-communication and, within this, of the ultimate, radical depth of human intercommunication as well. We may understand his funcion

[42] cf. K. Rahner, 'Christianity and the "new man" ', *Theological Imvestigations* V (London and Baltimore, 1966), pp. 135–153; also 'Christology within an evolutionary view of the world', op. cit., pp. 157–192; also A. Darlap, *Mysterium Salutis* I, ed. J. Feiner/M. Löhrer (Einsiedeln, 1967), pp. 99 ff., 59 ff., 147 ff.

[43] cf. the more precise treatment in the author's attempt at a speculative doctrine of the Trinity, *Mysterium Salutis* II (Einsiedeln, 1967), pp. 317–401.

[44] Besides the essays referred to in notes 25, 27 and 42 above, cf. also K. Rahner, 'On the theology of the Incarnation', *Theological Investigations* IV (London and Baltimore, 1966), pp. 105–120; also 'Current problems in Christology', *Theological Investigations* I (London and Baltimore, 1961), pp. 149–200.

[45] Esp. the essay referred to in note 27.

as Mediator in this way – or rather, we *must* do so – for the following reasons:

1. 'Grace', 'faith', 'Spirit', 'justification' were effectual even before Christ and took place throughout the whole length and breadth of history, even where there was no explicit preaching of the Gospel.[46]

2. *All* salvation occurs *intuitu meritorum Christi.*[47]

3. It is not the Christ-event which provides the foundation for God's will for our salvation, i.e. God's desire, effectual throughout the whole of history, to communicate himself;[48] the Christ-event is itself the 'effect' of the latter. *Because* God loves the world, he sent his Son.[49]

Christ's mediatorship can be said to 'effect' God's will for salvation in respect of an individual in so far as the highest and ultimate factor in any action must always be called its 'reason', in so far as the history of God's self-communication has become irreversible in this individual and has thus appeared historically as eschatologically victorious, and in so far as every individual person is seen as a member of mankind, to whom God's self-communication is addressed. Seen as a unity, the whole of this history of the salvation of mankind is the object, the goal and the 'reason' for the divine desire for salvation – if such a word may be used, bearing in mind God's sovereignty.[50] All factors of this salvation-history are, as such, factors of a *single* history willed by God in the decision to empty himself in self-communication, and they are all therefore mutually conditioning. But this mutual conditioning relationship itself has a structure, so we both can and must say that, in a unique sense, the highest and ultimate factor of this single totality, willed by God, determines and sustains everything else.

V

From this standpoint it ought to be possible to understand the relationship of Christ's mediatorship to those intercommunications which are

[46] For details cf. K. Rahner, 'The Word and the Eucharist', *Theological Investigations* IV (London and Baltimore, 1966), pp. 253–286; in this volume, 'Atheism and implicit Christianity'.

[47] cf. *DS* 1523, 1530, 1529, 1560, etc.

[48] cf. K. Rahner, 'Heilswille Gottes, allgemeiner', *Sacramentum mundi* II. *International theological lexicon* (Herder, 1968 ff.); also 'History of the world and salvation-history', *Theological Investigations* V (London and Baltimore, 1966), pp. 97–114; also pp. 115–134, and the studies referred to in notes 25 and 42 above.

[49] cf. John 3:16 and 1 John 4:9 f., and R. Schnackenburg's commentary in *The Gospel according to St John* I (trans. Kevin Smyth, London and New York, 1968), pp. 398 ff.

[50] Further remarks in the essays referred to in note 48.

also of relevance for man's salvation and which thus signify as many *mediations* of salvation.

If what has been said so far is correct and has been understood properly, we can make the following assertions:

1. *Wherever salvation occurs in the individual's salvation-history, it also mediates salvation for all others.* For a salvation-event of this kind, whether expressly or not, is in addition necessarily always involved in intercommunication: i.e. it is the love of one's neighbour, it is an event *within* the single totality of all salvation-history whatsoever, an event willed and effected by God, finding its context and its goal in this totality. Consequently these mediations are essential constituents of salvation-history. Every person who abides in faith and love is in this relationship because of all the other people, since each person is intended by God to be an 'element' – even though a unique and irreplaceable element – of the single salvation-history, and since God's Pneuma, imparted to us and forming the context and history in which salvation takes place, both presupposes human intercommunication *and* makes it more radical. According to Catholic teaching it is therefore obvious that mediations of this kind are not only the function of particular 'Saints';[51] they are effected by all faithful and justified people. Similarly, too, these mediations are not extraordinary, special functions of all believers, but they are identical with the latter's realisation of salvation which is always present, ultimately secure and perfected, before God and is sustained by his gracious will, which desires the single, *total* salvation-history and also the salvation-history of each one of its 'elements' as such. Since these mediations depend on, and actually *are* intercommunications, what has been said by no means excludes, but rather implies, the fact that these mediations can also become present to consciousness, indeed, that they *should* become so to some degree, thus taking the form, for instance, of explicit intercession and requests for intercession.

2. Since the world is the *one* world to which God communicates himself in his Pneuma; since in this world each person is present as he is *for* everyone else and *because* of everyone else; and since this world with its salvation-history is a real *history*, which is proceeding towards its goal and constantly lives in dependence on its goal; *this world of intercommunication, as history, has one apogee and only one goal: this is Jesus Christ, who,*

[51] cf. K. Rahner, 'The Church of the Saints', *Theological Investigations* III (London and Baltimore, 1967), pp. 91–104; also, 'Why and how can we venerate the Saints?', *Theological Investigations* VIII (London and New York, 1971), pp. 3–23; and 'All Saints', *ibid*, pp. 24–29.

as the God-given apogee of this history, is its sole and absolute Mediator. Far from excluding the saving, intercommunicative character of the world's salvation-history, it implies it. All intercommunicative mediations of salvation are dependent upon their *single* goal and their eschatological consummation in Christ, but for that very reason they *actually exist*; they are not merely secondary, ultimately superfluous consequences of Christ's mediatorship; they are the very preconditions which Christ's mediatorship creates for itself. In other words they constitute the conditions for the possibility of such mediatorship, conditions provided, of course, by God's sovereign grace itself in and through its will towards Jesus Christ – just as, conversely, Jesus Christ is willed 'for us men and for our Salvation'.

VI

In order to do justice to what has been said, two further things must be mentioned.

1. If Jesus Christ is not to become an abstract idea, a Christ-principle, and hence a mythological figure unworthy of belief, then this concrete, historical Jesus of Nazareth must be capable of being loved; he must not be merely another word for the incalculable sovereignty of the grace of the transcendent God. But how am I to accept and really love him as a concrete man (not merely accepting a theoretical truth about him) and how can *this* love of this particular concrete man be my salvation, if I am unable to love and be loved by other men, with whom I am in close, concrete proximity, in a mutual love (naturally in God's Pneuma and in relation to God) which is not only commanded but is *actually salvation* itself? I admit this quite openly: if I sometimes feel shocked by the overwhelming sort of Marian devotion in which a pious Catholic rushes to Mary's bosom, loves her, entreats and importunes her in utter confidence, as if nothing in religion were so important, then I ask myself in self-criticism whether it only shocks me because *I myself* am incapable of realising in a total and unselfconscious way this legitimate *concrete* form of human intercommunication which belongs to a living Christianity. For after all, my embracing of salvation in faith and love refers to Jesus (and not to an abstract idea of Christ), a Jesus who is at the same time the Crucified *and* the *Jesus* of Nazareth who stands 'at the right hand of God' (Acts 7:56), and who now lives in God as the concrete Man.[52] But if this is the case, how could I regard

[52] cf. K. Rahner, 'The eternal significance of the humanity of Jesus for our relationship with God', *Theological Investigations* III, pp. 35–46.

as reprehensible this direct, trusting love towards another person in God's glory.[53]

2. How, in an age of socialism, which by no means must be impersonal, or in the face of the Indian concept of the God-manhood of humanity as such, can the *uniqueness* of Christ's mediatorship be credibly proclaimed, unless one understands this uniqueness as that which gives the interdependence-in-salvation of all men its eschatological guarantee, its victory, its historical form and manifestation? How can this be done if it is only understood as the individualistic relationship of each person to the one Christ, as if each person in his own individual process of salvation could have nothing to do with anyone else?

Certainly, the Gospel says a hard 'No' to false self-interpretations on man's part, and makes it our duty to say no in such cases. But all the same this is only permitted when man's interpretations have the effect of closing everything down rather than opening up possibilities. But which case is it – 'opening up' or 'closing down'? – if we say that for man's salvation he needs to live in that *single* love of the Pneuma which joins all men together and hence makes each man of saving importance for each other man, provided that it is understood in faith that this single body of love has found its unique, victorious, eschatological consummation in Jesus Christ? This is an action of opening up, not closing down. Or should the members of the Body of Christ all be solely concerned with the Head of the Body and have nothing to do with each other? At least, not so far as their relationship with Christ, their salvation, is concerned? It is undoubtedly clear that all 'mediation' is a mediation to the end of *immediacy*, and not a 'medial' something which is inserted between and thus keeps separate the objects of mediation. And in a formally similar manner it applies also to the mediation of Christ's manhood to God and the mediations on the part of one justified person for another in relation both to Christ and God. If the man Jesus' mediation to God does not destroy God's immediacy but actually constitutes it as such, it cannot be held that any 'mediation' to Jesus Christ, even at the level of concepts, straightway eliminates the possibility of a relation of immediacy with him.

I am far from thinking that everything necessary has now been said on this issue. For supplementary material I refer to the studies already mentioned concerning the unity of the love of God and the love of one's neighbour, and the veneration of the Saints. One ought also to go into the

[53] However much the concrete practice of the veneration of the Saints becomes clouded over and succumbs to wrong tendencies, the fact cannot be obscured that this theological foundation is thoroughly legitimate and does not contradict the

many existential difficulties which man finds nowadays in respect of the veneration of the Saints, bearing in mind that nowadays these difficulties apply equally to the mediatorship of Christ. My sole intention was to say this: the saving intercommunication of all (justified) men is the existential ontological precondition for the mediatorship of Christ. The existential experience of this intercommunication is the perspective within which the experience, in faith, of Christ's mediatorship is alone possible; and the *converse* of this affirmation is also true. This saving intercommunication has its own history and achieves its victorious, eschatological consummation and its historical appearance (conquering unbelief – even the disbelief in this very intercommunication) in Jesus Christ who, as the eschatological meridian of this history, sustains it and is thus in this sense the *sole* Mediator. What in Catholic terms we call the mediations of the Saints is essentially nothing other than this saving intercommunication of everyone with everyone else. It can be further differentiated, in so far as we know in faith something of the particular function in salvation-history of a particular person, the Blessed Virgin for instance. But such differentiation changes nothing as far as its essence is concerned.

---

spirit of the New Testament. In their indignance at abuses, however, people have often eliminated what is essential as well.

PART THREE

Theological Anthropology

12

CHRISTIAN HUMANISM[1]

PERHAPS a question-mark ought to be put after this title, for as it stands it leads one to expect that a theologian is going to clarify and give reasons as to how Christianity and humanism form a unity, how humanism, when it is genuine, full-blooded and is really being itself, is actually Christianity. But the question which needs to be answered before making such a proud affirmation is so difficult, and has so many levels, that it seems to be more appropriate to present the thoughts of a Christian theologian who is *asking himself*, first of all, what the relationship is which exists between Christianity and humanism. In the first place it is no simple matter to say what Christianity or humanism really are. Consequently their relationship with one another is not so easy to define either. Even if one takes for granted ecclesial Christianity's understanding of itself with its authoritative theological affirmations, this very understanding can be still interpreted in many different ways, and depending on the particular interpretation one can arrive at very different definitions of the relationship between Christianity and humanism. Christian anthropology itself makes so many and such opposite assertions about man that, even if they are not interpreted as logical contradictions, they put such heavy demands on any particular man's actual ability to reconstruct a 'realisation' of these assertions, that in actual fact there are greatly differing interpretations of man even within Church orthodoxy, and consequently greatly differing attitudes to humanism. Augustine, Thomas Aquinas, Pascal, Teilhard de Chardin – all of them Christians – have very different Christian ideas of man and thus of humanism. And what of the very concept of humanism itself! Nowadays everyone wants to be a humanist. And at the same time there is less agreement than ever as to what a *man* really is.

[1] For the origin, purpose and the limits of this paper cf. the list of sources at the end of this volume.

I

Initially it seems quite easy for a Christian theologian to answer this question. He knows about man, he knows about God, and he knows about the God-man. And thus he confesses an absolute humanism. He can say that no-one can take man more seriously than the Christian. And he can say (which no pre-Christian or non-Christian religion and no modern ideology would actually dare to do) that Christianity acknowledges an absolute meaning and validity in *every* concrete human being and forbids anyone to try to escape into the void of the mere perishable and perishing world of time, laying upon him the task of believing that no-one can escape himself or be rid of himself, and that it is good to have to retain his own self. The theologian is aware that this *inescapable responsibility for oneself*, which Christianity proclaims, must take the shape of self-forgetfulness in the love of one's fellows, or else it becomes the hell of one's own egoistic isolation. This love of one's neighbour must be so radical and absolute, and must overcome subjectivity itself (as the possession of oneself) in its very essence to such an extent that it is henceforth only possible as something which *happens*, which comes to us from an absolute origin which is not ourselves, but which rather sends this love of our neighbour to us as its own love. In this way there exists an original and ultimate unity of the love of God and of one's neighbour,[2] whether explicit or unconscious, so that the love of one's neighbour is only sufficiently radical when it is an expression of the love of God, and the love of God only occurs (and man only knows who God is) when man loves his neighbour.

The theologian is aware that – if man is essentially a 'political' being[3] – this love of one's neighbour must not be the mere inclination of the affections or private intercommunication, which can be the most sublime form of egoism precisely because it can be so intimate and bring such happiness, but must become the sober service of 'political' love as well, whose concern is the whole of mankind, turning the most distant person into the nearest neighbour and having occasion to hold the nearest person sternly at a distance.

[2] cf. K. Rahner, 'The "commandment" of love in relation to the other commandments', *Theological Investigations* V (London and Baltimore, 1966), pp. 439–459; 'Reflections on the unity of the love of neighbour and the love of God', *Theological Investigations* VI (London and Baltimore, 1969), pp. 231–249.

[3] cf. K. Rahner, *Handbuch der Pastoraltheologie. Praktische Theologie der Kirche in ihrer Gegenwart*, ed. F. X. Arnold, K. Rahner, V. Schurr, L. M. Weber (Freiburg, 1966), Vol. II/1, pp. 31 f.; J. B. Metz, *Verantwortung der Hoffnung* (Mainz, 1968).

The theologian is aware that Christianity is Jesus Christ, i.e. that a man can be loved who, himself the servant of all and only genuinely loved *as such*, is God's own destiny, with the result that for all eternity Christianity can possess no theology which is not at the same time anthropology, the two uncompounded and inseparable.[4] Furthermore the theologian will demonstrate how, in this same Jesus Christ, the unity of the love of God and the love of one's neighbour, the presence of God and his love within man and in the love towards men, is eternally secured.

The theologian is aware that, since the necessary setting for the individual's salvation is the Church as the unity of mankind and its history *theology must always be 'political' theology*. He is aware that he may only look at the salvation of an individual as one which is not achieved fully except within the absolute future of the whole of mankind, as the ultimate result of the love of all the others in the absoluteness of God. In other words, the salvation of an individual soul does not consist in escaping from the history of humanity but in entering into the latter's absolute future,[5] which we call the 'kingdom of God'.[6]

The theologian is aware that, according to Christianity, salvation is achieved not only within the explicitly religious sphere but in *all* dimensions of human existence, i.e. even where man does not interpret his actions in a *consciously* religious way,[7] but where he loves in an absolutely responsible manner, serves his fellow-man selflessly and willingly accepts the incomprehensible nature and the disappointments of his existence, hoping ultimately to embrace its as yet unrevealed meaningfulness.

Thus he is aware that in this sense the whole of the human sphere is religious and the whole of the religious sphere is humane.

The theologian is aware that, if one assumes the power of sin, man's multifarious development not merely reveals 'friction phenomena' but is continually threatened by the absurdity of real sinfulness which we cannot ourselves eradicate;[8] from the example of the man who struggles and dies

[4] cf. further K. Rahner, 'On the theology of the Incarnation', *Theological Investigations* IV (London and Baltimore, 1966), pp. 105–120; in this volume: 'Theology and Anthropology'.

[5] For this concept cf. K. Rahner, 'Marxist utopia and the Christian future of man', *Theological Investigations* VI (London and Baltimore, 1969), pp. 59–68.

[6] For the biblical significance of this Christian fundamental category cf. R. Schnackenburg, *Gottes Herrschaft und Reich* (Freiburg,[4] 1965); H. U. v. Balthasar, 'Zuerst Gottes Reich' = *Theologische Meditationen* 13 (Einsiedeln, 1966).

[7] K. Rahner, 'Anonymous Christians', *Theological Investigations* VI (London and Baltimore, 1969), pp. 390–398 (literature).

[8] On this problem cf. K. Rahner, 'Guilt and its remission: the borderland between

on the cross Christianity knows that the most ultimate and radical love of others in God implies this very fate: one only passes from death to life by loving the other person; and in loving him one knows that it is only with God's help that one can avoid withholding oneself ultimately from the other person, that one must carry on loving, right to the very end of a pointless death.

II

So far so good. The theologian can be convinced that there is a Christian 'humanism' in the preliminary sense just mentioned: Christianity proclaims a genuine and radical 'humanism'; what it acknowledges concerning God, Christ, freedom, responsibility and judgment is not an arbitrary or superfluous superstructure of theology[9] or even a venom manufactured by man for his practical defence, but the ultimate and radical form of man's dignity, because the Christian message affirms man himself as really absolute and yet does not show itself unworthy of belief in the face of the brutal experience that man is a wretched animal and a merely ridiculous episode in natural history, such that it is in the end of no consequence what the individual does or what becomes of everyone.

The theologian can declare that he really does not see how, in the absence of this 'ideological' factor of the conviction of the absolute dignity of man and of humanity,[10] the actual course of the history of mankind, in which the latter reaches out in hope towards its future, is at all conceivable. He will declare, therefore, that anyone who is convinced of the irresistible nature of the process implicitly experiences and proclaims, in his own actions, this apparently 'ideological' factor as the innermost truth and reality of this world; that in other words he by no means understands it as a superfluous or harmful 'ideology'.

Furthermore the theologian could ask the non-Christian whether he would be able to maintain that a Christianity understood in this way is *not* a humanism. He could ask him whether he ought not to be glad that Christians endeavour to be human in this way, even if it is his own opinion that much of this Christianity is ideology or mythology, which it uses to interpret, clarify and render effective its humanism.

He might ask the non-Christian whether he knows of a *more radical*

---

theology and psychotherapy', *Theological Investigations* II (London and Baltimore, 1963), pp. 265–281.

[9] For the critique of ideology with reference to Christianity cf. K. Lehmann, *Handbuch der Pastoraltheologie* II/2, pp. 109–180 (literature).

[10] A theological interpretation of these fundamental concepts is attempted in *Theological Investigations* II, pp. 235–263.

humanism: whether, comparing theory with theory and not unfairly comparing humanist theory with the miserable practice of Christians, he is certain that his humanism is *better practically*, i.e. more effective. He could ask his liberal and enlightened brother whether even today he still regards him with suspicion as a clerical suppressor of the freedom of conscience and as a defender of the Church's positions of power in society, or whether it would not be better if the Christian and the 'liberal' were to work together so that the individual's personality and freedom are not smothered in the society of the future. The theologian could ask his Marxist brother where he sees the 'opium of the people', or 'for the people' in this Christian humanism, and whether, for example, it is really necessary for a politically powerful Marxism to persecute this Christianity in order to free mankind from servitude and self-alienation. He could ask him whether the freedom of *this* Christianity could not be guaranteed, even if, for various good reasons, one had certain reservations about the liberalistic concept of freedom; whether it is not good for a society (lest it should degenerate into a tyranny) if a Christian humanism endeavours to rescue men too, and if – instead of wasting much time in theoretical dialectic – it is left rather to actual practice and the future to show which side has the greater love, where the ever-living sources of strength are which defend mankind, and which theory is confirmed by practice.[11]

III

So far it seems that, for the Christian theologian, all is well. But in reality he has only just begun to embark on a dialogue with himself. He invites the Christian and the non-Christian to listen to this process of self-questioning in the hope that *both* of them will be able to make it their own.

The first question the theologian asks himself is whether he really knows *what* and *who* man is. Of course, thinking within the tradition he has received, he will say that he is able to utter a great many ultimate, radical things about man, even God's revelation concerning man; and that there is nothing clearer, more certain, more sublime and more beneficial than this very same Christian anthropology[12] with its highly concrete, material content.

[11] On the foundations and prospects of such a dialogue in theory and practice cf. K. Rahner, 'Reflections on dialogue within a pluralistic society', *Theological Investigations* VI, pp. 31–42.

[12] On the material content of a Christian anthropology of this kind cf. the remarks in *LThK* I (Freiburg,[2] 1957), cols. 604–627 (J. Schmid, A. Halder, K. Rahner).

On the other hand, drawing on the experience of the last hundred years, the Christian theologian will admit that in this age of a scientific anthropology, which no longer mythologises poetically and is no longer an exclusively theological discipline,[13] man has learned an immeasurable amount about himself which the Christian revelation has not taught him; and that for this very reason there already exists a humanism today (assuming that one does not look presumptuously upon this scientific anthropology as of no consequence from the human point of view). Nor can he interpret it as a self-awareness on man's part which was always present or which is itself a product of the message of Christianity. Hence it is doubtless true that theological anthropology finds itself in a totally new and threatening situation if, as is the case, it is placed side by side with a scientific anthropology which did *not* exist at the time when Christianity was alone in revealing and clarifying man's nature to himself. But all the same the theologian will still maintain that all the empirical, scientific anthropologies, which can only exist now in a permanent state of pluralism, can only bring man to himself *whole* and *single* provided that he hears the message of Christianity. Otherwise he necessarily cannot know what the *totality* of his variegated knowledge about himself means, nor why this known totality is of such absolute significance,[14] the significance without which man's understanding of himself cannot be a humanism at all.

But all this does not answer the question which the theologian puts to himself, whether he himself really knows what man is. For what does his own anthropology really tell him about man? That he is the being who loses himself in God. Otherwise nothing. For only what is implied in *this* statement or can be said about man in *this* connection, is a genuinely *theological* affirmation of his anthropology. Any other statement about

[13] We cannot trace the development of this concept here. Cf. O. Marquard, 'Zur Geschichte des philosophischen Begriffs "Anthropologie" seit dem Ende des 18. Jahrhunderts', *Collegium Philosophicum. Studien J. Ritter zum 60. Geburtstag* (Basle, 1965), pp. 209–239 (literature); in addition the essays by L. Oeing-Hanhoff, N. Hinske, O. Marquard and O. Pöggeler, *Die Frage nach dem Menschem. Aufriß einer philosophischen Anthropologie. Festschrift für M. Müller*, ed. H. Rombach (Freiburg, 1966); H. Pleßner, 'Immer noch Philosophische Anthropologie', *Zeugnisse. Th. W. Adorno zum 60. Geburtstag*, ed. M. Horkheimer (Frankfurt, 1963), pp. 65–73; A. Gehlen, *Anthropologische Forschung* (Reinbek bei Hamburg, 1961).

[14] Naturally these remarks depend ultimately on the particular concrete theological understanding of the relationship between nature and grace. Cf. *Theological Investigations* I (London and Baltimore, 1961), pp. 297–317; *Theological Investigations* IV (London and Baltimore, 1966), pp. 165–188.

man is only of theological significance provided that it can be referred back to this one, and provided that it is made clear (in whatever way, whether transcendentally or otherwise) that its denial would destroy man's being-in-reference-to God. But what does man know about himself in grasping this being-in-reference? What is there in this which he can apply to his theory and practice, if God is after all the ineffable, intractable Mystery? So long as it was thought possible to know something about God which constituted him as one quantity among others in the cosmos of extra-human realities[15] which mutually determine and explain each other, it was easy to believe that in saying that man is dependent on God, made 'after His image and likeness', one had made man intelligible for the purposes of his own *gnosis* and practice. But if, in our knowing and acting, we are only aware of God as our origin (our 'whence?') and our future (our 'whither?'), i.e. simply as a pure mystery[16] which is not a 'constituent' of the world of men – because otherwise God is confused with an idolatrous hypostatisation of a particular dimension of man – what is the good of saying to a man that he belongs to God? Ought not one to be silent before this ineffable mystery which silently overwhelms our existence? Not because religion is banished to the individual's interior sphere as was thought by naïve, old-fashioned Liberalism, which had no concept of man as a 'political' being, but because man is always tempted to live in a state of aversion to this seemingly unbearable and intractable mystery, in order to be at least a *man*?[17] Must not one say, 'What we know about man, we know from him himself and not from God; for we only know about God from our knowledge of man'? This applies equally to revealed theology, for this too not only works with human concepts originating from beneath and not from above (as far as their ultimate matter is concerned, which in part determines their usage), but actually only tells man that this unfathomable mystery as such is permanently present in Jesus Christ and wishes to communicate itself to us absolutely in the 'Spirit', creating a relationship of absolute immediacy with the incomprehensible God. Is theology in this case

[15] With respect to the preconditions for a relationship with God today cf. K. Rahner, 'The man of today and religion', *Theological Investigations* VI (London and Baltimore, 1969), pp. 3–20.

[16] cf. 'The concept of mystery in Catholic theology', *Theological Investigations* IV (London and Baltimore, 1966), pp. 36–73

[17] In this connection the following must be borne in mind: Does not this action of turning-away also imply the most radical turning-*towards*? Is not *theologia negativa* also a 'theology', an act which one must admit to oneself? How *could* such an act be avoided, since, in proclaiming that God is dead, one still presupposes him?

anything more than an *anthropologia negativa*, i.e. the experience that man continually loses track of himself in the uncomprehended and intractable mystery? And even if one emphasises that this *anthropologia negativa* does not turn God into a function of man but places man before the mystery which *absolutely is*, its *being* in no way dependent upon man but rather causing him to suffer the ultimate agony of his finitude, of what use is that to a humanism? Would not it still be the case that, in so far as they simply *live*, men live godlessly, i.e. secularly, and encounter God (whether he is named or unnamed) only in *death*? This is by no means an argument against theism. In the first place because man dies in any case and death is not an event at the end of life but *the* event of life itself, assuming that man is not thought of as vegetating like a mere animal, unaware of what is happening.

IV

In any case, however, as a kind of reduction of 'present' existence, which is capable of being manipulated and enjoyed, into the mystery of God, theism implies the elimination of each and every particular, concrete humanism in so far as it claims to be an eternal, *absolute* quantity; theism relativises every *concrete* humanism. And since in fact humanism is not the affirmation of an abstract formal idea of 'man' but the affirmation of a particular, concrete, familiar, beloved and cherished mode of historical existence, Christian theism, by contrast, is the very denial of such a humanism as an *absolute* quantity. Naturally this does not mean that it forbids a humanism of this kind. On the contrary, a genuine negation as an act can only take place with reference to a concrete affirmation. One can only negate by positing something, not by refraining from doing so under the misconception that one can achieve a pure negation. In this way every man necessarily carries out *his own* humanism, i.e. his concrete understanding and actualisation of existence. But it is precisely the latter which comes under criticism when man, in being a theist, lets it be swept away into the intractable, nameless mystery of God.

This Christianity does not erect a particular *concrete* humanism but denies it an *absolute* value; Christianity accepts the experience of its own humanism as one which remains constantly questionable.

Of course one *can* call the very affirmation of the dignity and value of man, of the responsibility of man's freedom, his spiritual and social nature – 'humanism'. In this sense one can call Christianity Humanism, and hence it can enter into a dialogue with the other humanisms as to whether the substance affirmed on one side is also affirmed on the other, how it is to be understood more precisely, and what it implies. But a dialogue of this sort concerning the formal, *abstract* aspects of a humanism will soon run aground: on both sides the understanding of this abstract *existentiale* itself is co-determined by the particular concrete humanism in relation to which one understands it, since one can never make an adequate concrete distinction between the horizon of understanding and what is understood within it. Hence the dialogue between the humanisms must consist, not in merely theoretical endeavours, but in their concrete confrontation, as the *practical* attempt to gain one's partner-in-dialogue for one's own concrete humanism, i.e. as (political) action, not pure theory.

This understanding of the humanist dialogue is most fundamentally appropriate for Christianity[18] if, on the one hand, it wishes to commend itself to others and if, on the other hand, it does not see itself as an abstract idea but as the absolute, concrete, historical fact of Jesus Christ and his Church – neither of which can be adequately theorised. As the fulness of the life of individual Christians and of their fellowship together, Christianity thus involves a *concrete* humanism, i.e. the historically given concrete humanity as it is lived out by Christians. To this extent, on the one hand, it seeks to win others to its concrete humanism, and on the other hand it is always ready, in the practical historical dialogue, to let its concrete humanism be subjected to radical change.[19] For Christianity as such – and this is the decisive point – cancels every concrete humanism by revealing its questionable nature before the incomprehensibility of God. Christianity's *concretissimum*, for which alone it stands, is Jesus Christ, who, in accepting death and suffering *for us* (and in no other way) has created our relationship of immediacy before God, and the Church, which looks for the Kingdom which is yet to be fulfilled and which is *not* identical with the humanism we ourselves have produced or shall produce in the near future.[20] Christianity renders every concrete humanism contingent, i.e. dispensable in favour of another, future humanism, by situating every one within God's open future.[21] In its conviction of man's

[18] cf. the author's essay referred to in note 11 above, and also the *Handbuch der Pastoraltheologie* II/1, pp. 102 ff., 254 ff., 265 ff.; II/2, pp. 168 ff.

[19] We draw attention to the fact that the Church itself needs dialogue *intra muros*; cf. the author's 'Concerning dialogue in the Church', in this volume.

[20] On the limitations of any intramundane future planning cf. K. Rahner, 'Experiment Mensch', *Die Frage nach dem Menschen* (cf. note 13 above), pp. 45–69, esp. 62–68; in this volume: 'The experiment with man'.

[21] In this sense Christianity is capable of the most radical elimination of what is

freedom, *rooted in* and *orientated towards* God, Christianity opens up the permanent possibility of an inhuman 'humanism'. But in consequence the only humanism which is inhuman is one which denies man's dependence on and relation to the intractable and incomprehensible One, thus positing itself as absolute and refusing to allow its own nature to be called in question by possibly taking a new decision to embrace *another* future, materially determined by history, which realises in concrete form the will to accept God's absolute future.

To the extent that Christianity, as the acceptance of the inconceivable mystery we call God, forbids man to try to understand and manipulate himself with reference to himself alone, at one and the same time it both calls into question each concrete humanism *and* also opens the way to an ever new, future humanism with its intra-mundane categories; for one can only be ready to realise God's absolute future if one is open to future intra-mundane humanisms. In spite of different emphases at various times the Church has always refused to decide between these two attitudes, which appear as opposites in Tertullian[22] on the one hand and in Clement of Alexandria[23] on the other. In fact they both belong to the nature of Christianity: the Church holds each concrete humanism at a distance as being contingent, questionable, provisional in respect of the future, and even sinful; and yet *at the same time* obliges the Christian to decide in favour of a concrete humanism, since only thus can he actualise a really serious Christianity, i.e. his will, in faith and hope, for God's absolute future. When today the Church declares that Christianity is compatible with any culture[24] and is not bound to any particular one, e.g. 'europeanism' or its imperialist and colonialist export version, it acknowledges (by implication) that a pluralism of humanisms is legitimate. Evidently this acknowledgment cannot refer solely to those humanisms which already exist, especially as the latter are threatened with being submerged in an intermingled world civilisation, but must apply above

---

ideological in intramundane future utopias; cf. *Handbuch der Pastoraltheologie* II/2, pp. 42 ff., 159 ff., 168 ff.

[22] cf. H. v. Campenhausen's short treatment in *Lateinische Kirchenväter* (Stuttgart, 1960), pp. 12–36; J. Klein, *Tertullian, Christliches Bewußtsein und sittliche Forderungen* (Düsseldorf, 1940).

[23] cf. F. Quatember, *Die christliche Lebenshaltung des Klemens von Alexandrien* (Würzburg, 1947); F. van der Grinten, *Die natürliche und übernatürliche Begründung des Tugendlebens bei Clemens von Alexandrien* (Bonn, 1949); W. Völker, *Der wahre Gnostiker nach Klemens von Alexandrien* (Berlin, 1952).

[24] cf. the statements of the Second Vatican Council: the Pastoral Constitution on the Church in the Modern World, Nos. 9, 53–59, 62.

all to one or more (that is an open question) *future* humanisms. And it is to this (or these) that men must open themselves creatively in a free historical decision. Christianity commits itself to and authorises the continually new humanism of the future, which is not actually Christian as such itself. It does not sanction a particular concrete humanism. But Christianity pronounces judgment on any humanism which sets itself up as absolute and thus explicitly or implicitly tries to inhibit man's openness to further concrete history and hence to God's absolute future.

V

The theologian must consider a further factor if he intends to concern himself with the problem of a so-called 'Christian humanism'. It is contained in what we have said already, but we must emphasise it more particularly here. Christianity is the religion of the Cross. Whether one calls it 'death' or the radical 'change' of which Paul speaks, it is a fact that in a Christian humanism man (man, humanity, individual and collective history) is subject to the law of death, and the sign of a genuine humanism is a Man nailed to a Cross. What does this signify for a Christian understanding of humanism? If there is no life without death, if death itself is a mystery,[25] all humanism whatsoever becomes a very obscure question. For how can man understand himself if he cannot understand death? It would be a very dubious kind of humanism which tried to pass over this question. The person who says that death is only a question for an egoistic individualism[26] has already given an answer and thus recognised that there *is* a question, for he cannot make us believe that one day this 'egoism' will die out, removing the necessity for this particular answer. Is it at all possible for man to be weaned away from this question so that it never occurs again, without altogether abolishing the very humanism which maintains and defends the dignity of man? Then what does Christianity say if it does *not* wish to avoid this question? And what does this imply for our understanding of humanism?

First of all I would like to make a preliminary observation, even at the risk of seeming callous and brutal, and although I know only too well

[25] On the following remarks the author refers to his study: *Zur Theologie des Todes* (Freiburg,[5] 1965).

[26] This answer can be found today among those Marxists who have cut themselves loose from crude materialism or an objectivistic concept of dialectic, and who now admit once again questions concerning the meaning of life and death as such (e.g. L. Kolakowski, A. Schaff, M. Machovec, E. Bloch).

that, as 'I' (though not as a Christian), I would not wish to be obliged to face up to what I shall now say. The Christian as such ought not to place *such* great importance on the death of an individual. Dying goes on everywhere, even in the brutal cases of children dying of starvation or people being strangled by cancer and so on. God evidently does not regard death as a scandal in the world which is *his* world, his creation, for which he is responsible. If one says that death is a phenomenon attributable to man's freely incurred guilt,[27] that is true, but it only begs the question, for in that case God must be held responsible for allowing this guilt to enter the world, since he could have stopped it from doing so without vitiating man's freedom. What I mean is merely this: Western humanism's high degree of embarrassed aversion to death[28] may well be very 'human'; to the extent that it encourages a certain sensitivity it may even be what is required of Christians as Christians here and now. But Christianity has not been issued with a straightforward and clear command to entertain this 'allergy' towards death at all times and in all places. If it is the case that Christianity in earlier times exhibited far less of this 'reverence for life' in home politics and war strategy, that the hectic Westerners who call themselves Christians in practice only act to a very limited extent in accordance with their theoretical death-allergy; and that wherever it wanted to seize the reins of power or actually succeeded in doing so, actual present-day Marxism calmly sacrificed, for the sake of the future, immense numbers of men, and not only in war, passively, but actively too, perhaps Christian, liberal and Marxist humanists ought to sit down and discuss soberly and honestly what value they *really* place on the death of the individual. Otherwise humanistic speeches about the dignity of human life will become degraded into propagandist party polemics. It is strange how quickly we acquire a good conscience when it is only our 'opponent' who must die. So the question is, what *precisely* is an honest *humanism's* attitude to death? But this is only mentioned here by the way.

But what is the *Christian* view of death, which is to be a co-determinant of a genuine humanism? In the first place death's plain, straightforward purpose is biologically to make room for more life, for other people. Not that this eliminates its questionable nature, as if it showed that the radical protest against death is unjustified. But initially it does make room for other people. And since it must be freely enacted by a person, death, even in its most primitive aspect as a biological phenomenon, has an inter-

[27] Details in K. Rahner, *Zur Theologie des Todes*, pp. 33 ff., 43 ff.

[28] cf. E. Waugh's well-known satire, *The Loved One*, for example; also P. Berger's investigations (e.g. *The Noise of Solemn Assemblies* [New York, 1961]).

communicative or 'political' character, i.e. it is possible for it to be a radical act of love towards the most remote neighbour. This is especially the case since in death one does not make room for this or that *particular* person, but for everyone.

However, in so far as humanism *is* actually and concretely *man himself* with his power freely to order the area of communal existence in his image and likeness, death, understood in this way and freely accepted, is also an act which relativises man's own concrete humanism; it liberates other men's future, which one constricts as long as one regards the whole sphere of history as occupied by oneself. If, therefore, the only genuine concrete humanism is the one which realises itself *by keeping itself open* to the open, unpreoccupied future of all men, death, the willingness to die, constitutes one of its internal factors. But if, as a future which man has to call into concrete existence, this open, unpreoccupied future only subsists in that absolute future which we call God, death and the will for this absolute future belong together. The man who dies *willingly*, i.e. letting perish what in experience he has possessed as his own (hence too his own humanism), and letting it perish without in the end protesting or denying its most inner and absolute validity, and without wishing to prescribe the way in which death is compatible with the absolute meaningfulness of the person; such a man simultaneously affirms God as the unprescribable absolute future, not created by him, *and* the right of other people to their own future. In other words he loves God and men in a radical act of accepting death. In this way the act of death becomes the radical act of the Christian *vis-à-vis* all humanism whatsoever: he relativises his own humanism and thus gives place to that of other men in a love which is selfless. So with regard to *humanism* too Christianity is in the right as the religion which faces the mystery of death.

In all this there are naturally many aspects of death which have not been made clear. But that is not our task at present.[29] Matters for further treatment would be the special quality of death as a result of human guilt,[30] death as the radical act of self-realisation on the part of a person in a state of radical suffering,[31] death as mystery,[32] death as participation in the death of Christ,[33] etc. Our only concern here has been to make it clear

[29] cf. the author's *Zur Theologie des Todes*; also K. Rahner, 'On Christian dying', *Theological Investigations* VII (London and New York, 1971), pp. 285–293.

[30] cf. note 27.

[31] cf. *Zur Theologie des Todes*, Part I; 'The passion and asceticism', *Theological Investigations* III (London and Baltimore, 1967), pp. 58–85.

[32] *Zur Theologie des Todes*, pp. 26 ff., 36 ff.

[33] Ibid., pp. 61 ff., 66 ff.

that, as the acceptance of the death of Christ and as the prognosis of one's own death, Christianity at the same time both calls in question each particular humanism by anticipating God's absolute future in faith and love, *and also*, precisely because of this, opens the way for the successively new humanisms of the future.

VI

Whereas until now Christianity as such has appeared above all to criticise the current humanism in favour of a future one, it must be emphasised more than ever that, although it has no clear, definite and concrete humanism of its own, Christianity does not give the Christian an excuse for being indifferent to a concrete humanism of the future. Naturally it was not until the most recent times that it became clear that the Christian has a duty towards a concrete future; then it was discovered that man – mankind – actually had the physical possibility of actively planning, shaping and directing the future – not merely individually, but collectively – by self-manipulation[34] and actively modelling his environment.[35] And at that moment the material unity of mankind from the point of view of its origin and absolute destiny (of which Christianity has always been aware) became a material unity within a concrete future which is to be actively created.[36]

Consequently mankind has both the ability and the duty actively to create this kind of forward-looking humanism. And the Christian *qua Christian* must make use of this permanently secular[37] opportunity. It is not possible at this point to define precisely how Christianity sees the relationship between a secular future which not only can be, but must be, created, and the absolute future which is God in himself.[38] But if we consider the Christian doctrine of the unity of the love of God and the love of one's neighbour,[39] which applies to the area of concrete human existence and not merely to the sphere of private intercommunication;

[34] cf. note 20.

[35] cf. J. B. Metz, 'Die Zukunft des Glaubens in einer hominisierten Welt', J. B. Metz/J. Splett (ed.), *Weltverständnis im Glauben* (Mainz, 1965), pp. 45–62.

[36] *Handbuch der Pastoraltheologie* II/1, pp. 191 ff., 237 ff., 259 ff.

[37] For an analysis of the process of secularisation cf. *Handbuch der Pastoraltheologie* II/1, pp. 222 ff., 234 ff., 267 ff.; II/2, pp. 35 ff., 208 ff., 239 ff. (literature), cf. also the essay 'Theological reflections on the phenomenon of secularisation', *Theological Investigations* X.

[38] Some remarks in the *Handbuch der Pastoraltheologie* II/1, pp. 33 f. The experiment with man, in this volume, pp. 219 ff.; *Theological Investigations* VI, pp. 59–68.

[39] cf. *Theological Investigations* VI, pp. 231–249.

if we bear it in mind that the real – not merely theoretical – act of opening oneself to God's absolute future can only be done by concretely anticipating the concrete future which is to be produced;[40] if we are clear that the emancipation of the secular world is not a process to which Christianity must of necessity become reconciled, but is itself an act of this very Christianity[41] arising from its understanding of God and the Incarnation of the Logos itself; then we are obliged to say that the creation of a humane future is not something optional for the Christian, but is the means by which he prepares himself, in actuality and not merely in theory, for God's absolute future.[42] If salvation itself – however much it must be accepted freely in a personal way – is a historically occurrent and a collective reality, i.e. a *unifying* thing and not highly individualistic, the actual mediation of this salvation cannot be solely a matter of the individual's inner life, but must itself be a historical and social quantity, service to one's 'neighbour', in whom all men are present.

Naturally the Christian knows that the love of his neighbour, of the other person, is only meaningful provided that this other person (and hence he himself too) has meaning and absolute significance. One cannot justify giving service to an empty and futile existence just because it is *someone else's* and not one's own. Therefore one can and must quite soberly take oneself seriously, in really loving the other person by service to him. But that does not alter the fact that it is only by loving other people that one enters into a right relationship with oneself. And if, in fact, it remains an eternally new question as to *what* it is that gives this other person a justified claim to be loved and recognised as important; if we cannot answer the question by referring to a creative love in the lover which *makes* the loved person worthy (for in this case the other person would be an invention of one's own); we must say that, for the Christian this embarrassment only constitutes the necessary spur to go on to grasp the mystery of God as the other person's true reality, rendering him worthy of love and revealing this love itself as incomprehensible. Thus it remains true that the other person's concrete future is the means towards the absolute future, which is one's own and everyone else's. The Kingdom of God only comes to those who build the coming earthly kingdom.

40 On the necessity of this truth which only reveals itself in action cf. also the more recent studies by J. B. Metz, *Verantwortung der Hoffnung* (Mainz, 1968).

41 cf. *Handbuch der Pastoraltheologie* II/1, pp. 234 ff.; II/2, pp. 239–267.

42 K. Rahner attempts to show that this perspective must be a part of the future Christian's piety: 'Christian living formerly and today', *Theological Investigations* VII (London and New York, 1971), pp. 3–24.

In doing this they use the continually new materials put at their disposal in succeeding ages which thus cause the plan itself to be changed continually. And the Christian knows no better than other men just what this concrete provision (created by man so that he may be ready for what *cannot* be created) looks like, what form it ought to take and how it is to be produced.[43] In this matter he is on the same level as everyone else. He is obliged both to enter into a dialogue with his fellow-builders of a common future, and also to involve himself in a struggle, for the concrete future, since it is not theoretically deducible, can only be decided and implemented as a result of a 'struggle' and even violence.[45, 46] In so far as for the Christian the provision of a concrete future is always situated within the incomprehensible absolute future, the Christian is precisely the one who knows least,[47] since he can only penetrate to the bottom of himself when he comes directly before his true foundation, the unfathomable God. All else remains preliminary. Hence, however, its absolute importance.

VII

In all this have we been talking about Christian humanism or the secular humanism of the Christian *qua* Christian? I do not know. But perhaps it will be permissible, all the same, to put a few questions to our non-Christian contemporaries who exist in such large numbers. Today the Christian lives among them, and in the future Christians will live everywhere as a *diaspora*.[48]

Must Christian and non-Christian humanists be enemies? I do not

[43] cf. 'Grenzen der Amtskirche', *Schriften zur Theologie* VI, pp. 499–520.

[44] On the necessity of this dialogue cf. the author's essay referred to in note 11 above.

[45] On this correct concept of power cf. *Theological Investigations* IV, pp. 391–409; on the essential concept of the 'area of freedom' cf. K. Rahner: M. Horkheimer, K. Rahner, C. F. von Weizsäcker, *Über die Freiheit* (Stuttgart,[2] 1965), pp. 35–44; also the remarks in K. Rahner, H. Maier, U. Mann, M. Schmaus, *Religionsfreiheit* (Munich, 1966), pp. 7–23. Cf. also the study on the subject of peace in this volume.

[46] What results from this is not a question of absolute non-violence but the limitation and the most humane form of violence. From this standpoint a more profound concept of 'peace' can be found, and a legitimate area can be discovered for a meaningful 'pacifism'. Cf. the studies in note 45.

[47] cf. J. B. Metz, *Gott vor uns. Statt eines theologischen Arguments: E. Bloch zu Ehren* (Frankfurt, 1965), pp. 227–241.

[48] cf. 'The Christian in his world', *Theological Investigations* VII (London and New York, 1971), pp. 88–99.

think so, provided that both sides realise that their obligations are to the future more than to the past. Must they be enemies because the concrete future which *one* wants to build is perhaps contrary to the plan of the other? But Christianity as such demands no *particular concrete* future and it is to be hoped that the non-Christian does not imagine he already has the future tucked away in his pocket like a complete five-year plan. This being the case, why should not they both plan together for the future which is unknown to both of them? Why not try together to come to a clearer awareness of those hoped-for aspects of the future which have as yet been anticipated only dimly – justice, freedom, dignity, unity and diversity in society? Does the Christian treat this future any less seriously than the non-Christian in seeing it as the means to God's absolute future? Or does not this very fact make the future as a matter of the highest seriousness *and* at the same time render it imperative to keep the future open to its further history? No doubt the Christian's secular humanism, in keeping itself open to God's absolute future, implies certain formal structures in this concrete, intramundane future too. But it also implies the provision of an area of freedom for the exercising of religious, and hence also of non-religious, decision,[49] since openness to the absolute future requires freedom for its realisation. Thus the non-Christian must be allowed an area of freedom to interpret himself in a non religious way. But why should not the non-Christian grant the same area of freedom to the Christian? In assuming that there *is* common ground for a dialogue between non-Christians and Christians,[50] we do not wish to say that there are no hard and fast differences and that all struggles and all historical decisions which involve the use of force could be avoided. Such a thing would be impossible even if the future were built solely by Christians.[51] For the collective, historical action which constitutes a particular future, even in the most moderate case, is not the result of pure theory but a *practice* which cannot be adequately deduced from theory. This practice always implies power and force as well, i.e. an alteration of the other person's historical situation even prior to his insight into it and free agreement to it.

[49] cf. E. W. Böckenförde, 'Religionsfreiheit als Aufgabe der Christen': J. B. Metz/J. Splett, *Weltverständnis im Glauben* (cf. note 35), pp. 298–314; in addition cf. note 45.

[50] At this point we must leave the question open as to how this dialogue is to be explained theologically in detail, since it is dangerous to see common ground *merely* in certain abstract propositions of so-called natural law.

[51] cf. the essay referred to in note 19 above.

However, if both sides could see this very issue in that clear-headed manner which is so foreign to the liberalistic approach; if they could admit it and mutually abide by it, it would be the most promising way of governing the form and scope of this abiding struggle so that everyone would always possess some tangible area of freedom with *tolerable* boundaries, and each side, having the courage to limit itself, would be positively concerned to guarantee the same measure of freedom for the other side. Not only because it is useful to have this guarantee when the other side has the upper hand, but because one's *own* principles demand it: because justice can only exist when the person in power used moderation; because one can only be a 'humane' human being by renouncing the desire to be absolute and by enduring the world's and man's pluralism however much one desires unity; because man's true victory is only won when the vanquished person remains as tomorrow's potential adversary, for otherwise the victor either discovers a new adversary among his own ranks or becomes stifled in that sterile, deathly particularism which no-one can shake off.

13

THE EXPERIMENT WITH MAN

Theological observations on man's self-manipulation

OUR topic here is man's self-manipulation today and tomorrow in so far as the question is also of theological relevance. It can legitimately be assumed that it *is* relevant because this self-manipulation is concerned with, or at least affects, man in his totality, and theology has to do with man's ultimate, total understanding of himself as a whole human being. I am aware that the frightening breadth and complexity of this theme are too much for me to deal with, especially as I have only a limited space at my disposal. Consequently I do not know whether, in the end, I shall have said anything really meaningful. But the main reason for my apprehension is this: in the first instance man's self-manipulation is a question for biology, sociology, medicine, pharmacology, psychology, technology and political science; for one can only raise the theological question when one knows what *can* be done – and how it can be done – in the field of self-manipulation. And for this knowledge one must turn to the specialists in these particular disciplines. So it seems at least. For one can only inquire *whether* (and according to *which* of the many possibilities) man ought to manipulate himself, provided that there is room left for such a question and that everything has not already been decided. Then, and only then, may the theologian too put in a word. And in doing so he must be quite sure that he has really comprehended and mastered the foregoing question and answer. Whether this is possible at all, however, is much more questionable than was thought, for instance, by those who drew up the so-called 'Scheme 13' of the Council. And it is no real consolation to have the impression that the representatives of these same disciplines are themselves insufficiently acquainted with the questions and results of their respective fields of study, and thus produce plans and utopias for human manipulation which are inadequate in the first place, in that they refer to man as a unity but do not really know him in his totality. In any case the theologian is in a grievous position. He is obliged to join in the discussion because it cannot be assumed that man's salvation is in principle independent of this self-manipulation, and the theologian's concern must be with the furtherance of man's salvation; and yet it is scarcely possible for him to speak at all.

Not only because, for him, man is turned into a question which he – precisely as theologian – must keep open to the infinite mystery, and thus he can never say in advance what concrete possibilities man himself, in the course of his history, will include in his formal theological outline of himself; but simply because the theologian – or rather let us say more cautiously, because *I* cannot flatter myself that I understand much of the perspectives, methods and results of those sciences which have taken the question of man, both in theory and in practice, to be a question of experiment with man himself. And yet it is precisely here that the theologian is supposed to make his contribution. Of course here we have struck a further problem, and one which we cannot deal with at all at this juncture, namely, the problem of the pluralism of sciences. Although they are concerned with one and the same human being, these sciences have grown to immeasurable proportions and can no longer be assimilated by any one individual. They constitute a pluralism which leaves the concrete human being more at a loss then ever, the more 'one knows' about man. It is a pluralism which will be overcome neither by modern computers, nor by scientific and specialist team projects, nor by an anonymous political organisation 'drawing all the threads of the sciences together'. So at least for the moment the theologian has no alternative but to try to say something, at quite a distance and in quite an abstract way, with reference to man's self-manipulation. And it must be, or will endeavour to be, something just plainly theological; the theologian will ask the theorists and practitioners of self-manipulation whether they may not find it of service in their own problems. Hence it is only a question of *rapprochement*, not a confrontation between the science and practice of self-manipulation on the one hand and theology on the other. So much by way of preliminary remarks.

I

1. *The new reality and the future of man's self-manipulation which has already begun.* Before turning our attention to actual theological propositions we must attempt in a few sentences to say what is meant by self-manipulation, that possibility of human activity which, however indirectly, is the subject of these observations.

Self-manipulation means that today man is changing *himself*. On the one hand, of course, there have always been quite small examples of the kind of active self-manipulation to which we refer. We shall have occasion to examine the theological and anthropological relevance of this simple fact. Man has purposely drunk wine to combat his melancholy; consciously used coffee as a stimulant; undertaken primitive attempts at human breeding; endeavoured to change his bodily form by means of various techniques, beginning with shaving; conceived the practice of education in terms of artificially superimposing knowledge instead of cultivating insight; attempted – even if in a clumsy way – to implement an institutionally controlled indoctrination, etc. And on the other hand this self-manipulation of man is still in its infancy, is still in many ways only a project, feeling its way, playing with vaguely apprehended possibilities; it is a scholars' utopia, created – with the scholar's characteristic ideological ruthlessness – by extrapolating whole systems for bringing happiness to mankind from mere initial items of knowledge. Most of it is still a dream or nightmare of the future and in reality no-one can say for certain whether it is even practicable, let alone whether it is desirable or morally justifiable. In any case, however, the situation is radically different from what it was. Man plans his own self; in much he is still groping his way, seeking the goals of his self-manipulation and only perceiving the possibility of realising them in the remote distance. But at the same time he has the feeling and actually experiences that the rate of his successes is increasing and that today's utopias can become tomorrow's commonplaces. Man is discovering that he is 'operable'.

This radically new period is approaching. It is approaching in all its dimensions. In spite of the many fluid boundaries which conceal the newness of this phenomenon from a naïve observer, it can be distinguished in many ways from the unreflected preliminary instances of self-manipulation which have occurred so far in human history. For it is multi-dimensional, its concern is with man as he is empirically experienced, not according to his spiritual and transcendental being as a free subject (later we shall have to deal in greater detail with what is meant here). It wishes to be consciously and methodically controlled according to genuine plans over a long period of time. Its concern is not with this or that *part* of man but with man as a totality; it wishes as a result of the new insights of all the anthropological sciences to penetrate to man's ultimate fabric in order to remodel it. It is not concerned with this or that man but with *man*, with mankind; it does not wish to conjure up a utopia of supermen within a profanised eschatology, but coolly to sketch, design and calculate a new, different man and then to produce him technologically in accordance with this plan. The concrete dimensions of this human production, the workshops of the factory of new human beings, merging into one another, are well known:

In the first place – to begin with that which is most external – there is the workshop of the hominisation of man's environment. Man no longer merely lives in an environment and cultivates it superficially, but actually creates it, looking at the given stuff of nature only as material for the environment which he intends to produce according to his own design. He is beginning to inhabit a world which he has shaped artificially; he manufactures synthetic products, erects 'machines for living' instead of houses; he makes use of atomic energy, which has been inaccessible until now and is not naturally available. Perhaps he will even extend his living space beyond the Earth, and no longer eat of the fruits of the earth but invent his own food. In all this man is already indirectly changing himself to a greater extent than he realises. In itself the active hominisation of the world is already a self-manipulation of man. He makes the Earth, and hence his own self, subject to him.

There is the workshop of biology, biochemistry and genetics. It is only just being constructed now, but at great speed; and already the biologists, overstepping the bounds of their theoretical science, are designing patterns for the biological self-manipulation of man; in the new laws on eugenics we can see them already becoming reality. We cannot describe these plans and possibilities in detail here: sterilisation laws for eugenic reasons to prevent the selection of negative hereditary factors; control of the birth-rate and the prevention of further population explosions by biochemical means; increasing the I.Q. level and the breeding of super-intelligences on a biological basis; the possibility of carrying out this breeding as a result of knowledge of DNA (desoxyribonucleic acid), thus penetrating to the innermost secret of heredity; knowledge of genetic codes; the setting up of insemination banks, making desirable stock available.

There is the workshop of medicine, pharmacology and, above all, psycho-pharmacology. Here man, clumsily botched together by nature, can be improved in an artificial environment and adjusted to the machines he himself has built. Here artificial kidneys and aortas are built, and transistors to regulate the heart-beat more effectively. Here men's spiritual, mental and moral problems are not made bearable and meaningful by appealing to his moral freedom, but his moral tensions are removed right from the start by drugs, morality is replaced wholly or largely by psycho-medical and psycho-pharmacological manipulation – which does the job much better – in so far as such action is still necessary for a man who has already been skilfully manipulated genetically.

Then there is the psychological workshop. But a psychology of the future, of course. Not like the churches of old, which – seen from a secular point of view – were psychological workshops where men were formed as free beings, after much wearying work of a piecemeal and dilettante kind, by an appeal to individual conscience. But a psychological workshop of the future, engaging in 'brainwashing' on a grand scale, fully acquainted with the use of the mass media, producing happiness and a feeling of well-being throughout the whole of man's body by means of electric brain-stimulation, and instilling into everyone an exemplary, socially desirable attitude by the modern psychological indoctrination which has no need of insight and freedom, so that the result is a frictionless society without any conflicts.

Then there is the sociological workshop. Here mankind's growth is calculated in advance, plans and laws are made to stabilise the earth's population at the desired level, exploiting fully the biological, genetic and medical possibilities available today or tomorrow. Here social medicine is organised; ways are found to match needs with resources, and to occupy man in his leisure time.

And finally we come to the innermost part of the factory: the political workshop. Here we find the World Government, in the hands of specially bred super-intelligences. Here the projects of the various workshops are co-ordinated, ultimate goals are established to which all the methods of treating man are to be orientated.

So far this factory for the new man does not exist. But it is as though buildings are being constructed simultaneously all over a great site, and one has the impression that these separate constructions will eventually grow into a single complex – into a hominised world. This is the one immense factory where 'operable' man dwells in order to invent himself.

2. *Theological comment*. What ought one to say as a theologian to all these states of affairs, possibilities, utopias, and dangers involved in man's self-manipulation? First of all two whole areas of discussion must be excluded for the purposes of this essay, although in themselves they are very important, namely questions of a *specialist and technical* nature, and the problems of *moral theology*.

(a) In the first place there are the specialist questions which must be answered by the relevant disciplines concerned with self-manipulation and which remain, for the time being, unanswered. For instance no-one really knows yet what the population explosion means as an issue affecting mankind. And yet this question is almost everywhere regarded as the point of departure for serious discussion of the utopia of man's self-manipulation. It is quite possible (no-one can deny it) that the growth of mankind may be governed by biological and psychological self-regulating systems, thus being kept to a tolerable level. Such self-regulating systems would obviate the need for manipulation in this area on the one hand, and on the other they would automatically be working towards a morality (for which man is subjectively responsible before God), so that the moral theologians would not need to be disturbed about the question either. It may well be that in spite of the amazing and rapid progress of biochemistry and genetics, a really practicable controlled human breeding, such as would alter man in depth and on a world-wide scale, is simply technically impossible. Nor does it look as though in the year 2000 or soon afterwards there will be a really effective World Government such as the prophets of man's producibility on a global scale require. So many questions are raised by the results of the relevant disciplines, so many problems arising concerning the long-term and secondary effects of the various procedures made possible by progress, that really practical and realisable planning is still largely impossible. These and similar questions must be excluded here, although they are to a large extent the preconditions for a theological approach, because they exceed the theologian's competence.

(b) The second question which must be passed over here is the moral theological question, although it is of great concern as a question of theology. I.e. the direct question as to what is permissible or even morally obligatory with respect to these possibilities and methods of self-manipulation in its various dimensions, and what is not permitted and why. At this point, of course, a thousand questions raise their heads: from the moral evaluation of a kidney transplant, the contraceptive pill, to the state control of fertility, the attempts to manipulate technically man's hereditary material, and all the other problems of social sexual morality which arise from these possibilities. So here we shall pass over the practical moral casuistry of man's self-manipulation, even if in what follows we cannot avoid referring to the hermeneutical framework for the treatment of such problems.

II

1. *Christian cool-headedness in the face of man's future.* Man is fundamentally 'operable' and legitimately so. If this proposition, which we shall elucidate directly, is assumed, the first thing which the theologian must

say to himself, to Christians and to the Church is that one is not to take fright at this self-manipulation of man. Of course possibilities of self-manipulation are becoming apparent today which are immoral and unworthy of man, and which may indicate a 'Fall' on the part of society. And we shall refer to the Christian's and the Church's duty to have the courage to oppose with utter resoluteness those kinds of self-manipulation which are the most recent forms of barbarity, slavery, the totalitarian annihilation of personality and formation of a monochrome society.

But it would only be symptomatic of a cowardly and comfortable conservatism hiding behind misunderstood Christian ideals and maxims if at the outset one were to simply condemn the approaching age of self-manipulation as such; to break out into lyrical laments on the theme of degrading barbarity, the cold, technological rationalism, the destruction of what is 'natural', the rationalisation of love, the heathenist lack of understanding in the face of illness, suffering, death, poverty, the levelled-down mass society, the end of history in a faceless fellahin society without a history, etc. Although we are unable to produce a concrete picture of the life of society and mankind in the year 2000, although we must take radical catastrophes and threats to man's existence into account, against which a Christian will have to fight with the greatest determination, tomorrow's world will be different from that of today. And in this coming world man will be the one who, both as an individual and as a society, plans, controls and manipulates himself to a degree which was previously both undreamed-of and impracticable. He *must* do so; he can do no other if he wishes to exist on the Earth side by side with many thousand millions of other human beings. He must *want* to be 'operable' man, even though the extent and the right way of carrying out this self-manipulation are still largely obscure, and although it is apparent that the Anglo-Saxon and Communist prophets of this future self-manipulation are themselves able to give only very vague details of this future. For whether one proclaims, with Huxley, that man's goal and future is pure 'fulfilment and self-expression', or says, with Elisabeth Mann Borghese, that at least everyone will have time to devote himself to what is true, good and beautiful; or whether one exalts the classless society where abilities, achievements and needs all finally coincide and where a common peace reigns in equality, freedom from illness, self-alienation and oppression – all these aims are highly abstract, imprecise and *uninspiring* too.

But it is true: the future of man's self-manipulation has begun. And the Christian has no reason to enter this future as a hell on Earth nor as an earthly Kingdom of God. Jubilation or lamentation would both run counter to the Christian's cool-headedness. For the Christian, both he himself and his world always remain (as long as history lasts) a world of creation, of sin, of the promise of judgment and blessing, in a unity which he himself can never dissolve.

2. *Self-determination as the nature and task of man's freedom as understood by Christianity.* According to Christian anthropology man really is the being who manipulates himself. Naturally, on account of the genuine historicity of his being and of his apprehension of truth, this fact has entered even into the Christian's awareness of faith in a quite new and penetrating way. But this fact, to which he is called at this present time and which confronts him as something new, can be recognised and accepted by him all the same as his very own, as the truth of old which has always been his and which gives itself to him anew in this form – if he accepts it.

According to a Christian understanding, man, as the being who is free in relation to God, is in a most radical way empowered to do what he wills with himself, freely able to align himself towards his own ultimate goal. He is able so to determine and dispose of himself that two absolutely different final destinations become possible: man in absolute salvation and man in the absolute loss of salvation. For what happens to a man in death and judgment (to use the language of the Catechism) is not an external gratuitous action upon him, a reaction to his previous dealings, but the manifestation of the naked reality of his own ultimate goal, with which he has identified himself. It is certainly the case that this absolutely inescapable transcendental self-determination occurs in dialogue with or against God; certainly its precondition is what we know as free creation and free grace; it is assuredly a freedom which knows itself to be continually exposed to the intractable nature of its situation, and thus knows that in all its activity it is also unavoidably passive. But this does not alter the fact – which is a commonplace to the Christian – that freedom is the power to determine oneself to an absolutely irreversible final state, that what a man will be for all eternity is what he has made himself. Man is the one whose freedom is laid upon him as a burden; this freedom is creative and what it creates is man himself in his final state, so that the beginning of this history of man's divinely appointed freedom – man's 'essence' as we say – is not an intangible something, essentially permanent and complete, but the commission and power which enable him to be free to determine himself to his ultimate final state.

In a correctly developed ontology of the subject and his dealings, as opposed to the 'thing' and its 'activity' (which unfortunately is taken for the most part as a model for the 'activity' of the genuine subject), it could be made plainer that in an anthropology based on a really Christian philosophy, a man's free action – which, in affecting the world, determines himself too – must not be imagined as an external epiphenomenon sustained on the surface of a substantial essence which itself remains untouched, but becomes part of the innermost determination of this essence itself. In contradistinction to 'things' which are always complete and which are moved from one mode of completion to another and thus are at the same time always in a final state and yet never ultimate, man begins his existence as the being who is radically open and incomplete. When his essence *is* complete it is as he himself has freely created it.

3. *Self-manipulation as a new manifestation in our time of man's essential freedom.* What is new in this issue is therefore not that man is *faber sui ipsius*, but that this fundamental constitution of man is manifested historically today in a totally new way. Today for the first time man's possibility of transcendental self-manipulation irreversibly takes on a clear and historically categorical form. I.e. until now man's genuine, radical self-manipulation (which is a constant factor, creating eternity) was operative almost exclusively in the field of contemplative metaphysical knowledge, knowledge in faith and moral action in reference to God. Therefore as soon as it arose, it disappeared, so to speak, into the mystery of God. This was all the more the case since the categorical and tangible aspect of this contemplation and moral practice (which was naturally always present) is constantly equivocal: it can be either genuine free action or the mere product of intramundane material causality. As mere equivocal objectifications they are therefore incapable of furnishing man automatically with a clear view of his own free self-manipulation. Now, however, man's transcendental self-manipulation has been clearly manifested, even if from the theological point of view it remains ultimately ambivalent.

No longer does man create himself merely as a moral and theoretical being under God, but as an earthly, corporeal and historical being. Passive biological evolution is being extended, at least to an initial degree, by an active evolution of civilisation. But the latter is not only external and supplementary: it is actually continuing its own biological evolution. This self-manipulation is not only carried out unconsciously, as was the case almost exclusively in the past, but deliberately planned, programmed and controlled. Man no longer makes himself merely with reference to eternity but with reference to history itself as such.

In this way, however, what he has always been now comes to light.

What he has always been at the root of his transcendental spiritual and intellectual essence as a free being now extends its influence to his psyche and his physical and social existence, and is made manifest expressly in these dimensions. To a certain degree his ultimate essence has broken through to the outer regions of his existence. To a larger, more comprehensive, radical and tangible extent man has become what, according to the Christian understanding, he *is*: the free being who has been handed over to himself.

Here we have not space to show how this modern man not only *corresponds* to Christianity's fundamental understanding of man but also how the historical breakthrough from theory to practice, from self-awareness to self-actualisation was essentially a *product* of Christianity, however much many Christians opposed this emancipating movement of history. For this possibility, which has arisen from modern rationality, science and technology, has grown historically because according to Christianity the world and nature are not something intangible, numinous and brooding in which man humbly experiences himself as hidden, but something finite, non-numinous and created; as a real partner of the God of the 'other world' man can and must stand over against *this* world as its lord.

4. *The question of the normative essence, the 'nature' of man.* It will be immediately apparent from what has been said that, as a result of this material and categorial self-manipulation – which has now become possible and which in the future will embrace a wide range of possibilities – theology is faced anew with the question of man's essence. For according to Christian theology man in his freedom can act contrary to his nature in an absurd and self-contradictory way. Ontologically and existentially this latter possibility is not of the same order, nor is it radically possible to the same extent, as action which *is* consonant with man's nature (a fact which must never be forgotten), but it *is* possible: the ambivalence of moral freedom in its potential for good or ill is reproduced in the categorial self-manipulation of man, even though it is not reproduced univocally and homogeneously (which needs to be considered in much greater depth) but only reflects this radical ambivalence in a partial and inconclusive manner. Consequently in the dimension of categorial self-manipulation the good is never as 'good' and the evil is never as radically evil as in the dimension of fundamental transcendental freedom.

But since a Catholic and Christian anthropology, on account of the *whole* man's unity and vocation to salvation, can never accept an absolute separation of the ethics of man's inner disposition from the ethics of his external actions and practical norms, the question arises as to *which* 'nature' of man must be the guide for man's categorial self-manipulation, lest he be put in a situation of radical, destructive self-contradiction. Although this question could never have been simply nonexistent, it was never put before men and Christians so clearly and urgently and in such a pointed manner prior to this historical age of self-manipulation.

This question arises from an apparent dilemma: if the 'essence' of man is taken in a purely transcendental and theological sense to be the personal spirit which, in freedom and radical self-possession, is confronted with the absolute mystery of God (as the One Who communicates Himself in love), and if this essence were *nothing else*, it seems initially at least as though – in the biological, physical, social and institutional dimensions – man's categorial self-manipulation would be unable to come into really serious conflict with his nature, or at most only in peripheral areas. For all practical considerations categorial self-manipulation would be thus irrelevant to the ethical and religious field. However, if one regards the nature of man as being everything which is on the one hand empirically observable and on the other hand not shown to be 'nonessential' as a result of the biological, psychological and other changes which happen to man apart from his reflex self-manipulation, man's categorial self-manipulation would have no morally legitimate object. At most it could gently reinforce the unmanipulated changes of 'nature'; it could not set itself any aims concerning the formation of man which had not already been set by 'nature' without man's assistance. But in this case the fundamental legitimacy of this categorial self-manipulation would itself be called in question and, in fact, denied. And that again is not admissible, if we understand it as a manifestation of that transcendental self-manipulation which – be it noted – has several very radically differing possibilities at its disposal, even in the area of what is morally good.

Formulating the dilemma here in such an abstract way was unavoidable. Ultimately, of course, it can only be an *apparent* dilemma, although it seems to call in question either the nature of man and the knowledge of this nature, or man's categorial self-manipulation, conceived as a fundamental possibility and task. (However, one has only to consider the well-known – too well-known – problem of biochemical birth-control for instance, to see clearly what is meant. We cannot enter into this special issue here, but however it ought to be dealt with in principle, there can be no doubt that in recent decades traditional text-book moral theology has often used a concept of 'nature' ('natural', 'according to nature') which ignores the fact that, although man has an essential nature which he must respect in all his dealings, man himself is a being who forms and moulds his own nature through culture, i.e. in this case through self-manipulation, and he may not simply presuppose his nature as a categorial, fixed quantity.)

In any case, as a result of man's categorial self-manipulation, today's theology has been presented with the pressing task of finding out just what this nature of man is which forms the horizon and limitations even of self-manipulation. Difficult and painful changes may be expected in this area. For in questions of concrete morality people have often spoken with reference to a condition of man which, though currently existent, was not of his essence; which, though stable until recently, has now been drawn into the changes involved in man's controlling of himself. Too often it has been said, for instance: this or that is contrary to the nature of private property, of money; contrary to the 'nature' of woman, the nature of the family; contrary to the natural function of a biological organ, etc., whereas in reality it was a question of a variable and relative quantity *within* man's constant nature.

We cannot devote any more space here to this complex question of the nature of man which lies at the bottom of the metaphysical and moral natural law, how it appears in a historically conditioned concrete form and yet can be recognised for what it is, how the possibility of knowledge of metaphysical essence is compatible with an inescapable historical conditioning of this knowledge, and how the theoretical and operative knowledge of man's essence form a fundamental and yet variable unity. We are only concerned with ascertaining what problems theology is presented with as a result of categorial self-manipulation. But in this connection we may make one further observation: nowadays the moralist often says (and practically speaking he is thoroughly justified in doing so) that a situation has now arisen in which man must learn that he *must* not and *ought* not to do everything he *is able* to do. At the same time the hard-headed sceptic will generally retort that on the whole one cannot expect man to *stop* doing what he *can* do, and that since man can do infinitely more than heretofore, what he does will be immeasurably more terrible and destructive. However correct these observations of the moralist and the pessimistic sceptic may be, two things must be added.

In the first place, if the radical ontological difference between good and evil is understood, i.e. if it is comprehended that evil is ultimately the absurdity of desiring what is impossible (because it has neither being nor meaning), then in the last analysis there is nothing which man is really able to do and yet *may not* do; and conversely, what he really *can* do, he *ought* to do without hesitation. The moralist who is really close to life, therefore, would have to show modern man that, wherever he ought not to act, it is ultimately pointless, even today, to do so (i.e. in a categorial and intramundane sense too).

Secondly, because man's creaturely and finite freedom is co-determined by that which it presupposes, which exerts its influence particularly in this very categorial area of freedom (and hence of self-manipulation), biological, psychological and sociological laws can be apprehended and accepted which, without vitiating the freedom of self-manipulation, act to a certain extent like regulating systems and in the long run and on the whole stop this self-manipulation from going off the path into an absurdity contrary to man's essence. As a few crude examples: every lie gradually reduces itself *ad absurdum*; where there are few children they become all of a sudden interesting and desirable again; the man who is too concerned with his own health becomes ill; when something new, which was fiercely striven for, is attained, it loses its impetus, becomes of necessity old and thus slowly abolishes itself; it is not only lemmings who jump into the sea when they become too numerous.

This is by no means an excuse for *laissez faire* and it gives no guarantee against a catastrophe, but it does constitute a consolation and an exhortation not to be too anxious. Apparently the 'essence' varies around a constant, innermost centre. And the *whole* essence consists of this centre together with the essential variations and aberrations and the attempts to express this constant essence in a new way. This applies to self-manipulation too. Especially since in this case, wherever the moralist believes he has located 'objective' self-manipulation running counter to man's essence and must combat it, he must be continually aware that it is only 'objectively' so; often and to a large extent – according to his own basic conviction – such instances, on a social and not merely individual scale, do not imply a genuine subjective state of sin before God. Objectively they belong to the same category as those instances where subhuman, 'innocent' nature permits itself to produce monstrous, aberrant things leading into biological and other culs-de-sac. Even aberrant categorial self-manipulation, seeming to spring from a really transcendental freedom *vis-à-vis* God, can be an ultimately harmless experiment on the part of nature, experimenting and slowly trying to bring forth what the genuine future holds in promise. This may be the case even where it seems as though it is only using man's intelligence and freedom for its own purposes, exercising its own essence and not man's free essence as such.

5. *The seriousness of irreversible historical decisions.* Having said all this we must not minimise the importance of the historical process involved in the initiation of man's self-manipulation. We are warned against this by a particular theological topic of Christian anthropology, which has probably never before been taken into account in this context, namely, the dogma of Original Sin. We cannot give a full account here of its actual content, but we merely draw attention to one of its particular principal aspects which is of significance in interpreting theologically the coming large-scale manipulation of mankind. The 'Fall' was actually the first act of self-manipulation by mankind, even if its context was essentially the dimension of religious, transcendental self-determination before God, and even if we leave open the question as to how far it had categorially tangible consequences, delivering man up not only to his own nature alone, which could conceivably be guiltless. But in this case of self-manipulation *sui generis* there is one thing which is an indubitable element of the dogma: the act had irreversible consequences, it inaugurated a process and mankind cannot get back beyond the beginning of that process. All future human history is ineradicably determined by this situation of guilt so long as history itself lasts. Although redemption embraces this fact of human history and ultimately sets its mark upon it, it does not abolish it.

In turn this implies the principle that even at the stage of self-manipulation mankind continues on its one-way, irreversible historical course. Where a collective self-manipulation on the part of the totality of mankind is concerned, it is at least in principle the case that an about-turn is simply no longer possible, even if the way is kept open to the most diverse future possibilities. For people unconsciously connect the idea of self-manipulation with the notion that it can do anything whatsoever *and can continue to do anything*; that every false manipulation can be rectified, at least in succeeding generations (and the self-manipulation ideologists are very little concerned for the individual living at any one time; he is only treated as material to be expended for the sake of the more distant future). However, the dogma of Original Sin warns us against this illusion; history will remain a one-way process in the future too; it will continue under the law incurred by its guilty beginning, involving death, futility, contradiction and suffering (however much the *forms* of the latter may change), such that no self-manipulation on the part of mankind can abolish this law. (Yet the Church and theologians must beware of thinking that they already know precisely what concrete forms this irreversible beginning will assume in the future; they must beware of prophesying that the poor, wars, TB, the class struggles, etc., will be perpetuated in their classical forms for all time.) Furthermore it may be that the projected large-scale manipulation of mankind will have irreversible and irreparable consequences which no further self-manipulation will be able to change. Such conceivable irreversible consequences cannot reverse the definitive victory, through Christ, of God's self-communicating dealings with mankind. But neither does this mean that mankind can experiment upon itself freely without fear of irreparable consequences. So long as mankind exists with its vocation to salvation, history (including the history of man taking himself in his own hands) remains a one-way street. Man's self-manipulation must not be thought of according to the model of a limited laboratory experiment where, for the most part, isolated processes can be performed and reversed at will.

6. *Planning the future and the absolute future of man.* Christianity is the religion of the absolute future. However, at the same time it stands in a quite definite and unique relation to the categorial self-manipulation of man and mankind. It is very difficult to define the highly differentiated relationship between anticipating the absolute, eschatologically occurring future in faith and theological hope on the one hand, and anticipating the intramundane future by means of planning and active self-manipulation on the other hand. So far this particular chapter of a Christian theology of history and the world has been almost totally neglected; consequently it is impossible here to give an account of it and thus provide a theological context within which man's active self-manipulation can be really theologically understood. At this point we can only make a few modest observations. We say that Christianity is the religion of the absolute future to the extent in the first place that God is not only 'above us' as the ground and horizon of history, but 'in front of us' as our own future, our destination, sustaining history as its future. For Christianity acknowledges the absolute, infinite God who is superior to the world, a radical and infinite mystery, as the God who in free grace communicates himself in his absolute mystery as its innermost principle and ultimate future, who sustains and drives history as his genuinely most intimate concern, not only distinguishing himself from it as its creator.

Secondly we say that man's ultimate design for the future, which God has destined for him and authorised, does not aim at what can be planned and executed out of the multiple possibilities of the plural world, but has already overtaken all such intramundane designs for the future, criticising them and unmasking them in their appearance of absoluteness, and thus (as we shall see) *confirming* them.

All human planning, every active human self-realisation involving the manipulation of a plurality of factors, is embraced by the fact (which can be neither planned nor manipulated) of the infinite mystery manifesting itself to us as love, which we experience and call God. Man is not only concerned with what he can *do* in the future; he experiences something which is not 'done' at all, but which is his destiny, the infinity of absolute reality, which is love. According to Christianity's experience of absolute future in Jesus Christ, the arrival of this future occurs essentially in the act of death. It occurs in this way and in no other; life is not thereby devalued, because in order to be able to die one must genuinely have lived life. But one only reaches the absolute future by way of death's zero hour, not because the former is death's gift, not because it could be calculated to be impossible in any other way, but because, beyond all deduction, absolute love was pleased to triumph in its greatest defeat.

If now this absolute future, confessed in hope by Christianity and to which the Christian, in planning his existence, opens himself, is related to the design for the future which is manifested and executed in the self-manipulation of mankind today (and it does not make any difference whether it is in a Western or Eastern form, in an explicit collectivism or one which is in practice so), the following brief remarks at least may be made:

7. *Shaping the future as a Christian task*. In the first place man's active intramundane self-planning in self-manipulation has fundamentally a positive relationship to man's openness to the absolute future in faith and hope. However 'secular' man's active self-manipulation is and remains (i.e. not positively deducible from the Christian design for existence as it is expressed in its ecclesial and verbal form), yet it must not be understood as an 'interim activity' (which, when pursued morally, receives a heavenly reward) lasting until the absolute future, the 'Kingdom of God' finally arrives in God's self-communication. But in its irreducible positive and negative duality it constitutes the necessary medium and historical form by which man is to embrace that 'openness' which is both active and passive, forming the precondition for the arrival of the absolute future.

Basically Christianity has always known and proclaimed this in teaching that, *inter alia*, the love of one's neighbour is the form and medium of the love of God and that this love must really be action and not ideology or the mere inclination of the affections. Only it must be borne in mind that, as a necessary medium for the love of God (and not merely as a secondary by-product of it), this active intercommunication can no longer be realised merely in the private interpersonal sphere involving each man and his 'neighbour'. Even if a person rejects a 'collectivism' in the pejorative sense of the word, he cannot and must not overlook the fact that mankind today must of necessity realise higher levels and forms of social existence (and has actually already begun to do so) if each person is to really and truly affirm every other person's existence. Mankind is beginning to enter upon a post-individualistic phase of its history. This new phase brings with it new changes and dangers to the genuine, unique personality and dignity of the individual. It must not annihilate this individuality, but actually provide it with a greater area of genuine freedom.

This means, however, that loving intercommunication itself takes on a new form; now it can and must be also a servant of the new forms of man's social existence, a servant of humanity. For now 'humanity' no longer exists merely as an idea, as an ideology, but begins to exist as a concrete reality. If 'society' is a reality in a quite new way, if it is slowly and inevitably reconstructing itself on quite new lines, it can be in a totally new way a partner in this task of loving one's fellows, which is the form and medium of that love in hope and faith through which the absolute future 'arrives'. Understood in this way, however, the love of others must *will* and *co-operate* in these higher achievements of society and humanity *as they are and must be in today's particular form*: i.e. mankind's self-manipulation with a view to the future.

Of course, the love of one's neighbour itself cannot provide the material principle from which to conclude the concrete aim and methods of this intramundane self-manipulation of mankind. The aim and methods remain secular, like the bread which in earlier times was given in love to the poor man lest he should starve. Nevertheless, mankind's active self-manipulation today and tomorrow can and must be the concrete, active expression of the love of one's fellows, making possible the 'openness' to God's absolute future, even if it cannot itself bring about this absolute future. As the religion of the absolute future, Christianity is and must be the religion which sends man into the world to act.

8. *Death as the permanent door to the absolute future*. At the same time, however, Christianity warns self-manipulating man that, in his movement towards the God who is in front of him, he is obliged to pass through death's zero hour. It is strange how little man's death and the death of history is talked about today in the customary future utopias. Death is pushed to one side; what is talked about is a kind of super welfare state with little work, a great deal of automation, the elimination

of illness, long life, complete equality of the sexes – their differences having been almost smoothed out; a society in which all internal and external conflicts have been eradicated by genetic and pharmacological manipulation and social training, where the altruistic instincts of insect-like state-builders are formed, where history, steered by a few wise men, has been actually brought to a standstill in a high-level euphoric fellahin existence. One has the impression that it could be a horribly boring existence: the ash of unchallenged equality and security, spread homogeneously over the fire of life, could either smother the fire or else have the effect of making it suddenly burst out at some point as a mass madness trying to break out of a deathly equality and security. Death and the readiness to die, which is what keeps life 'alive' in this aeon, and which alone is the door of eternal life, is being pushed to one side.

We have already emphasised the fact that the concrete forms of death, futility, suffering and pain do not authorise a conservative defence of the particular forms of death and conflict which currently set their mark on man's situation. Especially since this kind of pseudo-Christian defence, which was and is all too common, is mostly put forward by those who have to suffer least in this regard. There is naturally little point in the rich man extolling the blessings of poverty and the person in power in society praising the value of humility. It remains true, however, that self-manipulation and all its concrete and utopian aims are constantly subject to the law of death – which can be neither disposed of nor manipulated. And this experience of death (in this comprehensive sense) arises from the experience of self-manipulation itself. For every plan, every pre-set and pre-calculated system gives rise to new elements which were *not* planned and *not* scheduled, because it is constructed of pre-existing elements which can never be adequately penetrated and categorised. By definition, an absolute and absolutely transparent system, functioning without friction, could only be constructed by another one standing outside it; even a machine capable of learning and adapting itself can only do this within a finite area, so long as it is not identical with the universe.

And so long as man is a being of absolute transcendence, he observes all this in terror; he can only 'alter' it by anticipating it in a formal and empty manner in the world of theory. In actual practice he cannot alter it, however much of a concretely practicable nature may still lie ahead of him as an intramundane future which *can* be manipulated. He sees his limitation; namely, those things which *cannot* be manipulated, and death, *his* death, rising up out of the very midst of the things which *can* be manipulated. And he will always be asking whether this unfathomable thing which surrounds him is the void of absolute absurdity or the infinitude of the mystery of love, the absolute future which is reached through death, so that only by accepting it can man really discover and 'invent' himself. (This is always possible, even where categorial self-manipulation is in its infancy, and it remains the highest priority even where the latter has made the kind of progress which is inconceivable at present.)

This death is not only the zero hour through which the individual must pass on his way to the absolute future, but also the zero hour for mankind as a whole. If we like, we can demythologise the end of all history as proclaimed by Christianity. No stars need fall from heaven: it can be the end as a result of genocide; it can be a social end (as a result of atom bombs, for instance); a physical end in a world catastrophe; it could be (who can know for sure? – the Christian must take even absurdity into account) that mankind might actually regress biologically to the level of a technically intelligent and self-domesticated aboriginal herd or an insect-state without the pain of transcendence, history and the dialogue with God. I.e. it might extinguish itself by collective suicide, even if it were to continue to exist at the biological level. A Christian theology of history basically need not take fright at such an idea in itself (any more than at the idea of individual suicide or self-induced stultification), for it knows that the history of men always ultimately arrives at God, whether in salvation or judgment, or else it simply ceases to be the history of spiritual persons at all.

Man exists in an immediate relationship with God only by moving towards the future in front of him, but consequently he exists in this way *always*, at every moment of his individual and collective history. And this immediacy is always mediated by death, which keeps history alive for as long as there are men. For this reason too the celebration of the death of the Lord is the solemn anticipation of the arrival of the absolute future, and cannot be replaced by any festive proclamation concerning man's self-manipulation.

III

We must necessarily break off these fragmentary theological observations on man's approaching self-manipulation, well aware that the greater part has been left unsaid. The theologian himself ought really to say much more, quite apart from appropriate self-criticism on the part of the theorists and engineers of the self-manipulation of mankind in their own sphere. For instance the theologian ought to say more clearly why and how the most radical self-manipulation of man takes place either ontologically (and hence ethically) within a fundamental horizon, neither appointed by nor subject to man, or else it eliminates man as a denizen of history.

It ought to be made clearer that, having made this *a priori* Christian distinction, we do not know, nor can we predict, what concrete possibilities are in store for this self-manipulation. One ought to go on to consider the limitations of the official Church and its proclamation with particular reference to the giving of directions and advice for this self-manipulation, which as such always remains an adventure into the unforeseeable. One ought to complain that (as opposed to the official Church, which as such has no task here) Christians contribute so little courage and creative imagination to an ideology of the future for this self-manipulation, but are generally content to provide conservative admonitions and obstructions.

One ought soberly and courageously to consider, according to a supra-individual morality, what sacrifices could be expected of humanity today on behalf of humanity tomorrow, *without* being too quick to speak of immoral cruelty, of the violation and exploitation of the dignity of man today for the benefit of man tomorrow. Indeed one could ask whether the Church as such and ecclesially trained Christians have not been set the task (to be accepted in all humility) of playing a particular part in this future course of mankind; namely, a role which implies that *their* God (the God of history), who is always bigger than His Church, has entrusted a large part of history *not* to Christians but to others, who, in a more anonymous way, are all the same the executors of that history which is guided by God alone, ultimately opening out into His own eternal life.

These and other theological questions could be discussed in the face of mankind's self-manipulation, which has already begun. They would doubtless all come together in the simple experience that man really does *make* history (and thus himself) and that in this very activity he is not his own, but belongs to the mystery of love.

14

THE PROBLEM OF GENETIC MANIPULATION

WHENEVER a theologian is asked to state his position as regards the genetic manipulation of man he finds himself in a desperate situation. He is to give a moral evaluation of a particular phenomenon, but this evaluation refers to a completely new and previously nonexistent reality. In earlier times, by and large, the theologian himself had direct access to the matter he was to analyse from the moral point of view. Today man, in his scientific rationality, technology and self-manipulation,[1] is creating new realities, a second-order world, which is not immediately open to the individual unless he is actually a specialist in this field, a world with which he is really only acquainted in a rudimentary and second-hand manner. And it is in such matters as these that the theologian – himself a mere uninitiated layman in the field – is asked for guidance about their relation to humanity, morality and religion. How could the theologian avoid being in a desperate plight?

It would be wrong to attempt to smooth over these difficulties by saying that, as far as a *moral* evaluation of a particular issue is concerned, anyone (i.e. the theologian too) can still easily acquire as much knowledge as is necessary provided that he gets hold of genuinely specialist data. It is at least possible that the very 'detail' of which the theologian is ignorant, or of which he has only a vague notion, might be the decisive factor in his case; it might be the very detail which would alter the whole

[1] cf. on this concept K. Rahner, 'Experiment Mensch. Theologisches über die Selbstmanipulation des Menschen', *Die Frage nach dem Menschen. Aufriß einer philosophischen Anthropologie. Festschrift für Max Müller*, ed. H. Rombach (Freiburg, 1966) (This is the preceding article in the present volume.) Cf. also note 7 below.

This essay was originally intended for a symposium, which precluded the discussion of specialist issues of science or biology. For this reason there is also no reference to further literature. The literature mentioned in the notes is not intended to summarise theological research in this field up to the present time, but only to refer to the author's fuller remarks elsewhere on issues which could only lightly be touched upon here.

conclusion.[2] And even if the theologian takes care to keep himself informed, can he be sufficiently sure that he knows all he needs to know in order to be able to engage in discussion? Can he acquire an adequate view of the preconditions, possibilities (or practical impossibilities) and methods of real genetic manipulation of mankind in the immediate or distant future? Is it enough for him to rest assured in the conviction that he has formed his judgment in all conscience as best he can according to the present stage of scientific knowledge,[3] if it is obvious all the time that such a judgment is provisional, alterable by some further item of knowledge in the future? There is small comfort in this, if on occasion, as a result of such a provisional judgment, decisions and actions are taken which *cannot* (unlike the moral theological dictum pronounced in good faith by the naïve theologian) be subsequently reversed.

It remains true, therefore, that whatever is said falls within the proviso incurred by the theologian's predicament. We shall have to leave it to the actual process of investigation itself to reveal whether the theologian can perhaps come to grips with his situation in some other way, thereby arriving at a conclusion which he could resolutely stand by.

First of all, however, we must try to find some footholds in our problem; we must endeavour to find a way in to the issue in question. In the first instance we shall turn naturally to traditional moral theology, traversing its scope in order to gain some estimate of the peculiar character and the relative novelty and difficulty of our theme. The non-theological reader is asked to be patient, therefore, throughout the first sections. The following remarks are necessary in order to introduce the question in a theologically correct manner, to avoid the mistake of considering the problem quite apart from all tradition. In any case, to approach the central problem gradually by experimental means also helps

[2] A small example: for a few centuries Catholic moral theology has been convinced that the moment of union of the male and female germ cells is also the moment when an individual human being comes into existence. Will today's moral theologian still have the courage to maintain this presupposition as the basis of many of his moral theological statements, when faced with the knowledge that 50 per cent of all fertilised female cells never succeed in becoming attached to the womb? Will he be able to accept that 50 per cent of all 'human beings' – real human beings with 'immortal' souls and an eternal destiny – will never get beyond this first stage of human existence? In this particular case he can gain further knowledge and await developments; but what is he to do in other cases, where he merely suspects that neither he nor anyone else knows enough, and yet an answer must be given?

[3] For further information see the considerable material in P. Overhage's *Experiment Menschheit. Steuerung der menschlichen Evolution* (Frankfurt, 1967). The present author was not able to examine this book before writing this essay.

one to lay hold more accurately on the particular ethical theme we have in view.

I

In the face of the question of a 'genetic self-manipulation' of man, moral theology is immediately placed in an exceedingly embarrassing situation. At least *Catholic* moral theology, as opposed to that of Protestant theology,[4] will not be of the opinion, on the one hand, that the question can be directly answered from Holy Scripture, nor will it thereby assume from the outset that the actual decision in a case such as this must simply be left to the conscience of the individual. But if Catholic moral theology is looking for a fundamental, *material* solution, without being too quick to avoid the issue by means of 'situation ethics', it will encounter very considerable difficulties which may perhaps oblige us to rethink quite general problems of morality.[5]

It is impossible simply to dismiss the thought of man's 'genetic manipulation' as an unethical project. As far as a Christian understanding of mankind is concerned, man is not simply the product of 'nature', as if nature *alone* were able and authorised to determine and model man's being. Man is not only the being who is commissioned by God to further God's work of creation, the being who both may and must 'subdue the earth', i.e. his environment. Rather man is characteristically the being who has been handed over to himself, consigned to his own free responsibility.[6] In this sense he *must* 'manipulate' himself.[7] Freedom is the

[4] We cannot enter into a discussion of the attitude of the Christian churches and theologians. Practically all the Protestant churches (at least in Europe) reject genetic manipulation in the sense of heterologous artificial insemination and the arbitrary control or alteration of hereditary material.

[5] We need hardly say that this is not to set up, or hark back to, the old opposition between 'essential ethics' and 'individual ethics'. Cf. K. Rahner, 'Zur "situationsethik" aus ökumenischer Sicht', *Schriften zur Theologie* VI (Einsiedeln, 1965), pp. 537–544, 499–536 (with further refs.). See also note 17 below.

[6] cf. K. Rahner, 'Ursprünge der Freiheit': M. Horkheimer, K. Rahner, C. F. v. Weizsäcker, *Über die Freiheit* (Stuttgart,[2] 1965), pp. 27–49; K. Rahner, pp. 205 ff. above.

[7] The author may be permitted to use the concept of 'manipulation' in this rather wider sense (cf. note 1) although the editor and the other contributors to the original symposium (see the list of sources) have agreed on a narrower and more up-to-date usage. Our wider approach is a necessary preliminary in order to be able to show the deep *anthropological* implications of such a procedure. In any case, at the level of philosophical/theological reflection this fundamental concept cannot be simply defined technically once and for all without surrendering the universal vantage-point necessary to our observation. Furthermore, the really threatening aspect of "manipulation" can only be brought out by contrasting and distinguishing it from what is

inevitable *necessity* of self-determination, by which man (though starting out from a 'beginning' which is a prior datum and within a perspective of already pre-empted possibilities) *makes himself* what and who he wants to be and ultimately will be in the abiding validity and eternity of his free decisions. The fact that in earlier times this planned self-determination ('self-manipulation') took place almost exclusively on the individual, moral-transcendent plane of convictions and of conscience may perhaps initially obscure our view of the nature of man in this respect, but it does nothing to change the *fact* of this transcendental necessity: to the extent that man is 'handed over' to himself, he *is* 'self-manipulating' (within the limits set by his 'nature' and 'history'). Today this fundamental essence of his has now also broken through into history and society: today he is able to manipulate himself in tangible, bodily and societal terms, and – a radical difference here from earlier times – he can plan this manipulation rationally and steer it by means of technology.

Genetic manipulation is only one particular instance of this more general phenomenon. Consequently the formal, abstract concept of (genetic) self-manipulation does not automatically imply a morally repugnant act: man does not simply perform actions *external* to himself, merely suffering his own self passively: man is such that he actually 'performs' himself. Since the latter is in accordance with his nature, this kind of 'self-manipulation' is legitimate too, if it is true that a moral action is one which is in accordance with the subject's nature. The fact that today man is able to do this in ways which were previously not accessible to him does not change the abstract, formal concept of self-manipulation. This applies, for example, in the case of genetic self-manipulation if we take a preliminary 'abstract' look at it. For here, as in other methods of psychological, physiological and social self-manipula-

---

true and legitimate in the matter concerned; one must not use the word 'manipulation' *only* in its pejorative sense, at least at first. And finally, the theologian uses this wider sense because he may be said to have a reputation for entertaining a frozen, static concept of the 'nature' of man. If for once he begins in reverse, by proceeding from man's self-determination as his 'essence', it may emerge more convincingly and clearly from the process of investigation just *what* is meant by 'nature'. The use of the concept 'manipulation' in this essay is not to be separated from the actual context in which it occurs, so that the reader will only reach a full understanding of the concept if he himself follows the various diverse approaches to the issue which will be presented here. If he does this it will be clear that the author's intention is not to blunt the critical cutting edge of the contemporary usage of 'manipulation', but to approach these very problems from within a necessarily wider and more productive perspective.

tion, we must distinguish clearly between the process in its material content as such (i.e. the changing of hereditary material), and the conscious controlling of it, which does not automatically involve an artificial, arbitrary alteration which uses man himself as a means. For the moment we shall deal only with outlining the formal and abstract issues of the problem. The moral quality of control as such is determined by the moral quality of the process itself: if a thing is permissible, it may be expressly desired and consciously implemented.

Now a particular kind of 'change' of hereditary material is morally permissible. For it actually occurs legitimately, within certain limits, whenever a person chooses a marriage-partner, and whenever two human beings consummate their marital union sexually. Of course this kind of self-manipulation does not penetrate deeply into the human material as do psychological and pain-killing drugs and all cosmetic techniques in their different ways. But there are examples which show that, considered in the abstract, in this field of quite ordinary 'genetic manipulation' no moral objection can be raised on account of the conscious controlling of the process in itself. For example, no-one would think of raising a moral protest if a married couple were to opt for a particular coitus which they knew beforehand (supposing that they could) would produce a boy, rather than for another one, equally possible, but which would lead to the birth of a girl. But such a case would constitute materially and formally a 'genetic manipulation' according to our terms so far (which cannot embrace the concrete phenomenon of modern genetic manipulation in all its aspects). Thus the abstract concept of genetic manipulation is not subject to any moral reservations.

Clearly this does not take us very far, for it is plain that not everything that *can* be done is morally justifiable. In our case the moral quality of a *concrete* genetic manipulation depends on several factors:

1. It depends on the concrete subject of the manipulation: a married couple is something quite different from the state, for instance, or any other active subject taking such measures.

2. It depends on the concrete, premeditated result on the whole human being: to intend to produce a human being who would never be morally responsible for himself would be immoral, even if such a human being might be very 'useful' for the particular purposes of other men.

3. It depends on the concrete method employed in genetic manipulation: initially we cannot be certain that each *technologically successful* development can be fitted into the *whole* of human reality without being

contrary to the latter's nature. But unless this is safeguarded, any such development is thoroughly immoral.

All three aspects of the moral evaluation of concrete genetic manipulation can be reduced to a common principle: its *concrete* reality must be adjudged according to whether it is appropriate to or contrary to the nature of man.

At this point we encounter the real difficulties of the question. Is there such a thing as an unchangeable 'nature' of man against which we can measure the appropriateness or inappropriateness of a particular genetic manipulation? With all our knowledge of man's immense malleability in the biological, psychological, cultural and social spheres, do we still have the courage to talk about the 'nature' of man? Do we know precisely where the limits of man's nature are to be found? We are even more at a loss if it is true that man is not only placed in a process of natural historical development, but also can and must change *himself* if he is to come to full stature and find true selfhood. Even if there is such a thing as this 'nature', can we recognise it, if by 'nature' we mean, not the tangible, concrete constitution of man as he is at any one time, but what is thought to be perennially valid and hence normative throughout all historical change? If there is such a 'nature' of man, if it is somehow present to man's understanding of himself, whether propositionally or not, do we come across it in any other way than in a particular historical form, where we are unable to distinguish clearly and unequivocally between the nature 'in itself' and its concrete, variable form? Is it not the case that saying 'No' in the name of morality and humanity has often been merely the mistaken and ultimately ineffectual refusal on the part of historical man to change himself and experience a new form of his reality, a new form of his 'nature'? May not the reverse be true, in a way: can there be a moral judgment based not simply on the 'eternal nature' of man as a *primary* 'law of nature', but one which draws its imperative from the particular form of man's nature which is committed to him at any one time as his historical destiny, such that he cannot act with impunity contrary to it, even if he has the power to do so? How can we recognise the boundary between the foolish 'No' of man when he will not let himself be changed, and *this* 'No', through which man holds fast to a particular form which, though historically limited, is the currently imperative form of his historical nature? If man is essentially an inhabitant of 'civilisation' and never merely a factor of nature, is it not possible to think that now this 'civilisation' is shaping his very self and no longer only his environment? This too could be considered as 'genetic manipulation'.

At first sight it would appear that, in order to form an opinion of the moral quality of a particular instance of genetic manipulation, one would need to have a clear answer to all these questions, as well as the courage to give a definitive answer. At this juncture it will be obvious, however, that we can neither assume such an answer as given nor set out to provide one.[8]

II

Before trying to find a way of solving the problem under discussion without having to go into all the fundamental ethical questions which we have just raised, we must clarify certain fundamental problematical issues as they affect our particular question. Whatever the situation may be as regards the current judgments of modern men and specialists, man *has* a knowledge and understanding of his own nature, and this can exercise a *normative* function in his moral evaluations. But the question remains as to how far, if at all, this knowledge of the nature of man can take us in our particular inquiry. This dual statement must be expanded somewhat.

Man is essentially the *subject*: he is a person, aware of himself as a free being, and related, in this freedom, to the absolute mystery which we call 'God'. He experiences this *a posteriori* in his 'passive' subjectivity, in the flesh of history, in language and in the objective account of himself which he finds in 'civilisation'. Man's nature is constructed with a built-in transcendental necessity: man must inevitably affirm his own nature even in an action which seeks freely to deny it. Here we need not go into the question whether, further than trying to eliminate his nature as an individual – suicide being the most radical case – mankind as a whole could throw off its nature by implementing a process of 'civilisation in reverse', cultivating a species of intelligent animals which would live only unto themselves without being answerable for themselves. Such an action would be the most radical conceivable genetic manipulation. But *qua* action even this would be still the action of beings who would be denying *explicitly* what *implicitly* they cannot but affirm. The action itself, like individual suicide, would do nothing to deny the transcendental necessity of man's nature. For because of his subjectivity, i.e. his *a priori* limitless transcendentality, he cannot be mistaken for merely the highest 'stage' of animal development. Hence it is clear that what we call 'immorality' is when *this* transcendental nature is violated by man's self-determining action. Yet this does not imply straightway that what is moral simply coincides with what is appropriate to this *transcendental* nature.

[8] cf. further observations above, pp. 214–17.

We are left with a difficult question. Can we deduce a rule for distinguishing between morally justifiable and immoral genetic manipulation from this concept of morality as being in harmony with a transcendentally discoverable necessary nature? We can still see that genetic manipulation would be immoral if it tried to destroy or threaten man's nature as a free, subjective self-awareness in the flesh of history.[9] But the spokesmen of genetic manipulation would repudiate such a suggestion, even if one finds it hard to shake off the suspicion that the ideal they have in mind is of a gregarious animal who is, from the social, hygienic, economic and political points of view, at once the most co-operative and diligent *and* the easiest to manipulate.

However, does this definition of morality in terms of *primary* natural law help us any further in distinguishing *critically* between the various possible means and ends of genetic manipulation? Surely transcendental deduction cannot show a particular biological constitution of man to be so necessary that it had to be protected against genetic manipulation? For instance, no metaphysically-minded anthropologist would take it upon himself to prove that a particular brain capacity or the appendix etc. were necessary accompaniments of man's ontological, morally imperative 'nature'. This being the case, how can one know that a genetic manipulation which removes man's development from the biosphere where it was previously a phylogenetic development steered only by 'nature', and places it under the conscious control of 'civilisation' (e.g. by seeking to increase considerably the quantity of brain cells, or to adapt man biologically to his technological environment, etc.) is contrary to this 'transcendental' nature of man and therefore immoral? At this point the theologian who proceeds by means of ontological categories finds himself in severe difficulties, for there is little, indeed almost nothing, in man's biological constitution which he can recognise as necessary to his nature: on the contrary it is plain to him that a great amount, e.g. a particular colour or amount of hair, racial characteristics, etc., certainly does *not* belong to his nature.

The relationship of man's ultimate and really irreducible 'nature' to his concrete biological constitution is a highly complex matter from the theological point of view too. The man who only does research on the problem of the physical appearance of the first men will have to be very careful when it comes to making inferences *directly* to the metaphysical 'nature' of such beings merely from this external picture. And the con-

[9] At this point it is immaterial whether *this* kind of genetic manipulation is actually feasible *without* involving the liquidation of man's vital, personal sphere.

verse is true: the fact that 'man' came into being as such by a conscious awakening and in responsible freedom does not tell us anything of the 'phenotypical' appearance of such a real man.[10] All the same (and not least since it constitutes authoritative Church teaching) the doctrine of the unity of body and spirit (soul) compels us to maintain a very intimate connection between man's transcendental nature and his biological constitution.

Then how can man reject particular, calculated changes in his biological make-up as immoral? Would not such a judgment be perilously similar to those aesthetic judgments which arise as a result of familiarity and unfamiliarity, fashion, and the inherited ideas and prejudices of a particular historical period? For at this point one ought conceivably to scrutinise more closely the connection between the biological side of man and his psychic side (subjectivity and personality) in order to be able to judge the immorality of this or that genetic manipulation. For example one might say that a genetic manipulation was wrong if it destroyed or damaged considerably the vital substratum needed for genuine human intercommunication.

Or one could take a critical look at the 'aims' governing a particular genetic manipulation, in an attempt to uncover whether they conflict with man's nature as a personal being. One would have to ask the planners how they envisage carrying out such a manipulation in concrete terms, and go on to decide what would be implied by the particular *method*, whether the method – measured by the standard of man's personal subjectivity – is compatible with the subject's area of freedom (which must be guaranteed), his 'dignity', his 'privacy' etc.

The question remains, however, as to whether this kind of individual casuistics really succeeds in taking us any further towards formulating clear judgments. Just *when* would a biological alteration seriously damage a man's 'nature' as a person? What kind of manipulation ought one to accept under certain circumstances, especially when one considers that, after all, most human beings are only modestly equipped for their achievement of personality? *Which* of the aims of biological manipulation are *assuredly* contrary to man's nature, when one remembers how very limited a function the individual has to play in any case in the life of humanity as a whole? For it must be admitted – unless we deceive ourselves in a naïve individualism – that the individual is largely 'exploited'

[10] Further details in K. Rahner and P. Overhage, *Das Problem der Hominisation* (Freiburg,[3] 1965); P. Overhage, *Um das Erscheinungsbild der ersten Menschen. Mit einer Einführung von Karl Rahner* (Freiburg, 1959), pp. 11–30.

as such by society and humanity as a whole. If one appeals to the 'dignity' of the personal subject[11] against a particular method of genetic manipulation, if one appeals to his right to an area of freedom and privacy – and all these things arise, it is true, from man's transcendental nature – it must be recognised that they also constitute factors which are and have always been in competition with other necessary requirements of man – the claims of society, the rights of other men, and inevitable material and biological compulsions.[12] The more familiar factor, whose claims seem obvious as a result of custom, always inclines people to oppose the rights of a new and different factor.[13]

In consequence it seems that, from both the theoretical and practical points of view, we cannot get very far in the matter of morally evaluating the concrete forms of genetic manipulation, either as currently practised or as a future possibility, if we proceed by the methods of deductive, analytic and casuistic moral theology: the *abstract* concept of genetic manipulation cannot be shown to involve immorality *per se*. The critical evaluation of conceivable concrete forms of genetic manipulation rapidly disintegrates into a casuistics if it proceeds by using the abstract metaphysical nature of man as its term of reference. And in a casuistics of this sort it is to a large extent simply a case of one opinion against another. It is only the most extreme forms of genetic manipulation which exhibit clear-cut immorality, in trying unequivocally to liquidate or undermine man's nature, and of course it is not so much these instances which give rise to disagreement.

III

Is there another way of approaching the whole question? First of all some preliminary observations are necessary.

[11] cf. K. Rahner, 'The dignity and freedom of Man', *Theological Investigations* II (London and Baltimore, 1963), pp. 235–263. For the frequently used concept of the 'area of freedom' cf. M. Horkheimer, K. Rahner, C. F. v. Weizsäcker, *Über die Freiheit* (Stuttgart,[2] 1965), pp. 26–49, esp. 34–44; 'Vorbemerkungen zum Problem der religiösen Freiheit', K. Rahner, H. Maier, U. Mann, M. Schmaus, *Religionsfreiheit* (Munich, 1966), pp. 7–23.

[12] cf. K. Rahner, 'Theology of Power', *Theological Investigations* IV (London and Baltimore, 1966), pp. 391–409; also 'The peace of God and the peace of the world', *Theological Investigations* X.

[13] For example, think of the passionate protests which were once made against compulsory state vaccination in the name of the 'freedom of personality'. How *many* measures which are now accepted as normal in more highly developed human society were once rejected as immoral in the name of the free subject? And yet they are possible, even positively *moral* measures.

So far we have been able to manage with a very formal, abstract concept of genetic manipulation. But if now we are to go beyond a discussion of the moral *problems* involved in this concept and try to make a moral *judgment*, we shall have to be more precise about the particular genetic manipulation we mean. Up to now the concept 'genetic manipulation' has been necessarily ambiguous because of the concrete plans and utopias of the 'man-makers'. This creates new difficulties. For it is not easy to say what the spokesmen of genetic manipulation have in mind for the future. As a result of this any description of genetic manipulation for the purposes of moral theology will be inevitably somewhat arbitrary.

In the first place the following must be borne in mind: we are not concerned, at least not directly, with defining and delimiting a phenomenon in criminal law. Not everything that is immoral must also be the object of legal proceedings on the part of society as organised into a state. So here the question is not whether the state, for instance, should suppress private experiments on human genetic material in private laboratories. This does not mean that, even if we were to exclude this question or answer it in the negative, our whole issue refers only to the sphere of *private* morals. For there are many places where private and public life cross, many cases where society as a state influences the life of the individual, and, without having anything to do with criminal law and direct compulsory measures on the part of the state, they are yet dependent upon the latter; just as phenomena which are treated as, among other things, criminal social influences, are also subject to moral judgment. Thus the question could be raised, for instance, whether or not the state ought to make money available for experiments in state research establishments which have genetic manipulation in view, or whether it ought to permit or encourage aligned instruction and the implementation of genetic manipulation in places of public education, and so on.

But we are not to deal directly with these questions at this point. We are not concerned with either private or state eugenic measures in the usual sense (i.e. encouraging or suppressing particular desirable or undesirable marriage unions, marriage bans, private or state-organised birth-control, sterilising those who have undesirable hereditary characteristics etc.). We omit these questions simply because they do not constitute our present subject-matter. That is *not* to say that they are at the outset morally irrelevant, or that there is no danger at all of the state making immoral encroachments on the individual's sphere of freedom.

If we exclude these questions, the issues remaining to be discussed from the point of view of a *moral* evaluation of genetic manipulation are:

1. Biological experimentation with human genetic material;
2. Heterologous artificial insemination (A.I.D.).

As far as biological experiments with human genetic material are concerned, Catholic moral theology would have to distinguish between the moral evaluation of, on the one hand, obtaining the material in the first place, and on the other, the actual experiment itself. Since it is not certain, presupposing a distinction of this sort, that obtaining material for experiment is necessarily morally problematical, in practice the question of biological experimentation is reduced to the issue of the moral quality of the experiment itself as such. And in this case one would have to distinguish, in accordance with the perspectives and distinctions customary in Catholic moral theology, between experiments with unfertilised germ cells on the one hand (i.e. on separate male and female cells), and experiments involving test-tube fertilisations and further stages on the other.

The reason for this distinction is clear. Catholic theology presupposes that at the moment of union of the male and female cells a *human being* comes into existence as an individual person with his own rights. *If* this is the case, such a person is no more an inconsequential passive object for experiments than the prisoners of Nazi concentration camps were. The end does not justify the means. It would be to exploit a present human being for the sake of a future human being. A one-hour-old human being has as much right to the integrity of his person as a human being of nine months or sixty years.

Nowadays, however, the above-mentioned presupposition is no longer held with certainty, but is exposed to positive doubt. We cannot give reasons for this statement here: it must be assumed for the moment. Of course it does not follow from the fact of such an uncertainty that experiments with fertilised embryonic material *are* equivalent to morally indifferent experiments with mere 'things'. But it would be conceivable that, given a serious positive doubt about the human quality of the experimental material, the reasons in favour of experimenting might carry more weight, considered rationally, than the uncertain rights of a human being whose very existence is in doubt. This is not adduced to decide the issue one way or another, but only to show why this question too must be excluded from our consideration.

We are thus left only with heterologous artificial insemination as the concrete instance of genetic manipulation.[14] Homologous (inter-marital)

[14] cf. on the issue of heterologous artificial insemination the moral theological handbooks: B. Häring, *Das Gesetz Christi* III (Freiberg,[7] 1963), p. 367; J. Miller, *LThK* II (Freiburg,[2] 1958), pp. 104–105 (refs.); H. Thielicke, *Theologische Ethik*

artificial insemination may be left on one side since, whatever moral judgment one may come to, it is a quite different moral problem from the heterologous case since the father and mother are married and the child thus produced is the child of this particular couple. Heterologous insemination is, however, a highly complex issue. First of all its immediate concrete implications are clear. But when one looks at the aims of genetic manipulation it means far more: the obtaining of male sperm, its storage and checking, the age factor, etc., and ultimately the establishment of and the whole organisation of a 'sperm bank' as a public institution in society, documentation of the qualitative characteristics of the sperm, legal questions of the identity or anonymity of the donor, the extra-marital use of this material, the necessity of the consent of the male marriage-partner, the question of determining 'fatherhood' in such a case, and of course the resultant question of providing instruction and propaganda for heterologous insemination. Furthermore, the spokesmen of this insemination are concerned so to propagate it and to actually establish it as the general practice of a whole population as to achieve considerable results for humanity, such as long life, intelligence, hygienic stability among wide population groups, etc.

Finally, at the outer limit of our actual problem there arises the question as to whether, above and beyond the heterologous insemination controlled with eugenic aims in view such as is currently possible, it would be either possible or desirable to develop a fertilised embryo outside a human womb and successfully bring it to the state of a complete human being, and whether experiments should be initiated with this aim in view. This issue can, however, be subsumed and discussed here under the general heading of artificial heterologous insemination, which, understood in the way we have outlined, will be considered from now on as the object of moral evaluation.

Before proceeding to try to answer the actual question itself (as a question which concerns man's free and responsible action), we must make some observations on the following approach to a moral judgment on genetic manipulation. Epistemologically this particular approach is considerably different from that of the remarks we have been making so far.

III (Tübingen, 1964), pp. 768–788 (refs.). On the legal problems cf. D. Giesen, 'Die künstliche Insemination als ethisches Problem' = *Schriften zum deutschen und europäischen Zivil-, Handels- und Prozeßrecht* 18 (Bielefeld, 1963).

IV

In the case of those realities which have many layers and which cannot be adequately reached by analysis, there exists a *moral* mode of knowing. This moral knowledge itself has a structure which is both universal and not exhaustively analysable in conscious reflection. In a certain way it exercises a critical function in an area where 'is' and 'ought' *mutually* determine each other, but where what is 'objectively' right only becomes transparent to the person who has already embraced the correct attitude to it.

In other words, to adopt a term from the contemporary theology of faith, there is also a *moral* instinct of faith,[15] i.e. a universal knowledge of right and wrong belief. This 'instinctive' judgment cannot and need not, however, be adequately subject to analytic reflection. In the more concrete questions of morality this faith-instinct is clearly indispensable because such complex realities are involved which cannot successfully be subjected to analytic reflection – and yet they must be evaluated morally all the same. Wherever the judgment of this moral faith-instinct attempts to express itself in words regarding a particular issue, it naturally and inevitably works with the categories of rational analysis, 'reasons', conceptual arguments etc., and thus conceals its own character. But at bottom it knows that its judgments are not the resultant and formal logical sum of the rational considerations which it is able to 'objectivise'. Traditional moral theology has no name for the activity of this moral faith-instinct, although the instinct plays its part in the former. For instance, a merely 'rational' scrutiny of moral theological 'proofs' will often reveal – initially to one's great surprise – that, looked at purely 'logically', they already presuppose what they claim to be 'proving', or else they have recourse to Holy Scripture or the Church's magisterium as a final court of appeal, in spite of the fact that they were supposed to be dealing with questions of natural law, requiring an *inner* justification. What is really behind these 'proofs'? Under certain circumstances they are not as bad as they seem. They are ultimately an expression of the universal faith-instinct, which is by no means identical with its objectivisation in analytic terms.

Of course there are dangers in citing this kind of knowledge *sui generis*: it can be used merely to avoid producing what is sometimes

[15] For a view of the history of this idea and the problems and implications involved in it from the standpoint of dogmatics cf. M. Seckler, *Instinkt und Glaubenswille nach Thomas von Aquin* (Mainz, 1961).

actually possible, namely, a more precise rational, analytic justification; it can be used as an argument where it does not, in fact, exist, where there is merely false 'evidence' rooted in historically conditioned prejudices, whether those of tradition, society or class ideology. Consequently it is fundamentally legitimate to be critical of this approach, especially when one thinks how much mischief and crime was perpetrated during the Nazi period in the name of 'the healthy instinct of the people'. But such criticism must neither dispute nor disregard the reality and rights of this universal instinct in reason and faith, irrespective of what it is to be called and how it is to be described and analysed from the point of view of formal epistemology.

Furthermore, this mode of knowing is active in human life wherever someone is 'committed' to a particular attitude: it is even active where the rationalistic sceptic gives expression to his scepticism *vis-à-vis* all so-called 'taboos', as he calls those things he wishes to reject. Denying the existence and legitimacy of such a mode of knowing cannot get rid of it: it can only obstruct the process of critical reflection upon opinions, opinions which are themselves – explicitly or implicitly – dependent on the results of this mode of knowing. One can only proceed with caution with regard to something if one has not, at the outset, denied its existence. Nor does this mode of knowing mean to curtail or even replace rationality, for it possesses this very rationality as one of its own elements. But it is necessary because what is moral, the concrete action to be performed, corresponds automatically to the unity of experienced and conceptual reality. It cannot wait while conceptual analysis – an essentially endless process – makes its conclusions; it demands that one should enter into the darkness of reality (which is never completely transparent) and have the courage to take the step from theory to practice. This action is never the mere application of concepts to an empty world of matter, enjoying no reality but what the abstract concepts give it. This kind of universal moral instinct of faith and reason can calmly take 'risks' provided that it is self-critically aware that its judgments contain unreflected elements which are, as such, contingent, subject to change; and that consequently a *different* judgment may be shown to be correct at a later time. All the same, a particular contingent judgment of this kind can still be the only correct one *in its situation*. The making of it requires a universal knowledge of the current situation; this knowledge is correctly grasped in the 'instinctive' judgment which recognises what is currently and properly called for, and this results in an 'appropriate' judgment.

Since it is made 'in general' and 'in principle', the judgment made by a universal moral faith-instinct is not simply identical with what traditional moral theology calls a 'prudential' judgment,[16] nor with what I have described as an individual existential moral decision,[17] which cannot be adequately reduced to general concepts and their application to particular 'cases' and thus requires a 'logic of existential decisions'. The fact that there are these other phenomena in the moral field shows too, however, that what we have called the 'universal moral faith-instinct' must be present in the sphere of theoretical moral reasoning as well. For this *fundamentally synthetic* knowledge, formed by the unity of a prudential judgment and a unique moral existential situation, must clearly also be the case where the situation is 'per se' morally 'general' in nature, since this too is inaccessible to *adequate*, exhaustive reflection and analysis. Taking due account of this connection between the modes of knowledge, it is also justifiable to refer to the following moral phenomena as a demonstration of the mode of knowledge we have been discussing: the choice of a career or a marriage-partner is (or ought to be) a decision of solemn moral significance. Everyone admits – including the Church – that in considering the moral correctness of this kind of decision one may be aware of a large number of points of view and reasons for and against a particular decision; but in addition to all these factors the whole process of reflection includes a synthesising element, which cannot itself be reflected upon in isolation and yet must be present, so that, from among all the conflicting reasons for and against, one may observe the plain inner security which witnesses to a moral decision.

Here we cannot describe *how* this actually happens. It is certainly true that, in the examples we have quoted, the decisions involved are essentially individual in character (not least with regard to their objects). But we have already remarked that this same synthesising function of knowledge, by which we are able, so to speak, to see the wood in spite of all the trees, is also necessary where what is involved is only a *general* moral reality. And this latter is more complicated than the simple text-book model employed in the usual kind of moral theology.

The terrible consequences of ignoring the universal moral instinct of faith and reason, or of not having the courage to rely on it, can be seen

[16] For the more recent problems cf. F. Furger, *Gewissen und Klugheit in der katholischen Moraltheologie der Letzten Jahrzehnte* (Luzern-Stuttgart, 1965).

[17] K. Rahner, *Das Dynamische in der Kirche* (Freiburg,[3] 1965); 'On the question of a formal Existential Ethics', *Theological Investigations* II (London and Baltimore 1963), pp. 217–234; *Schriften zur Theologie* VI (Einsiedeln, 1965), pp. 499–536.

only too clearly, it seems to me, in a particular example of the most recent past. I refer to the simulated crisis of conscience concerning the production of a cheap Napalm bomb for the war in Vietnam, which Günter Wallraff fabricated and set before several prominent German moral theologians for their decision. We shall not relate the whole story in detail here. It is well known. In short it shows clearly that whenever a moral theologian merely dissects such a particular 'case' into a thousand aspects and individual problems and has the courage only to make abstract deductions from more general principles, merely engaging in 'casuistics'; whenever he fails to react simply and plainly from the instinct of faith to the single totality of the 'case', he arrives at 'solutions' which are simply blind to concrete reality; in plain language, they are *false*. Such 'solutions' do not exhibit the uncompromising simplicity of decisions which are truly Christian and human, and only reveal their own impotence. In order to see the helplessness of moral theology when it proceeds solely by analysis and deduction, one need only refer to the whole complex of problems involved in the moral evaluation, according to Catholic and Protestant moral theology, of making and using bio-chemical weapons. Even the Council was not able unequivocally to overcome this kind of mentality, which paralyses any action which could be said to be clearly Christian.

Of course, from the lofty standpoint of his subtle reasonings the 'speculative' moral theologian will object that this is to underestimate the complexity of the problem, that to adopt the method we have postulated is to make things too easy. But *vis-à-vis* this kind of moral theology which never finds a solution the following remarks must be made:

1. In moral questions a clear, decisive judgment cannot let itself be dependent on being accepted by everyone.[18]

2. Does not the moral theologian see that the uncertainty which is uniquely a concomitant of his rational-analytic method gives rise, in actual fact, to a practical judgment (which, to remain consistent, he must immediately pronounce to be an uncertain one); namely, the judgment implied by the activity of those men who *are* prepared to manufacture and produce the weapons referred to?

[18] How can a Christian who believes in all sober intellectual honesty that he is justified in submitting himself to the absolute claims of faith, suddenly find it within him to hold such a view in a question which involves the very life and death of mankind, simply because his judgment is not shared by everyone? On the theological problem concerned here cf. K. Rahner, 'Intellectual honesty and Christian faith', *Theological Investigations* VII (London and New York, 1971), 47–71.

3. Cannot the moral theologian see that his method *cannot* be the only valid one if it leaves men in the lurch in such deeply decisive life-issues? He ought perhaps to consider that what has thus become apparent is simply the insufficiency of his method, which is by no means an argument against the existence of another 'method'. This insufficiency itself proves nothing: whatever had to remain an open and controversial question in the past was simply not a matter of fundamental vital importance; and what *was* of fundamental importance was already held by the instinct of faith as a *fait accompli*, and was also self-evident in society's public understanding *before* the theologian began his speculative and analytic operations. As a result he could not have noticed that he was unwittingly working according to a method which he had not subjected to reflection, and that consequently he was achieving sufficiently certain results with a method which he imagined to be a merely conceptual and analytic one.[19]

4. A further factor must be considered. Nowadays, when disputed moral questions are discussed, one hears the argument – even among Catholic moral theologians – that 'it is quite conceivable' that, for instance, in a few decades almost everyone will have no objection to a particular course of action, and that it will be regarded as morally permissible or morally irrelevant. These moral theologians then conclude that therefore one cannot raise any fundamental objection to it in the name of humanitarian or Christian ethics (not even for reasons of 'pastoral' prudence).

We cannot give a detailed discussion of this phenomenon. But the following seems relevant in this particular connection: it is quite possible for certain moral states of affairs to become incapable of realisation as a result of historical development; they may then cease to be recognised as such, and an infringement of them will no longer be regarded as 'subjectively' immoral. Since moral knowledge and moral reality are closely interrelated it may happen that this particular moral 'object' *no longer exists* to make its demands felt, not merely that there is no 'knowledge' of it.[20] But all this is no argument for seeing the history of this disappearance of the moral 'object' (and the knowledge of it) from moral consciousness as *itself morally justifiable*, nor that such a state of affairs should be accepted or encouraged, especially at a time when the pernicious nature

[19] I presuppose here the analyses of the contemporary situation of the Church in a secularised, pluralistic and a-theistic world which I have given in the *Handbuch der Pastoraltheologie* II/1–2 (Freiburg, 1966).

[20] cf. initially K. Rahner, *Handbuch der Pastoraltheologie* II/1 (Freiburg, 1966), pp. 152–163.

of such a historical development can still be recognised and combated. To recognise the possibility of a partial moral blindness in the future, or even to foresee it, is no reason for bringing it about or passively permitting it to occur. It may well be that, in the providence of God, such a development in a particular culture or historical setting can have positive results (like polygamy had at one time). But the fact that good can arise out of evil by no means justifies the evil, and can only be a consolation for the person who looks on helplessly in the face of such a development. So we must be very careful and reticent about citing future moral sensibilities. We are to question the moral character not only of the actual result, but also of the historical process itself.

Here we must break off. This is not the place to elucidate further this fundamental question of method. We could not, however, simply presuppose or by-pass the question as if it were already settled, because all the answers which we are suggesting here can only be appreciated and understood from within this method. And above all, this means that all the 'reasons' which are intended to form the basis for rejecting genetic manipulation are to be understood, at the very outset, as only so many references to the moral faith-instinct (and as so many appeals to it, to have the courage to take a clear decision). For in my view the moral faith-instinct is aware of its right and obligation to reject genetic manipulation, even without going through (or being able to go through) an adequate process of reflection.

V

These more methodological remarks have already shown indirectly that the 'definition' of man cannot deal exclusively with the element of man's self-determination, however essential and decisive this particular constitutional element must remain when we talk about him. Man's finite nature implies that, however much he may conceivably (and even legitimately) submit his own self to planning, he is no less a being whose essence has been predetermined. He must accept this particular *existentiale* as well as the task of self-determination. We must now relate this fundamental anthropological and ethical insight to the concrete problem under discussion, and then draw the appropriate and necessary conclusions.

1. Man must freely accept his nature as being predetermined. For he has not called *himself* into existence. He has been projected into a particular world, and although this world is presented to him for his free acceptance or rejection, he has not *chosen* it himself. It is rather that the world

confronts him as something which has been determined from another quarter, *before* he embarks on his own history as a free being. Consequently the world can never be 'worked over' to such an extent that man is eventually dealing only with material *he* has chosen and created. Even if it were exhaustively calculated and planned in advance by the parents, the very stuff which is the precondition of the test-tube baby's freedom is (as far as the baby *itself* is concerned – and this 'self' is what is decisive) something already decided by someone else, something alien, like the genes one receives according to natural conception at the present time. It is part of the test-tube child's freedom to ask why he is obliged to shape his whole lifelong history out of the particular material which his parents have so wisely and thoughtfully selected for him by means of technology and planning. The question still remains as to whether, having had one's 'good fortune' planned and predetermined, one really considers oneself to be 'fortunate'. Accepting this necessarily alien determination of one's own being *is* and *remains*, therefore, a fundamental task of man in his free moral existence. All this can be understood, by 'transcendental deduction', as a necessarily given factor of man's nature. Wherever the *amor fati* – *fatum* in the sense of what is uniquely committed to the individual – is no longer achieved, and wherever this *fatum* is no longer accepted confidently in patience and humility as the gift of an *incomprehensible* love, man is subject to total neurosis, to a basic fear concerning his destiny which weighs more heavily on him than all the things which, as a result of this fear, he tries to escape from. Man's fundamental guilt is the consequence of his freely refusing to accept this gift.

2. However, although this *existentiale* and what it implies (the task of free decision) exercises its sovereign influence in the ultimate ground of man's being, it must also take on a corresponding 'categorial', tangible form in time and space, lest, banished from man's existence, it should be forgotten and ultimately freely denied by him.

Now man is in a certain respect most free when he is not dealing with a 'thing' but calling into being another, freely responsible person. If he is not to conceal or fall short of his nature, man must be presented clearly with the dialectically opposite position of his freedom as a man. And in concrete terms that means that the freedom to determine another person must remain a clear-cut and radical destiny, which one has *not chosen* but *accepted*. Procreation in particular must not become an act of neurotic anxiety in the face of fate. The other person must remain the one who is both *made* and *accepted*; both an elevating influence, because he has been chosen, and a burden to be accepted and carried. If man, when confronted with his child, saw only what he had himself planned, he would not be looking at his own nature, nor would he experience his true self which is both free *and* the object of external determination. Genetic manipulation is the embodiment of the fear of oneself, the fear of accepting one's self as the unknown quantity it is.

Someone might say that even genetic manipulation cannot really get rid of every indeterminate element in procreation and that therefore genetic manipulation does not run counter to what we have said. (In any case, surely certain 'eugenic precautions' are not really reprehensible?) In this case we must answer with another question: What, in actual fact, is the driving force behind genetic manipulation? What sort of person is driven to it? And the answer would be, in the first place, the *hate* of one's destiny; and secondly, it is the man who, at his innermost level, is in despair because he cannot *dispose* of existence. In genetic manipulation such a man clearly and unequivocally oversteps the boundary between legitimate eugenic precautions and the realm tyrannised by the desperate fear of destiny. Even in those cases where no precise boundary can be set, one can see that a particular action undoubtedly exceeds it. This is plain in the case in hand, since the concrete genetic manipulation is governed by the desire to banish the *fatum* from existence, at a particular point. To the extent that this intention does not quite succeed, it is contrary to the original desire, for this desire hates destiny and can only love – as the product of its own free action – what it has calculated and planned. It no longer desires to say 'I have gotten a man from the Lord' – from *God*, who cannot be manipulated and who must be concretely present in man's existence. The essence of this rather more theological conclusion can be seen just as clearly in the dimensions of concrete anthropology: *Does* man in the concrete – who is not a mere abstract concept – really wish, in accepting genetic manipulation, to accept what *cannot* be predetermined? Has he actually the courage to take a decision, the results of which are unforeseeable? Does he really want to enter into a future of open possibilities, full of both threatening and promising surprises? And if his will fails at this point, will he ever find it again in any other area of his existence? Or is he like a man who only wants to perform a particular function of his nature when it is too late for him to do otherwise, and who will thus not be really able to carry it out even then? These are the decisive questions.

3. Man has his own sphere of intimacy. Historically and sociologically its concrete form can vary considerably. But whether it is technologically

possible to abolish it is not the point, for this sphere of intimacy *should* exist, and ought to be resolutely safeguarded. It forms the innermost region of freedom which man needs in order to be really self-determining. At whatever point anyone else is able and is permitted arbitrarily to invade another person's private area of free decision, freedom itself ceases to exist.

Man is right to designate the ultimate achievement of sexual union as belonging to this area of intimacy. For human sexuality, as a free activity, both is and ought to be more than a merely biological function; namely, an activity of the whole human being: the appearance and realisation of personal love.[21] Now this personal love which is consummated sexually has within it an essential inner relation to the child, for the child is an embodiment of the abiding unity of the marriage-partners which is expressed in marital union. Genetic manipulation, however, does two things: it fundamentally separates the marital union from the procreation of a new person as this permanent embodiment of the unity of married love; and it transfers procreation, isolated and torn from its human matrix, to an area outside man's sphere of intimacy. It is this sphere of intimacy which is the proper context for sexual union, which itself implies the fundamental readiness of the marriage-partners to let their unity take the form of a child.

The fact that it is technologically *possible* to effect the changes involved in genetic manipulation while at the same time producing a new *human being* is no argument against the essential connectedness of the factors we have just referred to (the sphere of intimacy – the union of marital love – the child as the permanent form of this union). For the child produced by such a method is, in this sense, the child of the mother *and* of the donor. The latter refuses, however, to acknowledge his fatherhood in an act of personal love: he remains anonymous or at least does not wish to be the donor in respect of this particular mother; precisely through his anonymity he robs the child of the right and ability to fulfil the obligation of his existence, namely to accept himself as the child of these particular parents. Genetic manipulation of this sort is no more 'human', merely because it produces a human being, than a case of rape. The fact that a biological chain of cause-and-effect is not broken, even when the moral/human unity and the whole of really human meaningfulness receives a mortal blow (for the 'biological' side is intended to be an expression of this total meaningfulness), does nothing, in itself, to justify its own occurrence.

[21] cf. the Pastoral Constitution of the Second Vatican Council, *Gaudium en spes* Nos. 47–52.

4. What we have just said is directed against the *desire* (which is at least implicit in genetic manipulation) to plan man totally; it runs counter to the nature of man in the sense we have outlined. Consequently saying 'No' to this desire is not dependent on the question of its feasibility, and it is both possible and permissible to ask the further question, whether this desire *could* be totally realised, and what would be the moral implication of a failure in the execution of these plans.[22]

Initially we should have to answer the first part of the question in the negative. It can confidently be said that it would be impossible, from the technological point of view, to implement a genetic manipulation involving *all* future human beings, because, however much apparatus and 'automation' one had at one's disposal, the fact that one would have to deal with each human being as an individual[23] would imply such a vast quantity of active 'manipulators' that it would take up, *per absurdum*, the whole of mankind's attention and energy. But what would be the moral significance of the impossibility of producing the *whole* of future mankind by genetic manipulation?

In the first place it does *not* mean – as we shall show more clearly *a posteriori* – that a *partial* genetic manipulation is morally admissible, i.e. on the grounds that in any case 'not much' will happen. The practical impossibility of overstepping a particular quantitative limit is by no means a reason for morally justifying any action within that limit. If everyone told lies, for instance, the telling of lies would have no effect, because no-one would believe a liar any more. But that does not make a limited dose of lies a morally justifiable thing. Furthermore, if a *partial* genetic manipulation became normal practice, consciously recognised by society, it would create two new 'races' in mankind: the technologically manipulated, super-bred test-tube men who inevitably would have a special status in society, and the 'ordinary', unselected, mass-produced humans, procreated in the old way. But what new social tensions would arise from this, and at a time when racial discrimination and racial conflicts are laboriously being dismantled so that a gigantic, tightly-packed humanity can exist peacefully! Or is one to believe that this group of test-tube men, whose intelligence quotients would be clearly considerably higher from birth, would not aspire to such a unique position in society, and that the remaining herd of humanity (*without* 'pedigree')

[22] We need not go into the first part of the question in so far as the concrete details are concerned; that belongs to the field of natural science.

[23] Here we can pass over the question as to whether it is possible or impossible to synthesise the hereditary material itself in large quantities.

would obey them? But would the rest of mankind, remaining at least as intelligent, revolutionary and violent as *we* are, readily accept the leadership of pedigree test-tube men? All this would probably not happen provided that the number of genetically manipulated men were *very* small, and that for that very reason they could not lay claim to be the exclusive leaders of society. But in such a case the spokesmen of manipulation would not have achieved the very results they want, namely, to create mankind's elite of leaders, able to claim the right of leadership on account of their genetic qualifications. However, it must be declared immoral to plan to produce such conflict-laden material with its unforeseeable consequences. It constitutes a threat to man and to mankind.

5. Nowadays we are trying to extend and secure the individual's area of freedom. It is one of mankind's moral commissions. To pursue the practical possibility of genetically manipulating man is to threaten and encroach upon this free area. For it offers incalculable opportunities of man's manipulation – reaching to the very roots of his existence – *by organised society*, i.e. the state. This in turn subjects the state to the strong temptation of itself manipulating the genetic manipulation. And unless one adopts the radically false view (which is untenable from both the philosophical and the Christian standpoints) that what the state wants is automatically good and just, it must be acknowledged that, over and above the essential inner perversity of genetic manipulation, this gives the state the power of further immoral action in using it for its own purposes, to create men who suit its own predilections.

Let no-one say that *every* new and legitimate possibility always involves the temptation for man to misuse it, and that it is not thereby immoral, but must just be protected against abuse. The danger of misusing a newly created possibility may be taken into account *if* this new possibility is in itself justifiable and seems to be inevitable and required by man. But is this the case in genetic manipulation? What compelling aims does it have in view? That men should be able to grow a little older? But is that really desirable with the present size of world population, etc.? In any case, is this the right way – it is not the *only* way – to set about it? Or is the main aim that man should be genetically more intelligent and cultured? But is it true that higher intelligence is clearly correlated with a more highly developed humane sensitivity? Is the kind of intelligence which can be 'bred' in this way the kind we need today, i.e. the intelligence of wisdom, moral responsibility and selflessness? (For the other kind, the 'technical' kind of intelligence can be adequately increased by means of computers and cybernetics.) What is the point of genetic manipulation if not to extend the state's area of control and thus to diminish, instead of to increase, man's sphere of freedom? It would be wiser not to put weapons into the hands of one's aggressors.

6. In future man must develop a critical attitude towards the fascination exercised by every new possibility. Here, in general terms, we have a new moral commission.

Essentially it has always been possible to see that not everything which *can* be done, *ought* to be done.[24] The possibilities available to man in earlier days were, however, very stable, and as a result they had been tested countless times. The possibilities for evil (and they were relatively simple and clear-cut) were recognised promptly as such, since they were of a common and general nature, e.g. that 'cheats never prosper', tyranny is eventually self-destructive, excessive indulgence destroys the ability to enjoy, etc. The situation was simple: one knew what one ought not to do because one had already experienced the fact that such things were not really lasting possibilities in the long run, although one could 'get away with it' for a time. But the past did teach a sound doctrine: one should *not* do everything one is *able* to do; there are times when the attraction of the possible must be resisted.

Nowadays the situation is different. New and practical possibilities are set before us in relatively rapid succession, and they have vast and far-reaching effects. It is a strange factor of the dialectic of the accelerating movement of our history that these new possibilities can be discovered more quickly than their ultimate effects can be ascertained by practical tests. This is why it is so vital for humanity to develop a resistance to the fascination of novel possibilities. Of course there are 'feedback' effects in the field of social morality too, and they put a brake on the lure of novelty: the latest attraction in the form of the mini-skirt becomes monotonous when everyone is wearing it; and if almost everyone adopts the policy of limiting the size of the family because of the demands it makes, a large family will suddenly become an 'attractive' possibility and even gain a new social prestige. But there is no guarantee that such feedback effects can be relied upon in social morality in every case. The irreparable catastrophe can already have taken place before any feedback has had time to take effect. In certain cases to create immunity from moral diseases requires more time than the disease itself allows.

[24] Of course, in a real and most profound sense one cannot 'do' something which is really immoral, for evil, measured against the *whole* of reality (including man in all his dimensions and God as well), is always impotent and ineffectual. Cf. also B. Welte, *Über das Böse* (Freiburg, 1959).

Nowadays there are things with which one cannot have a preliminary run through, in order to gain experience for the next occasion and become wiser through trial and error. Or should one first of all arrange a 'trial run' for a total atomic war, for instance, before deciding to avoid a second one? Today we must be aware that a thing may have irreversible consequences.[25] This is a fundamental conviction of Christianity's theology of history; in spite of the multifarious possible recombinations Christianity sees the course of history as being ultimately a one-way street.[26] At all events, if the new humanity of the future is to survive, it must cultivate a sober and critical resistance to the fascination of novel possibilities.

Genetic manipulation seems to be, initially, a case in point. Are there any reasons against such a view? There could only be objections if there were considerable reasons *in favour* of genetic manipulation from other quarters. Like what, for instance? That we must bring the decline of intelligence and bodily health under control? But has anyone proved such a decline to be a fact? Or if it *is* partially the case, has it been shown that it could not be brought under control in another way? No such proofs are forthcoming.

7. There is another side to the fascination of novelty. The suggestion is that new possibilities will become actualities *all the same*; that nothing can resist them and that to offer any resistance is to be backing a loser; that one is being old-fashioned and stick-in-the-mud by not joining forces with the heralds of the 'new age'. On the contrary, it is one of the fundamental duties of a genuinely moral and Christian man to endeavour to do precisely this: to be *absolutely* faithful to a thing in a situation where is seems hopelessly doomed to failure. The biological end of an individual is not the only death of which one must not be afraid. There are other kinds of apparent death which one must not fear. History is not made by those who try to foresee what is 'inevitable' so that they can jump on the cart of fate in good time, but by those who are prepared to take the ultimate risk of defeat. No-one can say that genetic manipulation *inevitably* will come. The only person who 'knows' such a thing is the man who secretly *wishes* it to be so.

Is that kind of man a trustworthy prophet? Why should not mankind as a whole have to learn the lessons every individual has to learn in his

[25] cf. the previous article in this volume, pp. 205–224.

[26] For the significance of the dogma of Original Sin in this connection cf. note 25 above; also a study at present in preparation on the subject of *Evolution und Erbsünde* (Freiburg, 1968).

own life if he is to survive, namely, the lessons of sacrifice and renunciation?[27] After all we have said, the issue of sacrifice and renunciation is in this sense a 'rational' one and not the unreal fantasy of masochistic minds perversely obstructing their own progress. It is by no means certain that mankind will always be able to remain at the juvenile stage where it can only do the sort of 'mischief' which does not matter very much. That is surely another most valuable insight of our time. So then, if mankind as a whole must seek to learn the renunciation characteristic of maturity, it cannot be said that a rejection of genetic manipulation has 'no prospects' from the very beginning.

In conclusion let us recapitulate in order to understand the whole in the proper light. We do not claim that these observations against genetic manipulation are complete; rather they constitute an appeal to, and the inadequate objectifying of, a humane and Christian 'instinct' which can be discovered in the moral field. A moral awareness of this kind (which both is and does more than we have mentioned here) forms the context in which man has the courage to make decisions; thus a decision is also more than its rationale, because the act is always more than its theoretical foundation. This 'instinct' justifiably has the courage to say *Stat pro ratione voluntas* because such a confession need not necessarily be over-cautious about making a decision. On the contrary it can claim to be the first really to make room for the possibility of genuine criticism and to bring to light the justification, implications and limitations of a real theoretical foundation. All theoretical reasoning always says (among other things), 'We do not *want* to manipulate man genetically'; but this will is meaningful in spite of the fact that it neither claims nor is obliged to be exhaustively analysable by theoretical reason; measured against the opposite will, *this* will is more deeply meaningful and more genuinely human. It must accept the risks involved in history and the unpredictable,

[27] On this issue cf. the author's short contribution on the necessity of renunciation in *Festschrift für Wilhelm Bitter*, ed. G. Zacharias (Stuttgart, 1968) – given in this volume pp. 253 ff. From this standpoint one would have to go on to scrutinise the internal factors governing this intramundane 'design for the future', and its relation to the 'absolute future' and to the overcoming of death, etc. Cf. K. Rahner in the previous article, pp. 205–224; also his 'Ideology and Christianity; Marxist Utopia and the Christian Future of Man', *Theological Investigations* VI (London and Baltimore, 1969), pp. 43–58, 59–68; 'Christian Humanism', in this volume, pp. 187–204.

in order to find out whether it is stronger than its converse, and whether it can endow its theoretical meaningfulness with the particular radiance which is the exclusive characteristic of *performed* reality. Modern man is faced with making this decision.

Of course, in saying this we have raised yet another problem. Right from the beginning, rejecting man's genetic manipulation is not a merely theoretical declaration but a deliberate act. Consequently this theoretical discussion cannot be supported conclusively by the general, formal authority of the Christian churches alone. And so, as in many other cases in moral theology, we are faced today with a new, additional question of great importance: How, in concrete terms, can such a rejection (of genetic manipulation) be established in modern society as society's *own* maxim, its own inner attitude and 'instinct', in the face of society's 'pluralism'? However, this particular problem of moral and pastoral theology is part of a wider issue[28] which cannot be pursued further within the limits of the present discussion.

[28] Some pointers are given in K. Rahner, 'Reflections on Dialogue within a pluralistic society', *Theological Investigations* VI (London and Baltimore, 1969), pp. 31–42.

15

SELF-REALISATION AND TAKING UP ONE'S CROSS

PERHAPS it is possible to say something of 'psychological' importance even without psychology. Something said in a very abstract way can be concrete because it reveals more clearly what is universally valid but is easily obscured by things of secondary importance. Today one sometimes has the impression that people very often become unhappy because they want to be happy at any price. They are suffering from frustration anxiety: they think they might miss something, that something might escape them before they have to go; and at the same time they know that very soon they *must* go and that there is not much time left in which anything can happen to bring happiness. That is why they think that the most important thing is to take care not to let anything slip past them. But in reality this fear of not having consumed everything spread out on the table of life means that nothing is enjoyed: everything is merely 'crammed' in, the digestion is spoilt. In the last analysis everything has escaped one after all, and nothing is really experienced because one wanted to experience *everything*.

It is easy to see that this is not the way. Everyone knows that really. For one only needs to bear this in mind – and here we use abstract terms, so that we can see better; the possibilities available to free action are always greater than what can be realised; one can never be everywhere at the same time; to embrace one possibility is always to renounce another, unless one had an unlimited life-span. For man always looks beyond what he has realised, and what he sees is not only the promise of new things to come, but also the renunciation of much, indeed, of everything except that minute portion which can be realised; there is much which will not come again, because it would only have been possible in the place now occupied by what has *in fact* been realised. Narrow reality is death to infinite possibility; the latter dies unborn in the womb of reality. All this, as we have said, is easy to see. The consequence is clear too, namely that the ability calmly to let things go past is one of the great arts of life which are necessary to make our existence free and bearable.

But in reality this ancient wisdom of the necessity of 'proportion' does not banish our frustration anxiety. For something in us asks, Why should we calmly let what is possible go by, and only hang on to so little? Perhaps we have got hold of the wrong thing and have let the right thing, the thing which can unbind us and hence redeem us, pass by. How is one to know? One cannot seriously test every possibility *as such*; one can only test the things one has *really* examined; consequently one never knows, in being modest and restrained, whether one has put one's money on the wrong card or not. So instead, 'everything' – everything as far as possible, that is – must be tried, even if one knows that it is not really possible. Frustration anxiety continues to gnaw away; it knows it is senseless, but that does not kill it. The wisdom of keeping proportion becomes perverted into a cunning method of the part of frustration anxiety, scheming to extract as much as possible *all the same* from the empty wealth of possibilities. So in the end this itself becomes ineffective. All that remains is the desperate conviction that this is no good either. One is not alone in having frustration anxiety; one's own frustration anxiety has one too. It is not the force which keeps life moving, but it steers it, steers it into the void.

Are we then left with the only alternative of renouncing the thirst for existence, renouncing the will, 'seeing through' any initiation of action as the beginning of meaninglessness? But is it possible? Does it make sense? Is not this too another 'art of living' in disguise, is it not again merely another form of the blind impulse of life, trying in this way to reach its goal, in this case at least the happiness of silencing its own wishes? And does it really follow automatically or is it the absurd attempt, by saying a particular Yes, to utter a total No, and thus *secretly* to arrive back at a total Yes? For the activity of the will to live is itself still an act, and consequently it affirms what it wants to surrender. *Can* one really 'let go' of oneself right from the very root of one's being, in order to attain to the ability calmly to let go of the individual possibilities, except by being 'taken' from oneself? But by whom?

If death is life, i.e. if to relinquish the particular is actually not to lose but to gain everything, frustration anxiety is defeated. Not as if the void were in itself actually the 'fulness' – we do not really seriously believe that cheap dialectical trick of words. The 'fulness' is not to be pieced together from the sum total of particular finite possibilities, but lies ahead of us as the one, whole, 'absolute' future, which in Christian terms we are accustomed to call 'God'. He is ready to give himself to us if we succeed in 'letting go'. It is true that we do not immediately come to possess this fulness as soon as the absolute future (which contains the as yet unappropriated fulness and desires to give itself to us) enables us to let go. Whenever this marvel really takes place, and we simply let go, calmly in harmony with it, frustration anxiety is conquered at its very roots. Little reality is taken up as the promise of an infinite future, not as something which means the latter's death. We cannot 'ascertain' that all this happens to us in actual fact; we can only *do* it as the final act, an act which does not take pleasure in itself nor affirm itself consciously, an act which is *given* to us as our own particular act.

'God', 'grace', 'justification', 'freedom', 'faith', 'gift', 'task' (and all the other fundamental Christian concepts) are realities in this event of calm renunciation, and they are secretly understood as such. Everything implied by these words – the abandoning of oneself in the hope of finding the inconceivable fulness – takes place in the ultimately inaccessible depths of one's freedom when this freedom calmly 'lets go', i.e. lets the particular die, believing in hope that in this way (and ultimately *only* in this way) the whole, the fulness, 'God' will be received. This is not done only *in order to* receive the whole, for the particular too may and must be willed in a spirit of calmness.

In Christian terms this kind of renunciation in letting things die in faith and hope is called taking up one's cross. As an act of *free* acceptance it takes a step in the direction of death's inevitability and is thus a preliminary exercise in the acceptance of that particular death which is our unavoidable lot. Scripture calls this 'denying oneself and taking up one's cross'.

Where human qualities are *fully* developed, even if this cannot be subjected adequately to concrete reflection, the acceptance (of the cross) does not only occur in freedom's uttermost depths (together with its permanently ambiguous objectifications in the history of the individual); it does not merely 'occur', it also knows about itself, though in hope, not in the manner of reflection. Since man is an intercommunicative being and is only able to see himself clearly in another person, this acceptance knows about itself by perceiving another person – *the* Other Person – taking up his cross as *the* event of life. In him it can be seen that there is such an acceptance. As Christians we believe that we see Jesus of Nazareth as this Other Person taking up his cross. And in doing so we do not believe that he is only a sort of 'productive example' for us which really might just as well not be there. We believe rather that God lays the cross upon us and, within it, his own fulness, *because* he wills Jesus of Nazareth and has accepted and worked in him as his own life in time and history.

The true 'productive example' is the one which really empowers and enables us. For this reason Jesus of Nazareth is the 'source of salvation', the Redeemer. We Christians acknowledge him as the Crucified; we confess him as the 'Risen' one, since, in the unity of the experience of the Spirit, who sets us free to take up the cross, *and* of the testimony of his disciples, we believe that in this death the arrival of God's life itself has taken place in the *whole* of man's reality.

The person who, in a hope which no longer seeks to reassure itself, relinquishes himself in the depths of the mystery of existence, in which death and life can no longer be distinguished because they can only be grasped together, actually believes in the Crucified and Risen one, even if he is not aware of it (in conceptual terms). But to know of him explicitly is good and brings the promise of salvation. It is an assurance that one will be given one's own cross to take up as one's own, ultimate act of freedom.

Taking up one's cross has many forms. In what follows we shall dwell particularly on two of them. The first is to accept being disappointed – being 'undeceived' – by life. At the very latest this happens in death, provided that one does not actually try to deceive oneself about it – which never quite comes off. In this connection it must not be forgotten that dying already takes place in life, for life is itself *prolixitas mortis*, as Gregory the Great says. The second form, perhaps the most radical case of disappointment – of being 'undeceived' – occurs when one loves although this love does not, or no longer, 'pays off', nor tries to take pleasure in itself as a heroic selflessness. The attempt to produce this kind of pleasure – which is at bottom impossible – is the aim of all those glorifications of life to be found in sentimental novels *à la Reader's Digest*, where everything ends happily without any genuine dying. Is it not true that many exponents of psychotherapy use this same treatment? Cannot one avoid facing the fact that life is a *dying* if one arranges things cleverly?

There are probably only two ways of living: being driven by frustration anxiety, and the acceptance of the cross, which, whether acknowledged as such openly or not, is the Cross of Christ. Strangely enough, each of these ways of life can mimic the other. Probably it must be so; otherwise we could 'judge' ourselves. What the psychologist gets direct hold of is never one or other of these ways of living in itself, but at best its objectification, which is always equivocal. What seems to be a neurotic, even culpably incurred frustration anxiety, can be that very dying by which, in a hidden acceptance, the cross of life is taken up in suffering.

What presents a 'healthy' and 'balanced' appearance can be the result of a frustration anxiety which is driving the person to avoid taking up his cross.

Basically one need not be afraid that the acceptance of one's cross necessarily leads to passivity and resignation in the face of the concrete tasks of life. The man who does not fear death, or rather, who accepts the abiding fear of death, can enjoy the particular good things of life which come to him because they are a genuine promise of the absolute future. He is able to risk his whole self. He is free to love without sparing himself. He does not need to overtax this life's happiness and thus spoil it.

LIST OF SOURCES

THE SECOND VATICAN COUNCIL'S CHALLENGE TO THEOLOGY

A contribution to a projected symposium volume entitled 'The Future of the Church', edited by Mgr Otto Mauer (Verlag Herder and Vienna). Delivered as a lecture at the International Theological Congress of the University of Notre Dame (USA) on 23 March 1966. Also repeated to American students of theology at Munich on 14 February 1966 and, in altered form, in the *Kongresshalle*, Berlin, on 6 June 1966 at the invitation of the *Lessing-Hochschule* (Urania). First published in the American volume, K. Rahner, *The Church after the Council* (New York, 1966, Herder and Herder).

THEOLOGY AND ANTHROPOLOGY

A lecture delivered at the Theological Symposium of St Xavier's College, Chicago (USA) on 31 March 1966. First published in *Künftige Aufgaben der Theologie*, edited by P. Burke (Munich, 1967), pp. 31–60; also as a contribution to *Wahrheit und Verkündigung. M. Schmaus zum 70. Geburtstag*, edited by L. Scheffczyk, W. Dettloff, R. Heinzmann (Paderborn, 1967), Vol. II, pp. 1389–1407.

PHILOSOPHY AND PHILOSOPHISING IN THEOLOGY

A lecture given at the Conference of the Study Group of German-speaking Dogmatic Theologians in Munich from 3 to 5 January 1967. It was repeated at a conference of the *Katholische Akademie in Bayern* on 9 April 1967 at Munich. The lecture was subsequently expanded, and excerpts from it were delivered on 17 May 1967 at a meeting of the Munich Circle of Friends of the *Evangelische Akademie Tutzing* in a conference entitled 'Faith – Theology – Science' (a joint lecture with platform discussion of connected questions in collaboration with Professor

Dr U. Mann of Saarbrücken); at the invitation of the Faculty of Protestant Theology of the University on 20 June 1967 at Göttingen; as a lecture in English given in October 1967 in the course of a lecture tour of various universities and colleges in the United States. The study is likewise designed as a contribution to a symposium volume, *Die Zukunft der Philosophie*, edited by J. B. Metz and H. R. Schlette (Olten-Freiburg, 1968, Walter-Verlag).

THE HISTORICITY OF THEOLOGY

Delivered at Barcelona on 11 March 1966 as a lecture, on the occasion of the founding of the Spanish branch of the Paulus Society. In expanded form it again provided the basis of a lecture at a research discussion from 25 to 29 September 1967 at the Centre for International Research at the University of Salzburg (Director, Professor Dr Thomas Michels O.S.B.). First published in *Integritas. Geistliche Wandlung und menschliche Wirklichkeit*, edited by D. Stolte and R. Wisser, and dedicated to K. Holzamer (Tübingen, 1967), pp. 75–95.

THEOLOGY AND THE CHURCH'S TEACHING AUTHORITY AFTER THE COUNCIL

Delivered in English in October 1967, in the course of a lecture tour of various universities in the United States. First published in *Stimmen der Zeit* 178 (1966), pp. 404–420.

PRACTICAL THEOLOGY WITHIN THE TOTALITY OF THEOLOGICAL DISCIPLINES

A paper read at Arnoldshain on 5–6 April 1967 at a study group conference of the Ch. Kaiser Verlag (Munich), concerning the nature and function of practical theology. (Other contributors, Professor Dr E. Jüngel and Professor Dr M. Seitz.) The Kaiser Verlag is preparing a volume in which the other papers will also be published, together with a discussion.

THE NEED FOR A 'SHORT FORMULA' OF THE CHRISTIAN FAITH

An initial projection of the 'short formula' itself was published in the periodical, *Geist und Leben* 38 (1965), pp. 374–379, under the title 'Kurze

Inbegriff des christlichen Glaubens für "Ungläubiger"'. A version which was expanded so as to include several further aspects later appeared under the title given above in the periodical *Concilium* 3 (1967), pp. 203–207.

OBSERVATIONS ON THE DOCTRINE OF GOD IN CATHOLIC DOGMATICS

Lecture given at the University of Marburg on 16 July 1965 at the invitation of the Institute of Hermeneutics of the Theological Faculty of the University of Marburg (Professor Dr Ernst Fuchs). On the following day a fuller exchange of views concerning the contents of the lecture took place with Professor Dr Ernst Fuchs and Professor Dr Gerhard Ebeling. An invitation lecture at the College of Philosophy and Theology at Regensburg on 10 December 1965. First published in *Catholica* 20 (1966), pp. 1–18.

ATHEISM AND IMPLICIT CHRISTIANITY

Used as the basis of a lecture given in the course of a tour of several universities in the USA in October 1967. An initial brief version of this study was published in *Concilium* 3 (1967), pp. 171–180, under the title 'The Teaching of the Second Vatican Council on Atheism'. The Study as it appears in the present volume, in a considerably expanded form, was prepared for the major work, designed to appear in several volumes and in several different languages, entitled *L'Ateismo Contemporaneo* (Società Editrice Internazionale, Turin, 1967; German version published by Verlag Hueber, Munich, 1968).

'I BELIEVE IN JESUS CHRIST'

This essay was originally composed as a broadcast talk in the series *In Defence of Thought* (Interpretation of the Creed), and was transmitted by the South German Radio in the spring of 1967. First published in the edited series of broadcast talks entitled *Das Glaubensbekenntnis. Aspekte für ein neues Verständnis*, edited by G. Rein (Stuttgart, 1967), pp. 20–23.

ONE MEDIATOR AND MANY MEDIATIONS

Lecture delivered at Mainz on 24 June 1966 at the invitation of the Institute of European History (Professor Dr Joseph Lortz), and at

Munster on 17 February 1967 at the invitation of the Institute of Ecumenical Theology of the University of Munster (Professor Dr E. Iserloh). An expanded version of the study appeared as a published paper of the Institute of European History at Mainz, Lecture No. 47 (Wiesbaden, 1967). The version printed in this volume has again been revised, chiefly in respect of the notes.

CHRISTIAN HUMANISM

A lecture given at the Conference on 'Christian Humanity and Marxist Humanism' held at Herrenchiemsee on 29 April 1966 under the auspices of the Paulus Society. The manuscript was used in altered form as the basis of a lecture delivered on 15 November 1966 at the University Week at Düsseldorf, also at an Evening of the Society of Catholic Students at the University of Cologne on 5 December 1966, and at the invitation of the Reuchlin Society at Pforzheim on 15 December 1966. An initial version, including the most important points, appeared in *Orientierung* 30 (1966), No. 10 (of 31 May), pp. 116–121. The study also appeared in revised form and with added notes in the symposium volume, *Menschliche Existenz und moderne Welt. Ein internationales Symposion zum Selbstverständnis des heutigen Menschen*, edited by R. Schwarz (Berlin, 1967), Vol. I, pp. 131–148.

THE EXPERIMENT WITH MAN

This lecture was initially delivered at The Hague on 25 September 1965 at the invitation of the Dutch Society of St Adelbert. It was repeated at Munich on 3 November 1965, in the National Training College at Duisburg on 4 January 1965, in the Institute for Child Study of the University of Würzburg (Professor Dr J. Ströder) on 4 February 1966, in the Institute of Anatomy and Histological Embryology of the University of Innsbruck (Professor Dr G. Sauser) on 14 February 1966, at the Catholic Students' Union of the University of Munster on 18 February 1966, as an invitation lecture to the Faculty of Catholic Theology of the University of Vienna on 14 March 1966, at the Society of Training Colleges at Graz on 15 March 1966, at a conference of the Study Group of Medical Journalists at the *Akademie Tutzing* on 19 May 1966, and on the occasion of 'University Week' at Warendorf, Westphalia, on 8 December 1967. At the invitation of the Associazione Culturale Italiana the author delivered the same lecture in Italian at Turin, Genoa, Milan, Rome, and Naples (15 to 20 April 1966). In addition an English version was delivered at several American Universities and Colleges of Education in the course of a lecture tour through the United States in October 1967. First published under the title of 'Theologische opmerkingen over de zelfmanipulatie van de mens', *Adelbert* 13 (1965), No. 11 (November), pp. 197–208; first published in German as 'Experiment Mensch. Theologisches zur Selbstmanipulation des Menschen', *Die Frage nach dem Menschen. Aufriß einer philosophischen Anthropologie. Festschrift für Max Müller*, edited by Heinrich Rombach (Freiburg, 1966), pp. 45–69.

THE PROBLEM OF GENETIC MANIPULATION

An article intended as a contribution to a symposium volume projected by Professor Dr F. Wagner as editor, and entitled *Die Zukunft des Menschen. Zum Problem der genetischen Manipulation* (Verlag C. H. Beck, Munich, 1968).

SELF-REALISATION AND TAKING UP ONE'S CROSS

A contribution to *Dialog über den Menschen, Festschrift für Dr. W. Bitter zum 75. Geburtstag*, edited by G. Zacharias (Verlag E. Klett, Stuttgart, 1968).

In the list of sources given above no mention has been made of a number of excerpts or special papers which were printed in German. Broadcast talks are mentioned only when the article concerned was specially written for these. Nor has there been any special mention of the numerous translations which have been made. Only the work in which they were initially published is mentioned, whether this was in German or in a foreign language.

INDEX OF PERSONS

INDEX OF SUBJECTS